Interactive Web Graphics

with

Shout3D

Interactive Web Graphics

with Shout3D™

Rob Polevoi

SYBEX®

San Francisco • Paris • Düsseldorf • Soest • London

Associate Publisher: Cheryl Applewood

Contracts and Licensing Manager: Kristine O'Callaghan

Acquisitions and Developmental Editor: Mariann Barsolo

Editor: Kari Brooks

Production Editor: Nathan Whiteside

Technical Editor: Paul Isaacs

Book Designer: Maureen Forys, Happenstance Type-O-Rama

Graphic Illustrator: Tony Jonick

Electronic Publishing Specialist: Kris Warrenburg, Cyan Design

Proofreaders: Laurie O'Connell, Erika Donald, Nancy Riddiough, Camera Obscura

Indexer: Ted Laux

CD Technician: Keith McNeil

CD Coordinator: Kara Eve Schwartz

Cover Designer: Jorska Design

Cover Illustrator: Robert Polevoi; Shout Interactive, LLC

Library of Congress Card Number: 00-108242

ISBN: 0-7821-2860-2

Manufactured in the United States of America

10 9 8 7 6 5 4 3 2 1

Software License Agreement: Terms and Conditions

Acknowledgments

The decision to bring cutting-edge technology like Shout3D to a wide audience requires foresight and ambition. The people at Sybex were alert to the opportunity and supportive through every turn in the development of this book. My sincere thanks are due to Cheryl Applewood, who is building an impressive line of computer graphics titles at Sybex, and to Mariann Barsolo, who has guided this project from start to finish. And Nathan Whiteside and Kari Brooks are professionals who made the editorial process smooth and painless.

The folks at Shout Interactive and Eyematic Interfaces provided unstinting support. Jim Stewartson, Dave Westwood, Randall Ho, and especially Paul Isaacs (who performed the technical edit of the manuscript) have made certain that this book properly reflects the achievement that is Shout3D. These individuals are pioneers and leadership figures in the world of 3D computer graphics.

Dino Giannini provided much-valued assistance with his considerable modeling talents and his persistent testing. I can't thank him enough.

Andy King, my editor at internet.com, has supported my efforts to publicize developments in Web 3D on my 3D Animation Workshop Web site. He's a great guy.

And my family—Andrea and Hannah, Mom and Dad—I hope I am giving you what you all are giving me.

Contents at a Glance

Contents

Introduction

Shout3D is something very new and very exciting. It is a way of delivering interactive, animated 3D graphics over the Web, without plugins. The technology is completely transparent to the end-user, who simply watches a 3D window appear in a Web page.

This is no small achievement, and it opens the door to the long-promised emergence of interactive 3D graphics on the Internet. But the significance of Shout3D is actually greater still. The promise and future of 3D computer graphics is in realtime interactivity—whether in games, commercial visualization, education, or a host of other realms. In the past, the 3D artist and the 3D interactive programmer were necessarily different people. Shout3D offers a Java programming interface that is so clear and intelligent that 3D artists—modelers and animators—can learn to design and program the entire interactive experience. This new breed of 3D artist is poised to lead the revolution in 3D graphics heralded by the emergence of extremely powerful microprocessors and graphics hardware on the standard home computer.

This book is an invitation to those in 3D arts, graphics programming, and Web development to put all the pieces together and build the interactive 3D experience from start to finish.

Additions to Shout3D

This book was written during the development of Shout3D 2. Everything in the text is correct for Shout3D 2. However, some important additions to the Shout3D feature set have been added after the book was finished. Make sure that you look over the online documentation that comes with the package to get the complete picture.

Hardware and Software Considerations

Shout3D requires a computer system with a Web browser that supports Java 1.1; Microsoft Internet Explorer or Netscape 4 or above will do the job. You can use a Windows system or a Macintosh.

That said, some practical realities cannot be ignored. 3D models and scenes are best produced for Shout3D in 3D Studio MAX, for which Shout3D offers a custom export tool. 3D Studio MAX is only available for Windows systems. Indeed, most of the major

3D modeling applications are not available for Macintosh. Nor is the free Java Development Kit (JDK) from Sun Microsystems—the easiest way to get started writing Java interactivity for Shout3D—available for Macintosh.

The nature of the Web audience must also be considered. The large majority of end users have Windows systems, and it makes little sense to develop Shout3D content without at least significant access to such systems for testing. For analogous reasons, the developer must have Microsoft Internet Explorer installed (or rather, both IE and Netscape Navigator) to view content as it will be seen by most end users.

You can produce 3D content for use in Shout3D with any 3D package that exports to the VRML format. Users of 3D Studio MAX have a very significant advantage, however, because Shout3D provides a special export utility for this program that provides access to a much greater range of powers than generic VRML export.

A Few Typographical Conventions

Certain conventions in this book will help you work more easily with the content.

The CD icon appears in the margin whenever I reference something on the book's CD.

When an operation requires a series of choices from menus or dialog boxes, the ➜ symbol is used to guide you through the instructions, like this: "Select Programs ➜ Accessories ➜ System Tools ➜ System Information." The items the ➜ symbol separates may be menu items, toolbar icons, check boxes, or other elements of the Windows interface—any place you can make a selection.

`Monospaced` font displays fields, methods, and variables. This font also displays file, folder, and directory names, as well as parameters, which appear inside quotation marks.

Boldface code in code listings lets you know that something has been altered in that code sample.

➥You'll see a continuation arrow like this when a line of code has been broken, and it indicates that the line is continued from the line above it. We break the line of code only to fit within the book's margins. Remember, if you type in a line of code that is shown with an arrow, you should not break the line.

You'll find these types of special notes throughout the book:

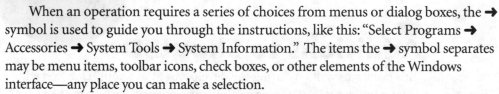

Tips indicate quicker and smarter ways to accomplish a task.

Warnings like this alert you to the potential for trouble and suggest ways to avoid it.

There are also a number of conventions involving capitalization, which are explained below:

Names of true Java classes are capitalized (Shout3DPanel), but when classes are referenced in a general way, they are lowercased (an applet class).

The first word in fields, variables, and methods is lowercased, but subsequent words are capitalized for readability (such as onDeviceInput(), fieldOfView translation).

The word "string" in programming is not generally capitalized. However, in Java a string is implemented using the String class (which, as a true Java class, is capitalized).

For the most part, Shout nodes should be capitalized because they represent Java classes. However, there can be exceptions when I am speaking about the concept implemented in the node. A good example is Light from Chapter 6. The Light node implements a light in a 3D scene. But I sometimes use the word in a way that means "the light being implemented," rather than its node implementation. For example, in the sentence "It doesn't matter how many lights you have in a scene," the main idea is that of a light source, not a Light Java class object.

What's on the CD?

The CD that accompanies this book contains everything you need for Shout3D development other than a 3D modeling package. Those who lack such a package, but who are nonetheless interested in programming interactivity using the Shout3D Java library, can make use of the model files that are provided with the projects on the CD.

The demo version of the most recent Shout3D 2 beta is on the CD and ready for installation on your system. You'll want to go to the Shout Web site at www.shout3d.com where you can download the demo of the final Shout3D 2 release, or you can purchase the full Shout3D 2 software package. Eyematic Interfaces is always upgrading the package, so be sure to check the Shout3D Web site for the most recent version to download.

Any free demo version of Shout3D is complete, but displays a banner across the bottom of the 3D viewing window with the Shout3D logo. If you license your copy for a given Web domain, the banner is removed. A license costs $199 ($79 for educational users). Visit www.shout3d.com for the details.

The CD also contains the latest version of the Java Development Kit for Windows from Sun Microsystems. Once again, this is the same package that is available for free from the Sun Web site. Visit `www.java.sun.com` to make sure that you have the most recent version.

You'll find all of the files for all of the exercises and projects in this book on the CD, organized by chapter. You'll also find a directory of bonus projects not covered in the text. These contain all of the files used in their development, including the original 3D Studio MAX scenes. There's a great deal that can be learned from the bonus projects, so be sure to look them over.

Contacts

You can reach the author at `robert@internet.com`. I also invite you to check in on my 3D Animation Workshop Web site at `www.webreference.com` (or more directly at `www.webreference.com/3d`) for tutorials and general coverage of the 3D world.

For direct contact with the developers of Shout3D, write Paul Isaacs at `pauli@shoutinteractive.com`.

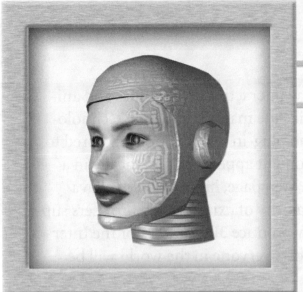

What Is Shout3D?

SHOUT3D

Chapter 1

Shout3D is a way to display interactive 3D graphics and animation on the Web. Unlike the major competing technologies, both old and new, no plug-in application is required to view Shout3D content. Shout content appears automatically in a window directly embedded in a Web page, in the form of a Java applet. As the overwhelming majority of existing Web browsers support Java applets, you can finally produce 3D content for the Internet with the assurance that almost everyone in the world will be able to see it—hassle free.

Shout3D uses 3D models and scenes created in standard 3D graphics and animation packages. Shout3D is based on Virtual Reality Modeling Language (VRML), the long-established standard for 3D graphics on the Web. As most 3D modeling and animation programs have tools to export their contents in the VRML (.wrl) file format, most 3D artists will be able to work with the packages they already know. However, 3D Studio MAX from Discreet is the most common platform for professional 3D work today, and thus Shout3D offers special support for this program. Instead of using the standard VRML export tools in MAX, Shout3D includes a custom export utility that provides access to a number of special features. In the future, Shout3D will include custom exporters for other standard 3D authoring packages; but for the present, MAX users will be able to produce the most impressive content. The Shout exporter permits the MAX user to utilize a remarkable range of MAX's powers in modeling, materials, and animation.

Shout3D is both a delivery mechanism for 3D scenes and a toolset for creating user interactivity. As a pure delivery mechanism, you can use Shout3D without any programming skills at all. An animation produced in MAX or another standard package can simply be run in an embedded window in a Web page.

If you want user interactivity, Shout3D's powers are essentially unlimited. Shout3D comes with generic applets that allow users to examine a 3D object from all directions or to navigate through a 3D scene. Once again, you can use these applets "as is," without any programming. But Shout3D comes alive when you access its remarkable programming toolset. Shout3D was created for the in-house use of Shout Interactive, the world's most outstanding developers of interactive 3D content. The Shout team required a toolset that would allow them to create the most ambitious interactive 3D content imaginable for entertainment, advertising, e-commerce, education, and games. Shout3D provides these tools to Shout Interactive, and now to the rest of us who are ready to embrace the opportunities of realtime interactive 3D on the Web.

Shout3D, This Book, and You

You might be a 3D modeler or animator interested (quite astutely) in bringing your skills to the Web marketplace. You might be a Java programmer thinking about bringing 3D graphics into your skill set. You might be a Web designer or developer, with either graphics or programming skills (or a little of both), interested in the possibilities for interactive 3D on the Internet. People from many different backgrounds will be drawn to Shout3D as the "next step" in multimedia for the Web.

Shout3D sits at the intersection of 3D graphics, Java programming, and Web development. This is frontier territory, as "cutting-edge" as it gets. It will be the extremely rare individual who already owns the range of skills needed to start filling the demand for professional-level interactive 3D Web content. The 3D artist must learn some programming and the concepts of interactive graphics. The programmer will have to learn about 3D graphics—and especially about how they are created in MAX or other standard professional packages. Both of these groups will have to learn at least a little about Internet technologies. The Web professional will have to take a stab at 3D graphics and at Java. And everybody is going to have to learn something about VRML, the ancestor technology on which the Shout edifice has been erected. Just as a marketable automobile is the merger of a range of electronic, mechanical, and design technologies, so is commercial interactive 3D Web graphics an integration of distinct technological threads.

This doesn't mean you have to be everything at once. Indeed, Shout Interactive itself is a team of 3D artists and programmers working together, as is typical of both Web development firms and interactive content firms. Many readers will simply be interested in exploring the possibilities of this technology without intending to implement it (or all of it) themselves. Yet I speak from personal experience when I say that motivated 3D artists who have never had any programming experience can learn Shout3D interactivity. And Java programmers are embracing Shout3D as a vehicle to enter the exciting world of 3D graphics. The skills of Shout3D development are those of a new era in Web graphics and can be expected to command top dollar.

The primary purpose of this book is to introduce interested readers to the nature and powers of Shout3D. Each reader may well be expected to take this knowledge in a different direction suited to his or her talents and inclinations. But success depends on a panoramic view—the big picture that reveals the contribution of all the various elements. In this field, and at the present moment, the perspective of the generalist is every bit as important as that of the graphics or programming specialist.

There is much about creating high-quality 3D content for use in Shout3D that involves little or no programming, but rather only modeling and animation in MAX or other 3D packages. And a great deal of simple interactivity can be worked out using JavaScript (the ubiquitous Web scripting language) or VRML rather than the true Java language. But the greatest value of this book will be for those who wish to learn the Java programming toolset that is Shout's profoundest asset and greatest contribution to the world of computer graphics. In short, this book seeks to provide the base for those who are looking to Shout3D with serious professional and commercial intentions. It is intended to serve those who want to understand where this important technological advancement can take them.

If you are a 3D artist who knows nothing of Java, or even of programming, this book will get you started. If you have programming skills, Java or otherwise, this book will put those skills to work in 3D using 3D resources provided on the accompanying CD. In fact, this book assumes nothing about the reader's background except intelligence and a genuine interest in understanding some amazing technology. Shout3D, like everything in Web 3D and Web development generally, is emerging under our very feet, and the desire to learn new skills is ultimately the only thing that matters in today's world. Once you get rolling, you can quickly determine what other resources you will need to build or strengthen your skill set.

Like Shout3D itself, this book is a brew of 3D graphics and animation, Java, 3D interactive programming concepts, VRML, basic Web technologies, and a few other things. This is a vast landscape that could never be fully addressed within a single cover. But our approach will be highly practical. We will be doing at least as much as we will be talking. We'll be getting our hands dirty and making things happen. When you start seeing results—when you start feeling the intoxicating sense of power and magic that comes from watching 3D graphics operate at your command—don't be surprised if this activity starts to dominate your thoughts and all your available hours.

What Is Shout3D?—A Longer Answer

Shout3D is a new technology for bringing interactive 3D graphics and animation to the Internet. It is, in every sense, revolutionary. Like all things revolutionary, its significance seems to multiply with every step that one takes to understand it and exploit its remarkable powers. It cannot be summed up in a catch phrase, nor can it be understood without direct immersion, for it represents a fundamental advancement in technology, offering limitless opportunities to creative minds. Shout3D is a new window on the Internet.

Let's take it a step at a time.

Shout3D Is Realtime Interactive 3D Graphics

Different readers will have different levels of understanding of the concept of 3D computer graphics. For now, it is enough to say that true 3D computer graphics involves the creation of *models,* which amount to virtual sculptures. These models are arranged in a *scene*, which amounts to a virtual space. The models are illuminated by various means and viewed through a virtual camera. The view seen through this camera is *rendered* into an image, as a sort of virtual photograph.

3D tools can be used to create a single rendered "snapshot" of a scene. But, more often, we make a sequence of rendered images to produce an animation. If a model or the camera moves between each rendering, the result is a sequence of changing frames in exactly the same form as a motion picture or video. By displaying a sequence of rendered images at an adequate speed, the viewer perceives only seamless motion.

You are probably familiar with the use of 3D animation in motion pictures and broadcast television. This type of animation is *pre-rendered*. That is, all the frames in the animation are rendered into images before the animation is used. Displaying the animation is simply a matter of displaying the images in order on motion picture film or videotape. The quality of pre-rendered 3D animation can be extremely high because the creator can use as much rendering time as necessary to generate beautiful images. Each frame in a high-end animation might take minutes (or even hours) to render on powerful computers, capturing subtle details and lighting effects in extremely complex scenes. Once the rendering is complete, the finished images will fly by the viewer at 24 or 30 frames per second on the motion picture or television screen.

Realtime 3D is another creature altogether. In real time 3D, nothing is pre-rendered. Using a computer, the viewer watches the rendering process live. Nothing is stored. The computer renders frames as fast as it can, and each rendered image lives for only a fleeting fraction of a second, only to be thrown away the moment the computer starts rendering the next one.

Why would we use realtime graphics? The first and most important answer is interactivity. A pre-rendered animation is fixed. You can view it, but you cannot affect it. If the viewer is given the power to interact with the 3D scene—moving the camera, moving the models, or whatever—there is no way of knowing in advance what will happen. Thus the 3D scene must render in real time, in direct response to the user's input. The impressive commercial success of the computer- and console-games industry has fueled enormous technological advances in realtime 3D graphics. Games are, by definition, interactive. Yet the opportunities for interactive 3D graphics extend far beyond gaming into areas of commerce and education that are only beginning to be explored.

There is a second reason for using realtime rendering, one that applies even where there will be no user interactivity. We have not yet arrived at the day when streaming video is entirely effective for most users of the Internet. Connection bandwidths are generally far too slim and the vast majority of users lack hardware powerful enough to run video in any case. This will no doubt change, but for the present it will often make more sense to take advantage of realtime rendering of 3D animation. The scene information necessary to render an animation on the user's computer is much smaller than a finished video of rendered images would be, especially for longer pieces.

Rendering 3D scenes is always a trade-off between speed and quality. To provide a sense of fluid motion, realtime rendering must take place at speeds of at least 10 frames per second, and preferably much higher. We've already noted how individual frames of high-end, pre-rendered animation will often take minutes (or at least many seconds) to render on powerful computers. What kind of results can we expect when a frame must render in one-tenth of a second or less?

In the past, the quality of realtime 3D rendering on personal computers was miserable, but the current situation is entirely different. Computer processing speeds have been spurting upward much faster than anyone anticipated. Of course, a word processor doesn't perform much differently on a 700MHz CPU than it did on a 233MHz version. But these improvements in speed have produced a startling difference in the performance of realtime graphics, as have the remarkable advancements in standard graphics cards. The gaming audience knows there may soon be little need for dedicated games consoles. Today's off-the-shelf home PC has the power to support realtime 3D, and tomorrow's version will be even stronger. The entire computer hardware industry is focusing on games and other realtime graphics as a motive for consumer upgrades.

To be sure, realtime 3D today doesn't have the full quality of pre-rendered 3D, but it's already quite good and is catching up very fast. Part of the answer has been, as noted, increased user processing power. Another factor has been remarkable technological advancements in realtime 3D. As you'll see, Shout3D can produce many impressively realistic effects that were unthinkable in realtime 3D in only the recent past. No one doubts that realtime 3D will support the highest desirable production values in the near future.

Shout3D Is Java Technology

This is a huge subject, especially for those readers who are unfamiliar with Java and perhaps with computer programming in general. Take it slowly and give these ideas a chance to sink in.

Java is both a programming language and a technology. It has come to be the most important programming language today, largely because it is purely *object-oriented*. Object-oriented thinking is everywhere in programming today, from Java and C++ at the high end to JavaScript and other simple-to-use scripting languages; but it's next to impossible to explain the meaning of this term to someone who does not already have considerable experience with an object-oriented programming language.

For the present, let's note that object-oriented languages involve the creation of objects (called "classes" in Java) as the basic unit of thought. Technically Shout3D is a library of Java classes to perform all the tasks needed to create and control a 3D scene and its display. There are classes to represent cameras, lights, and the models, and there are classes that provide tools for user interactivity. Learning Shout3D is, at bottom, a matter of becoming familiar with all of the classes in the library, their nature, and their functionality. Shout3D can do what its classes can do. Shout3D can be expanded by the addition of further classes to the library, making it easy to improve the package at any time. The online Application Programmer's Interface (API) documentation—called "Javadocs"—in your Shout3D package is a detailed guide to all of the Shout3D classes. The sooner you start wandering through this treasure chest of powers, the sooner you will come to grasp the full significance of the Shout3D vision.

I cannot stress enough another point about object-oriented languages: If object-oriented programming means anything, it means the power to build right on top of what you already have. To take the most obvious example, the Shout3D library includes a class named Shout3DPanel. This object is nothing less than a true 3D realtime rendering engine that runs in a window on a Web page. Without any knowledge of programming at all, you can use this class to display a 3D animation created in a standard 3D animation application; however, the standard Shout3DPanel does not provide for any user interactivity. If you want to add interactivity—perhaps the power to start and stop the animation by clicking the mouse—you don't have to open up and rework the Shout3DPanel class. You simply create a new class and indicate that the new class is an extension of the Shout3DPanel. The new class can be written only to provide for the interactivity, which may require just a few simple lines of code. Because the new class extends Shout3DPanel, it will automatically have all the powers of that class with the additions you have made. You don't have to understand how the underlying Shout3DPanel class works to add the new features you desire.

I said that Java is both a language and a technology, but what does this mean? If Java were only a programming language, it would be impressive enough. It could be used as most major programming languages are used. Programmers could write their code in the Java language and then compile it into a form suitable to whatever platforms—processor and operating system—they wished. But Java is designed for use in a different way. Java does not run directly in an operating system, but rather in special software called the Java Virtual Machine (JVM). To run a Java program on your computer, you must have a JVM installed, and it must be the one appropriate to your operating system. Any Java program will run on any JVM. That means once you've written and compiled a Java program, you can feel confident it will run on any computer that has a JVM. You never have to worry about different versions for different platforms.

This creates an ideal way of distributing programs over the Web. The Netscape and Microsoft Web browsers have long come equipped with JVMs. Applets are special kinds of small Java programs designed to run inside a Web browser. They are placed on Web servers just like any other kind of file, and when they are downloaded with a Web page, they use the client's JVM to run.

Shout3D content is delivered in applet form. Anyone with a browser that comes with a JVM—nearly everyone out there—will be able to run the applet. There is no need for any additional or plug-in applications; the JVM, already resident on the client's system, does all the work.

This issue is so important that it's worth addressing in a little more detail. All computers with a standard browser will have a Java runtime installation. By this I mean that they will have the JVM that actually runs the Java programs and will also have a standard library of Java classes that the JVM uses. When a user comes across an HTML page with Shout3D content, the server will deliver both the *content* and the *player*. By *content*, I mean a file containing the 3D scene information, and perhaps additional files of images and sounds needed in support of the scene. The concept of the *player* takes some getting used to. You might at first think of the player as an identifiable viewing application, like Windows Media Player or even a Web browser. But this is Java, so you have to learn to think more creatively.

To deliver the player, the server will simply download a set of Shout3D Java classes. Most of these will be the standard ones that come with Shout, but may include some you've built yourself—such as where you've added interactivity by extending a Shout3DPanel class. Between the Shout Java classes that are downloaded from the server and the standard Java classes that are already on the client's system as part of the standard Java installation, the JVM is able to build the desired application as a window in the browser screen.

The standard Shout classes that are always downloaded amount to a little more than 100KB. At first glance it would seem impossible that a realtime 3D rendering engine can be built out of so little. But that's the beauty of Java technology. This 100KB of downloaded material leverages the large Java class library that already exists on the user's system to build the application. This is why powerful applets can be created by delivering only small amounts of code. A huge Java resource base is already resident on the client's system, waiting to be put to work.

Shout3D Is Founded on VRML

The VRML (generally pronounced "vermil") is an international standard for delivering interactive 3D graphics on the Web. It was the product of visionary minds that plotted a 3D experience for Web users long before it was a practical possibility. The VRML movement (and it was definitely a movement) attracted a wide range of creative and committed people, and the current situation in Web 3D cannot be understood without a little VRML background.

VRML, like Java, is both a language and a technology. The word "language" is a bit too strong, as VRML is nothing like a true programming language. Rather, VRML is a kind of file format. It is in regular ASCII text, so it's entirely readable by regular human beings and editable in any word processor. This text, or code, describes a 3D scene. It defines every detail about every model in the scene, the relationship between the models, the location and nature of lights and cameras, and the animation of the models, lights, and camera. So VRML might properly be called a "3D scene description language."

VRML as a technology is best understood as a specification. The VRML specification document describes everything an application must be able to do in order to display an interactive 3D scene. A VRML viewer (sometimes called a player or a browser) is a program that displays VRML content. It reads VRML files and generates the scene described in the file on the viewer screen. Thus, the complete VRML specification describes all the powers required of a VRML viewer program and defines the scene description language the program must read and process. Any VRML viewer application that is completely compliant with the specification can display any VRML files that are written in a form that is also compliant with the specification.

As a practical matter, the VRML initiative fell almost entirely into the hands of a single company, Silicon Graphics Inc. (currently known only as SGI). SGI got VRML started by offering the use of its Open Inventor file format as the basis for the VRML language. From that point forward, SGI, through its Cosmo Software division, took the lead in developing a VRML viewer (Cosmo Player) for free distribution and powerful VRML authoring tools (Cosmo Worlds) for content developers. In the summer of 1998, SGI was struggling with financial crises related to its primary business of computer hardware manufacturing and decided to dispose of Cosmo Software and its entire VRML-related enterprise. This abandonment was effectively fatal to the VRML movement, and although the surviving VRML community continues to pursue initiatives through its Web 3D Consortium, VRML no longer defines the direction of developments in 3D graphics for the Internet.

Some important consequences of the VRML era are still with us, however. One of the most significant is the fact that most 3D graphics and animation packages have some vehicle for exporting content in the VRML file format (.wrl). This means that 3D artists generally have readily available means for producing VRML content. A closely related issue is the sheer number of people with significant exposure to VRML and its concepts. There is a lot of knowledge and experience out there that can and should be leveraged on the subject of interactive 3D for the Web. VRML, especially in its second manifestation (VRML 2, or VRML 97), embodied some very sophisticated principles of general applicability. And, of course, there is a lot of legacy VRML content out there on which to build.

While many of today's new initiatives in Web 3D are completely unconnected to VRML, Shout3D is an evolutionary step that maintains deep roots in VRML. It builds from VRML, yet has made critical improvements. From one perspective, Shout3D can be considered just an improved type of VRML viewer. VRML (.wrl) files generated from standard 3D packages can be played in a Shout3D applet. Thus we have VRML without the need for the large plug-in applications (such as Cosmo Player) that were once needed to view VRML content. VRML content now runs automatically in a Web browser.

But Shout3D departs from the present VRML specification in important ways. For one, Shout3D does not support all the features required by the VRML specification. Some of these features were considered unnecessary, especially in light of the additional download size they add to the Shout3D player component. When a working VRML file fails to run in Shout3D, the reason is almost always that it includes some VRML element that was not continued in Shout.

On the other hand, Shout3D provides a large range of critical features that are not found in VRML. In most cases, these have been added to support demand for features not supported by the original VRML specification. 3D Studio MAX users who could not export some of MAX's higher quality models often fueled this demand. But many of these new features can be used apart from MAX; for example, Shout provides VRML-like nodes for panoramic environments and progressive anti-aliasing. Shout's .s3d format is an extended VRML file format. It maintains the structure of a VRML file but may contain Shout-only elements.

Perhaps the most significant departure from VRML was a different view on how to best author for user interactivity. VRML attempted to provide for all kinds of user interactivity as standard features of the language. Yet for truly commercial projects, these standard features were insufficient and VRML developers were forced to rely on additional programming of their own, layered on top of the viewer application. From long experience with developing high-end interactive content, Shout Interactive decided to create a clear and more workable division between the 3D scene information and the programming code for interactivity. In Shout3D, user interactivity can be handled completely and independently in Java (or JavaScript), leaving the .wrl (or .s3d) file to contain only the 3D scene information. Not only is this approach much easier to understand than mixing scene and interactivity information in the VRML file, it allows for the direct utilization of the full powers of the Java language for interactivity.

However, Shout3D did not completely cut the cord with VRML's standard interactivity features. Some of these have been preserved, including (for those familiar with them) the Touch Sensor and the concept of Routes. This enables developers already familiar with these basic features to continue to use them with Shout, and it allows more legacy VRML content to run in the Shout3D applet. This practical compromise with the past and present gives Shout3D some important strengths. In fact, the more advanced Shout developer can return to the VRML approach by creating custom nodes. This important technique uses Java programming to develop tools and complex effects that can be added to a scene simply by typing their names into the scene file.

VRML is the mother of Shout, providing it with a tested framework and a host of practical advantages. Yet Shout is evolving quickly to meet the expectations of a new audience and will undoubtedly distance itself more and more from its VRML origins. This is an organic process in the native sense of the term—rooted in the past but quick to adjust to a rapidly changing environment. For the near future, a Shout3D developer must have a sound, basic understanding of VRML and how to edit VRML files where necessary. This will be especially true for those who cannot use Shout's MAX exporter, for most VRML export utilities have personality quirks. This is no mere burden, because it is almost impossible to understand the basic concepts of a 3D scene without hands-on exposure to VRML files. We will have many opportunities in this book to look at VRML files and understand how they are used to create a scene graph in Shout3D.

Shout3D Is Cheap

Shout3D is a remarkable bargain. The entire package can be downloaded and used on a "demo" basis for free. The free version comes with a logo strip that obscures part of the applet window with the Shout logo and a link to the Shout3D Web site. When you are ready to post Shout content on the Internet, the cost is only $199 ($79 for educational users) for a license code that removes the logo strip. The fee applies to all uses on the same Web domain, so you can have as much Shout content as you want on any one site for $199. (You can even put your content on the Web for free if you don't mind the logo strip!)

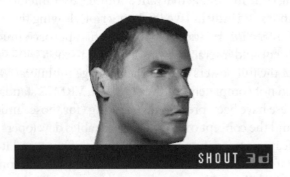

Shout3D Is Important

3D computer graphics is a field that continues to expand so rapidly that even those involved in it on a full-time basis cannot hope to keep abreast of every new idea and development. Realtime interactive 3D is approximately in the state that "traditional" 3D graphics found itself a decade ago—only beginning to gel behind standards. Realtime interactive 3D for the Web is quite literally in its birth throes. Competing technologies are emerging from every direction, and it's far too early to pretend to predict the success of any one, or even the general impact that 3D may be expected to have on the Internet. In this climate, one might reasonably be expected to question which specific technologies to explore or embrace.

Shout3D differs from its competitors in fundamental ways. Of course, the ability to deliver 3D content on the Web without the need for user plug-in applications is an extraordinary advantage. For a great many developers and sites, user plug-ins are simply not an acceptable option, and the Shout approach will be the only realistic alternative.

Moreover, Shout is Java. That means the full and unlimited power of Java programming can be brought to the process of developing Shout content. Shout is no mere proprietary solution to the question of delivering 3D graphics on the Web. It is a pure merger of 3D graphics and Java, two of the most important currents in contemporary technology. Indeed, many people will agree that the Shout3D applet is the most important application of Java technology on the Internet they have ever seen. It surely will fuel many impressive developments in the use of Java applets for interactive Web graphics and interfaces. Immersion in Shout means immersion in Java, a profitable use of one's time that can be turned in many exciting directions, both on and off the Internet.

Yet for those of us who love 3D computer graphics, there is perhaps an even more significant element. The world of 3D graphics has always been divided between programmers and artists. Neither has been in much of a position to understand the other. Shout3D has created a programming toolset that is fully within the reach of the intelligent and motivated artist. We are entering a new era of interactive art and design, one that will reward those who can think in terms of both graphics and programming. The new 3D artist will be able to conceive and execute the entire interactive experience. Shout3D fashions the tools of interactive programming in a form that is elegant, coherent, and rich. Exposure to these tools will reshape the mental framework of 3D practitioners, broadening their horizons into new regions of creativity. In this regard, Shout3D may be the most important development in computer graphics in many years.

This book is designed to introduce you to new vistas and lead you down the trail far enough to begin your own profitable explorations. It will be fun, exciting, and challenging.

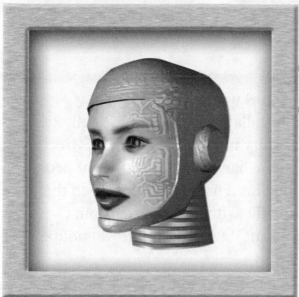

Your Shout3D
Installation

SHOUT3D

Chapter 2

Working with Shout3D begins with learning your way around your Shout3D installation. When you install Shout3D, you get a directory named Shout3d_2.0, which is divided into subdirectories. If you're like the vast majority of people, you'll wander through it looking for a program to load—in the case of Windows users, it will be the file with an .exe extension. You'll find one in the form of the Shout3DWizard, but it will not be quite what you expect.

Shout3D is a toolset, not a program like 3D Studio MAX. With the minor exception of the Shout3DWizard, you will not be working through the interface of a standard authoring application, nor are all of your tools in the Shout3D installation. For those who will be programming custom interactivity in Java, the Java Development Kit (JDK) or another Java development environment will be just as important as your Shout3D installation. But the tools that are unique to Shout3D are obviously only in the Shout3D installation. In this chapter, we'll get oriented in the Shout3D installation and get a strong sense of how all the pieces fit together.

View from the Top

I'll assume you've unzipped your Shout3D installation as instructed in the README file that comes with the package. This does nothing more than create a Shout3d_2.0 directory, with files and subdirectories. No application has been installed in the conventional sense.

Stop reading right here and start poking around through these directories. It's not a matter of pretending to learn where everything is—which is impossible to do in a short time—but rather of taking the first steps toward intuitive navigation through the directories and subdirectories. It takes practice, so get started as soon as possible. The process is analogous to learning the graphical interface of a standard application.

After you've spent some time wandering about and getting the lay of the land, consider some general observations. The installation is divided into four directories. The 3DStudioMax_plugin directory contains the MAX exporter utility. If you have MAX, you simply copy the plug-in file in this folder into your MAX standard plug-ins directory, and the utility becomes an element of MAX. Other than to consult the MAX exporter documentation, you'll never have cause to visit this directory again.

Thus the working Shout3D installation consists of three directories:

docs

Shout3d_runtime

Shout3d_wizard

The docs directory contains the documentation, including a QuickStart tutorial, a User's Guide, the much more technical Shout3D Specification, and the Shout online Javadocs documentation. These are all in HTML form for easy reference and cross-referencing. The index.html file in the top-level directory of your Shout3D installation contains clear and handy links to all sections of the documentation. You may want to drag an index.html file shortcut onto your desktop so you can quickly access any part of the Shout3D documentation. The Shout3d_wizard folder provides access to the Shout3D-Wizard, a simple Java application to help you prepare and publish Shout3D applets that we will consider later in this chapter.

The Shout3d_runtime directory is where all the action is, and you'll need to understand it rather well. Let's jump right in.

The Runtime Directory

If you work in Shout, you come to live in the Shout3d_runtime directory. When we speak of a *runtime*, we refer to the software environment that is used to run an application. Thus the Java Virtual Machine that is included in the standard Web browsers is often called the "Java runtime." The Shout runtime contains the files that create a Shout applet within the Java runtime. This is true whether the applet is being viewed from your local drive or over the Internet. In fact, to deliver Shout content over the Internet, you simply copy selected contents of the runtime directory to the server.

The runtime directory is divided into codebase and demos folders. The demos directory contains only HMTL files with <APPLET> tags in them. Everything needed to create and support these applets is in the codebase directory. Thus the codebase directory contains all of the Java classes that these applets may require, the model files describing the 3D scenes used by the applets, and additional resources such as bitmap images and audio files. The codebase directory contains everything you'll need during the development process, and you'll be adding to it as you work. When you publish on the Web, you copy a stripped-down version of this codebase directory to the server. This copy will have the same subdirectory structure, but it need contain only the specific model files and resources required by the particular applet being published.

Instead of a demos directory, you upload only the specific HTML file you need. The <APPLET> tag in that file has a CODEBASE attribute that indicates the location of the codebase directory on the server. In the same way, the <APPLET> tags in the HTML files in your local demos folder point to the location of the codebase directory in your local Shout installation.

For example, look at the <APPLET> tag from modswing.html in the demos directory.

```
<APPLET CODEBASE="../codebase" CODE="shout3d/Shout3DApplet.class"
➥ARCHIVE="shout3dClasses.zip" WIDTH=320 HEIGHT=240>
<param name="src" value="models/modswing.s3d">
<param name="background"
➥value="images/shared/wooden_stage_bg.jpg">
</APPLET>
```

The CODEBASE attribute points to the codebase directory in the Shout installation. The HTML file is in a sibling directory to codebase, so the path leads from demos, up to Shout3d_runtime (the parent directory), and back down to codebase. The path "../codebase" indicates a route passing through the parent of the current directory.

There's no requirement that the directory referenced in the CODEBASE attribute be named codebase. *You can call it whatever you want (e.g.,* mycodebase, shout_codebase) *when you upload to a Web server.*

Applets and Other Java Classes

Let's continue with this <APPLET> tag to understand the codebase directory more completely. The CODEBASE attribute references the directory that contains all of the Java classes that may be required by the applet. The CODE attribute points to the location of the Java class file that constitutes the specific applet. This applet class will be found in one of two locations. The basic Shout3DApplet is in the Shout3d folder of the codebase directory. Look in that folder to confirm this for yourself. Note that once codebase is established as the CODEBASE directory, all of the files referenced in the <APPLET> tag are specified relative to codebase. The sole exception to this is the value of the "background" parameter. If a value is provided for this parameter, it will always be a file that is referenced like all other textures in Shout3D—relative to the directory in which the model file (i.e., the value of the src [source] parameter) is located.

All other applets, including those you develop yourself, are stored in the `applets` folder. For example, `onePyramid.html` in your `demos` folder makes use of the ExamineApplet to permit the user to rotate the camera.

```
<APPLET CODEBASE="../codebase" CODE="applets/ExamineApplet.class"
➥ARCHIVE="shout3dClasses.zip" WIDTH=320 HEIGHT=240>
<param name="src" value="models/onePyramid.s3d">
<param name="headlightOn" value="true">
</APPLET>
```

This is good time to look over the `applets` directory. Observe that there is a matching panel for each applet, and that there is a .class and .java version of each. The .java version is the source code written by the developer. Open one of these files in a text editor to see what Java code looks like. These text files are compiled to produce the .class files that are actually used by the Java Virtual Machine.

The applet class file referenced in the `CODE` attribute of the `<APPLET>` tag is the primary Java class file. Think of it as the class that marshals all the other classes it needs. Many of these classes are in the standard Java installation that will be found on any system that has a Java-enabled Web browser, but others must be found in the Shout3D class library. Poke around in the `Shout3d` folder in the `codebase` directory to get a sense of this library. Notice that there are no .java files within the `Shout3d` folder, only .class files. This is because Shout3D does not include the source code for the Shout3D runtime library. Java files are only provided for those classes that serve as demos and examples for Shout3D developers.

Different Shout3D applets will require different subsets of the Shout3D class library. This could mean that the applet makes a separate trip to the server to download each class it needs—an unpleasantly time-consuming process. To speed things up, a representative collection of classes that are used by most applets is packaged in a .zip file and is referenced in the `ARCHIVE` attribute of the `<APPLET>` tag.

You'll find more Java classes in the `custom_nodes` directory. These are extensions to the Shout3D library. There are a handful of examples in this folder, and we'll add to these in the course of this book. The power to create custom nodes to extend the powers of Shout3D is one of the most impressive features of this technology, and one that reflects a basic strength of Java.

Model Files and Resources

Thus far, we've been looking at Java classes in the `codebase` directory. The rest of the directory is devoted to resources—images, audio files and, above all, the 3D scene files.

These are all in the models directory. Wander through this folder to get the idea. You'll find scene files in .wrl, .s3d, and the compressed .s3z formats, either in the main directory or in subdirectories organized for specific projects. You'll find bitmap images in JPEG and GIF format. And you'll find a few audio files in the .au format, the only format available to Java applets.

The android subdirectory is illustrative. It contains two scene files in .s3d format. android.s3d is a textured model of a spacegirl's head, created in 3D Studio MAX and exported using the Shout3D plug-in. Open this file in a text editor, like WordPad, and get a sense of the VRML-like structure. It's essentially a VRML file with some additional nodes that are unique to Shout3D. Take some time to see if you can figure out what's going on, because learning to read scene files is a basic and essential skill. You'll see that the scene is divided into a number of objects (head, eyes, ears) in separate Transform nodes. Note how materials and textures are applied to each piece of geometry and how, in the case of the head, the mesh can support multiple materials and textures (for face, mouth, etc.). This is how Shout3D implements the Multi-SubObject material definition in 3D Studio MAX. The appearanceIndex, which you can find within the head Transform, assigns different appearances to different polygons of the head. Note also how you can map many different material parameters at once, including diffuse color, specularity, bump, and opacity, for very sophisticated effects.

Look over the list of JPEG bitmaps in the android folder. These are the images listed in the various texture fields in the scene file. Look for some of these in the .s3d file and note how they are described. In each case, they are named without a directory, for example, as android_neck.jpg. This is because they are located in the same directory as the scene file. If they were not, the field must state the complete path to the image, relative to the location of the scene file.

When working in MAX, it's unlikely that you will be using bitmaps that are already located in the intended directories within the Shout3D installation. You'll generally need to copy the images precisely where you want them to reside after export to Shout3D. You may also need to hand edit the scene file to make sure that it indicates the proper path to these image files.

The other scene file in this directory is an animated version of the same model, using MAX's morphing tools. Look at this file in a text editor and notice the addition of the morphing and interpolation nodes.

Now that you've paid your dues, go to the demos directory and run the HMTL files in the android subdirectory there. Make sure that you look at the source code for these HTML files, either through your browser or by opening the files in a text editor. You'll see how these files reference the appropriate scene files in the src (source) attribute.

Other Codebase Directories

The javax and shout directories contain Java classes required by the Shout3DWizard. You'll never be using them directly, so ignore them.

The interactiveRenderDemo directory contains classes required by for the Interactive Render Demo in the demos directory. Once again, you won't need anything in here for your own work.

The Demos

The demos directory is the sibling of codebase within the runtime directory. Anyone with a serious interest in learning to develop Shout content should spend a great deal of time exploring the examples found here. Look at a demo and then open the associated scene file in a text editor to try and understand what's happening. As you learn Shout3D, you'll want to study the applet and panel classes used in these demos. The source code is found in the applets directory.

You'll find two Web pages in the docs directory named demos.html and newIn2.0.html that review the demo projects in a general way.

Publishing on the Web

Publishing Shout3D content on the Internet is a matter of getting the appropriate files, in the correct directory structure, uploaded to a Web server. We'll first try it "by hand," and then we'll see how the Shout3DWizard can automate and improve the process.

Preparing Files for the Server

Rather than waste time with an abstract explanation, let's prepare the android project for posting on the Internet. We'll need the android.html file, currently located in the demos/android folder. Before you upload it, you have to consider where the codebase directory will be located on the server, and make sure that the CODEBASE attribute in the <APPLET> tag reflects the proper path from whatever directory the HTML file is in.

For example, assume that you place both the android.html and the codebase directory in the same directory on the server (whether the root directory or some subdirectory). The attribute should read:

```
CODEBASE="codebase"
```

If the codebase directory will be placed in a directory that is a sibling to the directory in which the HTML file will be placed, the proper path is:

```
CODEBASE="../codebase"
```

If the HTML file will be placed within the codebase directory itself, the attribute must indicate that you are currently in the codebase, like so:

```
CODEBASE="."
```

In short, you must indicate how to get to the codebase directory on the server from the directory in which you place the HTML file.

Let's turn to the codebase directory itself. We will only need those files in the codebase directory that are actually used by the android project, but they must by kept in their proper subdirectories. The easiest way to do this is to copy a complete version of the directory to another location on your system and delete unnecessary files. It doesn't hurt anything to have unneeded files, but let's do it right.

Start by deleting the Shout3DWizard and vrml2tos3d application files from your copy of codebase. These files are obviously not needed to display the applet. Leave the shout3dClasses.zip archive where it is.

Open android.html in a text editor and consult the <CODE> element. This project uses the ExamineApplet, so delete all of the files from the Applets folder except ExamineApplet.class and ExaminePanel.class. Next, open the scene file, android.s3d, in a text editor and review it to see if there are any custom nodes. You probably can't do this at your current state of knowledge, but if you had created the scene yourself you would definitely know whether you had used any custom nodes. The scene doesn't use any custom nodes, so you can delete the entire Custom_Nodes folder from the copy of the codebase directory.

The models directory is easy. Delete everything except the android folder. You can delete morph_android.s3d from this folder, because we are using only the nonanimated android.s3d. If you wish to eliminate the android subdirectory and move all its contents directly into the models directory, you'll have to change the src attribute in the <APPLET> tag in the HTML file from:

```
<param name="src" value="models/android/android.s3d">
```

to:

```
<param name="src" value="models/android.s3d">
```

You can delete the javax and shout directories entirely. That leaves only the Shout3d folder, which contains the Shout3D class library. The safest approach is to leave this library complete, especially if there is a possibility that you will be adding other projects to this codebase later. But you may also choose to eliminate elements of the class library that you are certain not to need. This saves the hassle of uploading these files to the server, but users will never download any unnecessary classes, so there's no performance penalty for uploading the whole class library. We can safely delete the Hanim and Sound folders, as this project makes no use of these classes. Make sure to leave all of the classes that are directly in the shout3d directory (as opposed to in its subdirectories).

At this point, you should have a copy of the codebase directory with the following elements:

The archive named shout3dClasses.zip.

An applets folder containing the ExamineApplet and ExaminePanel classes.

A models folder that contains only the android folder or the files from the android folder.

The Shout3d folder, with or without the sound and hanim subdirectories.

To see if this setup works, copy the android.html demo directly into your copy of the codebase directory. Open this file in a text editor and set the CODEBASE attribute to indicate that the codebase directory is the current directory—the one that the HTML file is already in.

CODEBASE="."

Make sure that your src parameter uses the correct path to the .s3d file—either models/android.s3d or models/android/android.s3d, depending on whether you have retained the android subdirectory within the models directory. Load android.html in a Web browser to make sure everything is working. If it's not, check your Java Console for error messages. It will often be obvious from these messages that you have failed to type a file name correctly or are using an incorrect path. The Java Console is an absolutely essential tool, and can be found through your browser menu bar. If you don't find it under View in Internet Explorer, add it though Tools ➜ Internet Options ➜ Advanced.

I've included a copy of the codebase directory we've just constructed on the CD for your reference.

If the scene appears and is working properly, you can be certain that it will perform the same way if all of the files and directories are uploaded to the Web server. The only thing you may wish to change, depending on how you like to structure directories on the server, is to move the HTML file out of the codebase directory. If you do, make sure the CODEBASE element in the <APPLET> tag reflects the correct path from the HTML file to the codebase directory, as discussed earlier.

Go ahead and upload the codebase directory to your Web server. Hopefully, your FTP utility allows you to upload entire directory structures. If it doesn't, you'll be stuck having to create all of the directories and subdirectories on the server by hand, and upload files to each of them separately.

If you are uploading to a Unix server, you may encounter problems if you don't make certain that the permissions of all these new files and directories are set to allow all users to access them.

Now try loading `android.html` from your server into a Web browser. If the code-base directory was properly installed and the HTML file correctly points to that code-base, things should look the same as they did when you loaded from your local drive. If not, check the Java Console. Almost certainly, you failed to upload all the necessary files in their proper directories.

Make sure you always test your content in both Microsoft and Netscape browsers, using as many different versions and platforms as possible.

Using the Shout3DWizard

The Shout3DWizard plays two roles. First, you can use it to preview .wrl or .s3d files without having to write or edit an HTML file to hold the applet. The Wizard's preview tool creates an HTML file for you. This is a simple convenience but not a critical one, as it is easy to edit an existing HTML file from the demos directory in a text editor for this purpose.

The more important function of the Wizard is in packaging your project files for publishing on the Web. In this regard, the Wizard performs many of the steps that we performed "by hand" in the previous section. But the Wizard can also perform optimization functions that reduce unnecessary download time. At a minimum, it will compress your .wrl or .s3d scene file into a zipped .s3z version. You'll often be surprised how greatly this step reduces file size. But the Wizard can also, optionally, be used to create a custom .zip archive that contains only the precise Java classes required by your project. We will see how this works as we go along.

Launching the Shout3DWizard

The Shout3DWizard is a Java application. Windows users can launch it from a small application, Shout3DWizard.exe, in the Shout3d_wizard directory.

The Windows executable is not the Wizard application, but just a means of launching it. Being a Java application, it must be run within the Java virtual machine. Its supporting Java classes are found in the javax and shout folders within the codebase directory. You will never have occasion to use these classes directly, but you may wish to poke around in these two directories to get the idea.

The Shout3DWizard should start correctly from the executable, but some systems may have problems. On those systems, you'll need to load the application directly from a Java command line, assuming (as it's fair to assume) that you've installed the Java Development Kit (JDK). (Installation of the JDK is covered in Chapter 6.) To load the Wizard in this way, open a Command prompt panel and cd (change directories) such that the current directory is:

```
shout3d_2.0\shout3d_runtime\codebase
```

The file Shout3DWizard.class is located in shout\tools\wizard\. Thus, the command (from within the codebase directory) to run the application is:

```
java shout.tools.wizard.Shout3DWizard
```

Type this command exactly as written (it's case sensitive) and press Enter. The Wizard will launch.

Regardless of how you launch the Wizard, a small panel will appear.

Setting Applet Parameters

Once the Wizard is loaded, use the File option on the menu bar to load a scene file, whether .wrl or .s3d. By default, the file selection dialog opens in the models directory.

Open the android folder here and select android.s3d. The title bar should now indicate that this file has been loaded.

Click the Publishing Options button to roll out the full panel. The panel is not resizable, so you'll have to scroll to see all the options.

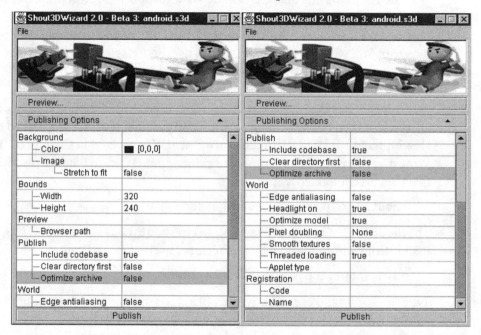

Take a good look at your choices; they divide into three categories. Preview ➜ Browser path applies only to previewing, and you'll rarely need to consider it. It allows you to set a path to a specific Web browser for previewing. By default, you'll be previewing through your default Web browser. If it's not working, or if you want to preview in a different browser, you can set the path to the browser application here. Just click the empty box to the right of the words "Browser path" and use the resulting file dialog to select your browser.

The entries under Publish relate to packaging your projects for uploading to a Web server. We'll consider these in a moment.

All of the other choices set attributes or parameters for your applets. It's important to understand that these choices simply write text in the <APPLET> tag in the HTML file produced by the Wizard, and that the result is no different than if you edit this tag in a text editor. But the Wizard provides the convenience of alerting you to all of your alternatives.

All of the applet parameters are described in the online User's Guide in your Shout3D installation (Part 3: Publishing Shout3D Content with the Shout3DWizard). This is a handy and complete reference on this subject.

You'll start with the choice of applet. Click in the empty box to the right of Applet type. A file selection dialog box will open in the applets directory. Although it doesn't tell you, the default applet type is the basic Shout3DApplet, which has no interactivity features. To find this class explicitly (as you will sometimes need to do) move up to the codebase directory and down into the shout3d directory. Load the file named Shout3DApplet.class. This is just for practice, so open the dialog again and get back into the applets folder.

The applets folder contains all of the applets that are extended from the basic Shout3DApplet and therefore have more features, typically involving user interactivity. Most of the applets here have been written for use in specific projects and can't be used with just any scene file. If you develop your own applets, you'll add them to this directory and they will, more likely than not, be coupled with specific scenes or with scenes containing some specific elements. However, there are a few applets that are intended for general use with a wide variety of scenes. The WalkApplet provides "walk-through" navigation in a scene, and is well demonstrated in the walk_demo.html file in the demos directory. It has a number of special parameters to customize it that are discussed in the online Shout3D User's Guide (Part 7: Features of the Bundled Applets).

Even more important is the ExamineApplet, also discussed in the User's Guide. This applet allows the user to view a scene from any angle and to zoom in and out, using the mouse and keyboard. The applet was designed to automatically adapt to objects of any size; therefore, you can always put a scene into an ExamineApplet without worrying about camera placement. If you do include a camera in your scene, the ExamineApplet will keep your specified direction of view but will relocate the camera so that the initial view contains the entire scene within the applet's boundaries.

Choose the file named ExamineApplet.class as your applet type. Be sure not to choose the file named simply ExamineApplet or ExamineApplet.java, as this is the source code for the applet, not the compiled version. And don't use either of the corresponding ExaminePanel files.

Next, scroll to the top of the panel and consider your applet dimensions. If you would like to try dimensions other than the default of 320×240 pixels, enter some other values.

Click the Preview button. It may take a moment, but a Web browser window will open and the applet will load.

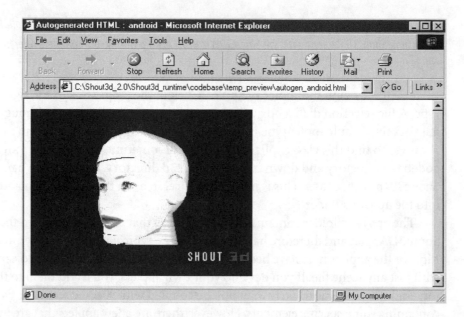

The lighting is a bit rude, but we'll correct it shortly. First, note the address of the file in the browser. The Wizard has created a Temp_preview folder in the codebase directory. Find that folder and open autogen_android.html in a text editor. You'll find the following HTML code:

```
<HTML>
<HEAD>
<TITLE>Autogenerated HTML : android</TITLE>
</HEAD>
<BODY>
<APPLET CODEBASE="../" CODE="applets/ExamineApplet.class"
➥ARCHIVE="shout3dClasses.zip" WIDTH=320 HEIGHT=240>
<param name="src" value="temp_preview/android/android.s3z">
<param name="headlightOn" value="true">
<param name="backgroundColorR" value="0.0">
<param name="backgroundColorG" value="0.0">
<param name="backgroundColorB" value="0.0">
<param name="regcode" value="">
<param name="regname" value="">
<param name="antiAliasingEnabled" value="false">
<param name="bilinearFiltering" value="false">
<param name="loadResourcesInSeparateThread" value="true">
```

```
</APPLET>
</BODY>
</HTML>
```

Note how the applet type and dimensions set in the Wizard have been used in the attributes of the <APPLET> tag. These attributes are common to all Java applets. Beneath them is a list of parameters that are unique to the Shout3DApplet class, and therefore to all applets derived from it, such as the ExamineApplet. The src parameter is essential because it indicates the scene file to be used by the applet. All of the other parameters are optional. If they are not provided, the applet will use default values. We can change these values by editing the text and saving the file, but let's adjust them using the Wizard.

The most important parameter (after src) is headlightOn. If the scene has no lights in it, you need to add a headlight. This is a light pointing in the same direction as the camera. The android scene already has lighting in it, so the headlight is unnecessary. Use the drop-down list in the Wizard to change this parameter to false. Preview it again. It should look much better.

When the lighting in a scene is all wrong, or nonexistent, make sure you check your headlight parameter.

3D scenes can look terrible against a black background. Click the small color sample to the right of the Color label to get a color picker tool. Select a light background color and preview again. Much better!

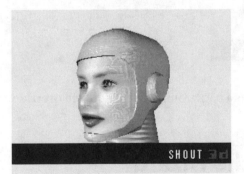

The moment we lighten up the background, the edges of the object are revealed as jagged. Return to the Wizard and set Edge antialiasing to true. Preview it again to see the improvement. This kind of antialiasing is rather crude, but operates quickly enough to work in real time. Thus you can rotate the object and its remains constantly antialiased. Shout3D offers a much higher quality antialiasing feature, called Still Camera Progressive Antialiasing, which must be added to the scene file and is not available as an applet parameter. While this other method produces higher-quality images, it doesn't operate while the camera is moving. We'll try it out later in the book.

Experiment with the other parameters, and consult the User's Guide for more information on this subject. Take the time to open the HTML file in a text editor to see how the parameter changes are reflected. Pixel doubling can be a very useful feature. The render is built from one-quarter as many pixels, but each pixel is multiplied into a 2×2 square to restore the original panel size. The result is a cruder image running at a better frame rate, which may be useful for games or other highly interactive projects.

To test it out, get your applet previewing, click inside the image space, and press the 'f' key on your keyboard to display the current frame rate. Rotate the camera to see how the frame rate changes and to get a sense of the average rate. Now use the Wizard to set Pixel doubling to "regular." Preview it again. The new version will be much blurrier, but will evidence a considerably faster frame rate (especially on a very old system like the one used for the following screenshot). The "smooth" option blends pixel values for a visually superior, although somewhat slower, result.

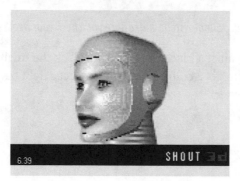

Note that you can use an image as a background, and that it will override any selected color.

Publishing with the Wizard

We tried publishing "by hand" earlier in this chapter to make sure we understand what's necessary to get Shout3D content on the Web. As a practical matter, it makes more sense to use the Shout3DWizard for this task because it saves time and provides important optimizations that speed user downloads.

Basic Publishing

Let's continue with the android project currently in the Wizard. Set your parameters the way you want and preview to confirm that everything is OK. Now it's time to publish.

When you publish from the Wizard, all of the necessary files and directories will be placed in a published directory in your Shout3D installation. Consider the publishing choices in the Wizard panel. First you must decide whether to include the codebase. The codebase is obviously necessary to run your content, and the default is true. You would set it to false only if you already had a complete codebase installed on the server from a previous project and wished only to add new content files.

You can also choose to clear the published directory of any current contents before publishing new contents. The default setting of false allows you to add multiple projects to the same published directory, consolidating multiple pieces of content for posting to the Web server.

There are two elements to the optimization process—optimizing the scene file and optimizing the archive. We'll consider the second option later, so make sure that Optimize archive is set to false for the time being. By default, Optimize model is set to true. This option will covert your .wrl or .s3d scene file to a compressed .s3z format.

Let's give it a try. Click the Publish button at the bottom of the Wizard panel. After a little while, a published directory will appear in your Shout3D installation. Open this directory to review the contents. You should find:

A complete copy of the shout3d directory containing the entire Shout3D class library.

An android directory containing android.s3z and all necessary image files.

A complete copy of the applets directory.

The standard archive of classes in shout3DClasses.zip.

An HTML file, autogen_android.html.

The first thing to do is open the HTML file in a Web browser and confirm that everything is working. Once you've done that, open the HTML file in a text editor. Typically, you won't be uploading this file to the server, but rather copying its <APPLET> tag into some larger HTML page. Take a look at the <APPLET> tag:

```
<APPLET CODEBASE="." CODE="applets/ExamineApplet.class"
➥ARCHIVE="shout3dClasses.zip" WIDTH=320 HEIGHT=240>
```

```
<param name="src" value="android/android.s3z">
<param name="headlightOn" value="false">
<param name="backgroundColorR" value="0.85490197">
<param name="backgroundColorG" value="0.827451">
<param name="backgroundColorB" value="0.8392157">
<param name="regcode" value="">
<param name="regname" value="">
<param name="antiAliasingEnabled" value="false">
<param name="bilinearFiltering" value="false">
<param name="loadResourcesInSeparateThread" value="true">
</APPLET>
```

Note first that the CODEBASE attribute is set to the current directory. This makes sense because the published directory is, in effect, the codebase directory, containing a stripped-down version of the codebase directory in your Shout3D installation. That means that the HTML file is within the codebase directory. By contrast, the HTML files in your Shout3D installation are typically found in the demos directory, which is a sibling to (and not part of) the codebase directory. Take a moment to make sure you understand this distinction. It accounts for the difference between the way that the CODEBASE attribute is handled in the original android.html demo and the published version here.

Next, note how the src parameter is set to only the .s3z file. Compare the file sizes of the original android.s3d and the compressed android.s3z. The compressed version is less than one-quarter as large.

The <APPLET> tag is ready to be cut and pasted into your intended HTML page. Depending on the file structure used on your Web server, you may be able to include that HTML page in the codebase, just as the autogenerated HTML file is. But it's likely that you'll need to put the HTML page containing the applet elsewhere, and thus you'll need to edit the CODEBASE attribute of the <APPLET> tag to point to the correct relative location of the codebase.

The next step is to review the applets directory in the published codebase. The Wizard copies the entire directory, and thus it makes sense to delete all of the files other than ExamineApplet.class and ExaminePanel.class before uploading to the Web server. You may also choose to prune down the shout3d directory a bit, as we did when we "hand published" this project earlier in the chapter. In fact, the entire package should look the same as when we created it by hand, except that all of the content files are packaged in an Android folder rather than a models folder.

You can now upload the entire `published` directory to your Web server. You probably will want to use another name for this directory on your server, but make sure to preserve the correct names of all of the subdirectories and files. If the content loads correctly from the `published` directory on your local drive, but fails to load over the Internet, the problem is almost certainly the CODEBASE attribute. Make sure that the <APPLET> tag in the HTML file on your server contains the correct path to the codebase on the server.

Optimizing the Archive

The standard Shout3D archive, `Shout3DClasses.zip`, contains a well-chosen selection of Java classes from the Shout3D library. In any given case, however, it's likely to be missing classes you need or to contain classes you don't. Any classes missing from your .zip file will be downloaded automatically from the `shout3d` directory in your codebase, but this is inefficient because each such class requires an extra trip to the server. The ideal situation would be to create an archive that contains every class, and only those classes, you need for a particular project. This .zip archive loads in a single transaction with the server, greatly reducing download time, and the archive will then contain no unnecessary baggage.

Change the setting of Optimize archive in the Shout3DWizard to true. Click the Publish button. The Wizard will do some thinking and a preview window will appear with your content. Test it thoroughly to determine whether all the functionality is present. In this case, that means dragging the mouse to rotate the camera, and zooming by dragging vertically while holding down the Ctrl key. If everything works, the archive has captured every necessary class. Close the preview window and the Wizard will write to the `published` directory. Open this directory to find a customized archive named `android.zip`.

The custom archive may end up larger than the standard archive, but that's because (hopefully) there's no need to grab other classes from the `shout3d` directory. You still have to upload the Shout3D class library to your server. Because of the different ways in which the Java classes are loaded in different browsers, you cannot be certain that all the required classes will be loaded from the archive. You will often find that a browser needs to grab a class from the full Shout3D library, even if it's already present in the archive.

An important advantage of archive optimization is that you can more precisely determine the size of the user download—a matter of considerable importance when dealing with Webmasters. If the archive is complete, the total download is the size of the archive plus the size of the scene file and its resources (image and audio files). This figure can never be completely correct because, as I just mentioned, a browser may need to separately download some classes that are included in the archive.

If you open the HTML file, you'll see that the ARCHIVE attribute points to the custom .zip file, instead of the generic `shout3dClasses.zip`. Load the HTML file in a browser to confirm that everything is working. If it is, you can upload everything to your server, as before.

The Wizard is a useful and essential tool, but it's important to understand that, with the exception of its critical optimizing functions, it performs tasks that you should be able to perform directly. The serious student of Shout3D will want to be able to edit <APPLET> tags in HTML files and assemble content for publishing "by hand" to be sure that he or she fully understands these processes. When you know what you're doing, you can rely on the Wizard with real confidence.

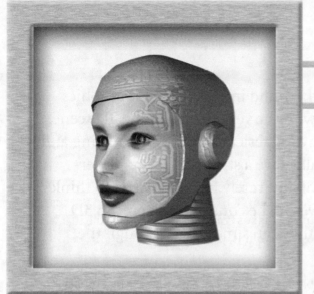

Understanding 3D Scenes in VRML

SHOUT3D

Chapter 3

R eaders without any background in 3D computer graphics must become familiar with the very nature of the 3D scene. Readers who already have experience with 3D modeling and animation software will generally have a strong intuitive understanding of the 3D environment, but rarely have had need to think in the more precise ways that we will be considering here. So 3D artists should not assume that they can simply leaf through the material in this chapter.

A 3D scene is described in a file. Most 3D scene description files are in a binary form unique to the particular application that was used to create them, although some of these formats have become standards that can be used to move content from one 3D package to another. Shout3D uses the VRML file format (.wrl), which is a human-readable format in ASCII text. It can be examined and edited in any word processor. Shout3D also uses a format immediately derived from VRML, named .s3d. Its primary purpose is to allow the addition of scene features that have been added by Shout, but are not included in the VRML language. But the .s3d format describes 3D scenes in the same way as a .wrl file.

There are two reasons that the serious Shout3D practitioner must learn about VRML. The first is simply that users who produce content in .wrl format (rather than directly in .s3d using the Shout3D MAX exporter) will often find themselves needing to make minor hand-corrections to the .wrl file to get it to perform properly in Shout. The VRML export tools of all 3D applications, including the very impressive ones in MAX, have personality quirks. They might remove or reverse certain elements that were in the original file before exporting to .wrl format, or they may automatically include certain VRML features that are unnecessary and not supported by Shout3D. Users who rely on VRML export from a favorite 3D package for use in Shout must master enough VRML to figure out what standard editorial changes are necessary to get clean .wrl files for use in Shout.

The second reason is far more important, and it applies even to those who will be using the Shout3D MAX exporter (and therefore will not need to edit .wrl files). The scene file (whether .wrl or .s3d) contains all of the elements and structure of the 3D scene. User interactivity is a matter of giving users access to the elements of the scene so they can change their values. And animation that is programmed in Shout3D's Java classes (rather than key-framed in MAX or another 3D animation package) also requires an understanding of, and access to, the elements of the scene. If you can't find your way around a scene file, you will not be able to author meaningful user interactivity or crdate programmatic animation.

When the Shout3D player reads in a scene file, it builds a Java version of the scene out of Java class objects in the Shout3D library. But each of these Java objects (except for those added by Shout3D that don't exist in VRML) has the same name and structure as the VRML objects in the scene file. Thus, the internal scene in memory that Shout3D actually renders (and which the user may be permitted to control) is a direct reflection of the contents of the .wrl or .s3d file.

Rather than burden you with a lot of theory, we will work directly with exercises that will get you going "hands-on." Inherent in this approach is an invitation to explore in any direction you choose. Feel the excitement and take time to play. When you finish this chapter, you will know a great deal that will serve as the basis for your understanding of interactive 3D graphics.

Objects in 3D Space

A 3D scene consists of objects in space. The space of the entire scene is called *world space*. The idea that a scene would require more than one kind of space is definitely novel to people first approaching 3D computer graphics, but the notion of multiple spaces coexisting in a scene is based on concepts of measurement—which is what space is really all about.

In the middle of Tokyo, there's a bridge that is used as the reference point measuring distance throughout the city. Just so, in a 3D scene, a certain location is arbitrarily chosen as the origin. The position of any point in the world space of the scene is determined by reference to this origin point. As we are working in three dimensions, the position of any point is determined by three coordinates (x,y,z), which are the distances from the origin in each of the three dimensions. In VRML and in the vast majority of 3D programs, the x direction is horizontal, the y direction is vertical, and the z direction is depth. (3D Studio MAX inexplicably violates this rule by making z the vertical and y the depth, but the Shout MAX exporter correctly reverses these.)

The Simplest Possible Scene

We'll start with a cube-shaped object as it might appear in any standard 3D modeling and animation package—in this case 3D Studio MAX. The center of the cube is positioned at the origin of world space. Its coordinates are therefore $x=0$, $y=0$ and $z=0$, generally written as (0,0,0). A grid displayed as a ground plane helps to visualize the 3D nature of the scene. A cube isn't a very interesting model, but we need to work with something simple to learn the fundamental concepts.

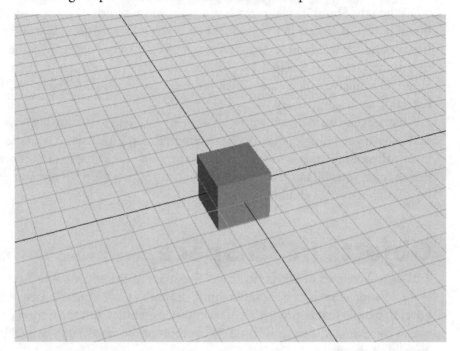

The scene is composed of a single object. To be more precise, the scene consists of a single geometric object, because the lights and a camera (through which we are viewing the scene) are also objects in the scene, but they are not visible objects. Let's put these invisible objects aside for the time being and consider only the geometric object—the cube. This object has three distinct features. It has a specific shape. It has a specific color (which you won't be able to determine in the black and white image). And it has a position and orientation in the space.

In VRML, as in almost every 3D scene description format I'm aware of, this collection of attributes is organized in a characteristic way. The geometric shape of the object is called its geometry. The color and other surface attributes (such as shininess) are called appearance. Together, the geometry and the appearance are called a shape. This is confusing because most people would not think of the "shape" of an object to include its color, but accept this as a convention in computer graphics. (We'll run across many other confusing conventions.) Thus we have a structure of:

```
shape   {
    appearance
geometry
}
```

The position and orientation of a shape in a scene is controlled by a *transform*. The idea of a transform is absolutely central to 3D computer graphics, perhaps the most important single concept that one must master. A shape is nested within a transform, like so:

```
transform   {
    shape {
        appearance
        geometry
    }
}
```

As such, these elements of the scene have no specific meaning. By giving them concrete values, a scene comes into being. For example, the values in our current simple scene might be indicated as follows:

```
transform   {   #position is (0,0,0) in world space
    shape{
    appearance   #color is red
    geometry     #cube measuring 2x2x2 meters
    }
}
```

The Same Scene in VRML

Let's move on to the description of this same scene in real VRML code. Listing 3.1 is named onebox.wrl on the CD, and you can examine it in a text editor (such as WordPad).

LISTING 3.1 ONE RED BOX (*ONEBOX.WRL*)

```
#VRML V2.0 utf8

Transform {

    translation   0 0 0
```

```
children  Shape {
  appearance  Appearance {
    material  Material {
      diffuseColor   1 0 0

    }
  }

  geometry  IndexedFaceSet {
    coord  Coordinate {
      point  [ -1 1 1,
               -1 -1 1,
                1 1 1,
                1 -1 1,
                1 1 -1,
                1 -1 -1,
               -1 1 -1,
               -1 -1 -1 ]
    }

    coordIndex  [ 0, 1, 3, 2, -1, 4, 5, 7,
                  6, -1, 6, 7, 1, 0, -1, 2,
                  3, 5, 4, -1, 6, 0, 2, 4,
                  -1, 1, 7, 5, 3, -1 ]

  } #end of IndexedFaceSet
} #end of Shape
} #end of Transform
```

There is a great deal to learn in this simplest bit of code, so please take some time to ponder it. I've highlighted the key terms we've already learned and added some comments (with the # symbol) to the final lines to help you understand the nested bracketing structure.

We'll be playing with this .wrl file for much of this chapter, so you don't need to work through all the details right now. For the present, let's see if we can grasp at least a few critical points. First, notice how some of the words are capitalized and others are not. The capitalized words, such as Transform, are *nodes*. Nodes are the basic elements of the scene description. Lowercase words are *fields*. Fields are the specific features of a given node. Note in particular how some of the same words appear both as nodes and as fields (e.g., Appearance and appearance). This is one of the most confusing aspects of learning VRML scene structure, so don't worry about it right now.

The whole scene consists of a single Transform node. The scene begins with a Transform node and its opening brace and ends with the corresponding closing brace. A Transform node has two basic features. It indicates what objects fall under its control, and it specifies what values to apply to those objects. In our simple example there are two fields. The translation field determines the position of the object. It is at (0,0,0) in world space. The children field contains all the objects that are controlled by this Transform node. In this case (as is very common), only a single Shape node is controlled by the Transform.

Let's stop right here and get practical. We'll load this scene into a Shout3D applet and play around with the values to see what happens. To do so, copy the Listing 3.1 file (`onebox.wrl`) from the CD into the `models` folder in your Shout3D installation. You'll also need an HTML page to hold the applet. Copy `onebox.html` from the CD to the `demos` folder in your Shout installation. This HTML file reads as follows:

```
<HTML>
<HEAD>
<TITLE>onebox</TITLE>
</HEAD>
<BODY>
<APPLET CODEBASE="../codebase"
➦ CODE="shout3d/Shout3DApplet.class"
➦ ARCHIVE="shout3dClasses.zip" WIDTH=300 HEIGHT=300>
<param name="src" value="models/onebox.wrl">
<param name="headlightOn" value="true">
</APPLET>
</BODY>
</HTML>
```

This will load the .wrl file into the standard Shout player without any user interactivity. Note that the headlight is on, as indicated by the value of "true" for the `headlightOn` parameter. This saves us the trouble of adding lights in our scene file because a light object will be automatically created when the scene file is read into the Shout3D player.

Run the HTML file in your Web browser. You'll see a bright red square in the middle of the applet window.

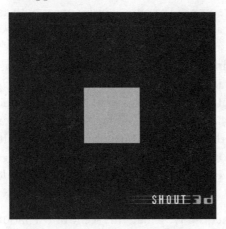

This certainly doesn't look very three-dimensional. The reason is that (just as with the lights) we didn't create a camera through which to view the scene. Because we didn't do so, Shout created a default camera directly in front of the object, looking at it face on. The default camera is located at (0,0,10) in world space, meaning that it is ten units in front of the world origin (0,0,0) and pointed directly at the origin. You will almost never create scenes in which you don't explicitly create a camera—positioned and directed specifically for your needs—but we're trying to keep our scene file as simple as possible. Cameras are called Viewpoints in VRML, and therefore also in Shout3D, so from now on we'll use the correct term.

Sometimes you'll load a scene into Shout and the display will be completely black. Very often this is because the default Viewpoint ends up being located inside your geometry. After you make this mistake a couple of times, you'll remember to create a camera and position it explicitly when authoring your scene in your 3D modeling and animation program.

Changing Position

Now we're ready to do some experimenting that will really open your eyes. Open up the .wrl file in a text editor and change the values in the translation field of the Transform node. For example, change the *x* value by changing the field from 0 0 0 to 2 0 0.

Save the file (always in ASCII text format) under the same name and refresh or reload the page in your browser. Voila! The cube has moved to the right.

Take some time to play with all three numbers—*x*, *y*, and *z*. Try both positive and negative values and different combinations. Note how changing the *z* value makes the cube appear larger or smaller as it moves closer to or farther away from the default Viewpoint position. In fact, if you move the cube too close the Viewpoint (0,0,10), the cube will disappear because the Viewpoint will be inside the cube.

All this is very simple, but nonetheless extremely important because you can now understand how a 3D scene can be made interactive. Right now you are changing the values in the original scene file, and you must reload the scene to see any difference. But what if, after the scene were loaded into memory, the user were given the power to change these positional values while viewing the scene. This might be through text input boxes or by mouse clicking or dragging. However it is done, user control is possible because the values in fields can be changed after the scene is constructed in memory.

Rotation

Our cube would reveal its three-dimensional geometry if we could rotate it a bit. But if you look at our .wrl file, you won't see any mention of rotation. What gives?

VRML relies a great deal on default values. If a default value is used, the corresponding field doesn't need to be written into the scene file. In this case, our cube was not rotated from its default orientation when I created the scene, so rotation information was omitted. This makes for the shortest possible scene description file. Had it been rotated to begin with, there would have been a rotation field listed under the Transform node. To rotate it now, we'll have to add the field by hand.

Set your translation (position) values back to 0 0 0 and type a new line beneath the position field. The two lines should read:

```
translation    0 0 0
rotation       0 1 0 0
```

Rotation is a very deep subject in 3D graphics, as any 3D animator knows well. For now, let's just get the basic idea. VRML (and therefore Shout3D) uses the axis-angle method of describing rotations, a method common to 3D programming, but one not often used by 3D artists. Shout3D provides excellent tools for handling rotations in ways that 3D artists are more comfortable with and converting them to axis-angle form. But for right now, let's work directly with the axis-angle approach.

In the axis-angle approach to rotations, the first three values define the axis of rotation. The fourth value is the amount of rotation around the axis. This method is therefore most comprehensible when we rotate only around one of the major axes. To rotate our cube around its vertical axis, we choose the *y* direction only. Thus, the first three numbers are 0 1 0 (*x,y,z*). The fourth number, as we said, is the amount of rotation around that vertical axis. This value is expressed in *radians*, not in degrees. A radian is 57.3 degrees. Radians are commonly used in graphics programming as an angular unit of measure, and it's easy to convert between degrees and radians. To rotate the cube one radian around the vertical axis, edit the field to read:

```
rotation   0 1 0 1
```

The strange number of 57.3 degrees comes from the fact that there are 2π radians in a complete revolution of 360 degrees, and $360/(2\pi)$ is about 57.3 degrees.

Save the .wrl file and reload or refresh. The cube should now be rotated as follows. Things are looking a little more three-dimensional!

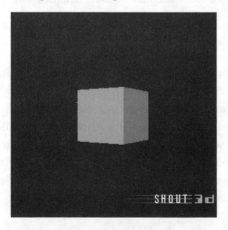

Experiment with different axes. Rotate around the *z* axis using 0 0 1 as the first three values. Rotate around the *x* axis using 1 0 0. Try different values in the fourth slot for different amounts of rotation. As you do this, think of the general significance of being able to change these values dynamically after the scene has been loaded into memory. A user can rotate an object if these values can change in response to, say, dragging the mouse. Everything that we are now learning about the scene description file (the .wrl or .s3d file) will apply just as much to the Java construction of this scene information created in memory when the scene file is loaded.

Scaling

The concept of *transformation* in 3D computer graphics includes three elements—translation (position), rotation (orientation), and scale. By default, the scale of an object is set to 100 percent of the size specified by its geometry. Thus, as I didn't scale the cube when I first created it, the scale field was left out of the Transform node in the .wrl file. To experiment with scale, reset your translation back to 0 0 0, and set your rotation to 1 radian around the *y* axis. Then add a scale field. You can scale separately in *x*, *y*, and *z*, so let's try doubling the height of the cube by scaling it to 200 percent in *y*. Your code should look like this:

```
translation   0 0 0
rotation       0 1 0 1
scale          1 2 1
```

Note how the number 1 (or 1.0 if you wish) indicates 100 percent. Save the .wrl file and reload or refresh your browser. The new taller object should look like this:

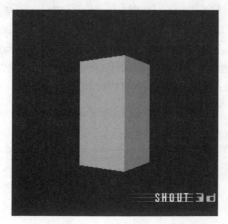

Play around with different scale values, and while you're doing so, take the time to consider something rather deep and important: Translation occurs in world space. Given the location of our default camera, increasing the x translation value always moves the object to the right. Decreasing the y translation value always moves the object down. But scaling is different. The object scales in its own *local* space, not in the world space of the scene. If you increase the x scale value, for example, the cube expands outward toward its own "left" and "right" directions, not in the horizontal directions of the scene. Take a look at the object with the following Transform values:

```
translation    0 0 0
rotation       0 1 0 1
scale          3 1 1
```

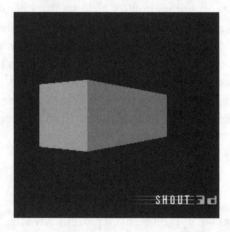

Where am I getting all these field names, like rotation *and* scale*? All this information is in the VRML 97 Specification, included on the book's CD. Make sure you take a look through Part 6, the Node Reference, to get a sense of all the VRML Nodes and their fields. A quick glance at the information listed for the Transform node will reveal other fields we haven't touched. Then look at the Transform class object in the online Javadocs. You'll see that the Shout3D Transform class contains the very same fields.*

Within the Individual Object

Thus far, we've been working with the Transform node. This is definitely the most important node in a VRML scene description. Most of what we typically consider animation amounts to changes in the translation and rotation values of Transform nodes over time. But let's move down now into the Shape node. Remember that the Shape node defines both the geometry of the object (what most people would call its "shape") and the surface appearance of the object (including color and related elements). We'll start with the geometry.

Understanding the Geometry

The geometry field of each Shape node itself will contain one of several types of nodes that define different kinds of geometry. VRML contains some nodes that automatically provide basic shapes such as spheres, boxes and cylinders. These are typically called *geometric primitives*, and they are useful because you can define their dimensions very easily. For example, a cube with the dimensions 2×3×5 can be written in a VRML file as a Box node.

```
Box {
size 2 3 5
}
```

But this kind of very simple geometry is of limited use. It is much more useful to consider the most important type of VRML geometry node, the IndexedFaceSet. This is a polygonal mesh described as a network of points in space (vertices) connected together to define surfaces.

Most 3D modeling is a matter of designing and developing polygonal meshes using interactive tools. Even the more sophisticated NURBS modeling tools are ultimately a way of creating polygonal meshes. No one creates 3D models by writing program code. The code in a model file, whether in VRML or any other format, is created by the modeling program as the modeler works in a graphical modeling interface. But we need to understand, at least in a basic way, how a polygonal mesh object is coded in an IndexedFaceSet. And we also need to understand the range of information that can be contained (and modified) in an IndexedFaceSet beyond the bare bones description of the geometry.

Here is the geometry field of our Shape, isolated from the rest of the `onebox.wrl` file.

```
geometry  IndexedFaceSet {
    coord Coordinate {
        point  [ -1 1 1,
                 -1 -1 1,
                  1 1 1,
                  1 -1 1,
                  1 1 -1,
                  1 -1 -1,
                 -1 1 -1,
                 -1 -1 -1 ]
    }

    coordIndex  [ 0, 1, 3, 2, -1, 4, 5, 7,
                  6, -1, 6, 7, 1, 0, -1, 2,
                  3, 5, 4, -1, 6, 0, 2, 4,
                  -1, 1, 7, 5, 3, -1 ]

} #end of IndexedFaceSet
```

The concept here is easy, though the structure of the code takes a while to get comfortable with. Let's get right to heart. Our cube, like any polygonal mesh, must be described as a collection of polygons. With a cube, this collection is composed of six quadrangles (quads), one for each face. Consider that each quad will share vertices (corner points) with two other quads. We could describe each quad by listing the position of each of its four vertices, but this would waste file size because we'd have to repeat the same values three times. A much better idea is to make a list of all of the vertices used in the mesh. Then another list can be used to indicate how the listed vertices should be connected to create the quadrangular faces of the model.

The Vertex List

Look first at the list of numbers within the field called `point`. There are eight lines, each consisting of three numbers. These are the eight vertices at the corners of the cube. The location of each vertex is specified by its (x,y,z) coordinates. These coordinates are in the local space of the object, not in the world space of the scene. They are measured from a local origin in the middle of cube. We'll understand this idea quite clearly in a moment.

Edit the .wrl file we've been working with to eliminate any scale field in the Transform (if you put one there) and create a rotation around the vertical axis of 1 radian. The translation field should be set to the world origin.

```
translation  0 0 0
rotation     0 1 0 1
```

Save the .wrl file and load (or reload) the HTML file. You should see the same rotated cube you saw a short while back.

Now edit the point field to change the *y* value of the first vertex from 1 to 2.

```
point [ -1 2 1,
        -1 -1 1,
         1 1 1,
         1 -1 1,
         1 1 -1,
         1 -1 -1,
        -1 1 -1,
        -1 -1 -1 ]
```

Save the .wrl file and refresh your browser. You'll see that one of the vertices on the top of the cube has move upward, changing the geometry.

It's clear now how the vertex list in the point field defines the location of each vertex. To get a good feeling for the distinction between the local space in which the geometry is constructed and the world space of the scene, change the translation values in the .wrl file to move the cube around in the scene. As you do so, it should become obvious that the vertex that was set to (−1,2,1) in local space can be in any place in world space.

When we translate the object, we are actually translating the center of the object's local coordinate system—its local (0,0,0). For example, when we set the translation field to 0 2 0, we are placing the center of the cube at that location in world space. The locations of each of the vertices are relative to this new center position in world space.

The Faces List

The IndexedFaceSet must not only specify the locations of the vertices on geometry, but also how these vertices are connected to create the polygons that constitute the surface of the mesh. This is where the coordIndex field comes in.

```
coordIndex   [ 0, 1, 3, 2, -1, 4, 5, 7,
               6, -1, 6, 7, 1, 0, -1, 2,
               3, 5, 4, -1, 6, 0, 2, 4,
              -1, 1, 7, 5, 3, -1 ]
```

Note how the coordIndex field is a list (an *array*) of numbers (integers). There are four integers followed by a −1. This pattern recurs six times. These are the six quad faces of the cube. The numbers are indexes into the list of vertices we just worked with. There are eight vertices, and as is standard in all computer programming, they are numbered 0 through 7 (rather than 1 through 8). So the first quad of the cube is constructed by connecting the first vertex in the vertex list (0) to the second (1), and then to the fourth (3), and finally to the third (2). The −1 is a delimiter, a signal that says this polygon is finished and the next number will begin a new polygon.

Other Important IndexedFaceSet Features

Between the vertex list in the point field and the polygon list built from it in the coordIndex, the entire geometry of the cube has been specified. This is the main purpose of the IndexedFaceSet node. But the IndexedFaceSet node contains many other important fields that have been omitted in our simple .wrl file. For example, if our object were texture mapped, such that an image was applied to its surface, the texture coordinates would be listed in a field of the IndexedFaceSet. If colors are assigned to specific vertices to use vertex color techniques, this information is also contained in the IndexedFaceSet node. Generally you will not need to edit this information by hand, but there are a couple of fields that definitely deserve your attention right from the start.

For the overwhelming majority of the objects, the geometry defines some kind of closed surface. It would be inefficient to render both sides of the polygons on a mesh when only one side is visible. Thus, by default, an IndexedFaceSet will only render the front faces of its polygons. Sometimes it's necessary to reverse the direction of the faces, so that the opposite sides of the faces render. The ccw field in the IndexedFaceSet determines the direction of the rendering faces. By default, this field is set to TRUE. To see the inside faces of our cube, edit the .wrl file to include the ccw field and set it to FALSE. You may want to reset your first vertex to its original position as well. The complete .wrl file should look like this:

```
#VRML V2.0 utf8

Transform {

  translation   0 0 0


  children  Shape {
    appearance  Appearance {
      material  Material {
        diffuseColor   1 0 0

      }
    }


    geometry  IndexedFaceSet {
      ccw   FALSE
coord  Coordinate {
      point  [ -1 1 1,
               -1 -1 1,
                1 1 1,
                1 -1 1,
                1 1 -1,
                1 -1 -1,
               -1 1 -1,
               -1 -1 -1 ]
      }
```

```
coordIndex  [ 0, 1, 3, 2, -1, 4, 5, 7,
             6, -1, 6, 7, 1, 0, -1, 2,
             3, 5, 4, -1, 6, 0, 2, 4,
             -1, 1, 7, 5, 3, -1 ]

        } #end of IndexedFaceSet
     } #end of Shape
  } #end of Transform
```

After editing, save and reload. You will now be looking directly into the cube, viewing the inside faces on the back. The top and bottom faces aren't visible from this angle. Your scene should look like this:

Reversing the direction of faces is typically called "flipping normals." A normal is an imaginary ray pointing in the direction that a polygon is facing for rendering purposes. Flipping the normal to the other side of the polygon reverses the definition of the front and back faces. Flipping normals is often necessary to correct errors, but is sometimes required for design purposes. For example, to create the interior walls of a room, the normals must face inward.

Another critical element of the IndexedFaceSet node gets to the heart of why polygonal models "work." Our cube is truly intended to look as though it was constructed out of a network of flat surfaces. But what about the vast majority of models that contains curving or rounded surfaces? These must be built out of polygonal geometry, but the renderer is capable or creating an illusion of smoothness by shading between the vertices.

Take a look at two identical models of a sphere. The one on the right clearly shows the polygonal mesh, but the one on the left is shaded by the renderer to appear smooth.

The difference between the two is due to the `creaseAngle` field in the IndexedFaceSet node. The `creaseAngle` is the largest angle between two adjacent faces that will be smoothed. Like all angles in VRML and Shout3D, it is specified in radians rather than degrees. The sphere on the right uses a `creaseAngle` field set to zero. There is, therefore, no smoothing at all. The sphere on the right uses a `creaseAngle` set to 3.14 (pi) radians, which is equal to 180 degrees—the largest possible angle. Thus, the entire object is smoothed. This is a much higher number than necessary in this case because there are no angles even close to 90 (much less 180) degrees in this sphere. But you will often find it convenient just to set the `creaseAngle` field to its maximum possible value to assure that an object is completely smoothed.

Understanding Appearance

In 3D graphics, we think of the geometry of the object independently of the color of its surface. Geometry alone cannot produce a renderable object, because rendering is the process of building a picture of the object using colored pixels. This statement must be qualified a bit because, as mentioned in the previous section, some kinds of color and texture information are placed in the IndexedFaceSet. But we can start from the proposition that the surface colors that an object produces when rendered are severable from its geometry.

The word "appearance" is one of the many terms that we'll come across that has a specific meaning in computer graphics that differs from conventional understanding. We've already noted that the Shape node includes color information that would hardly square with the common meaning of the word "shape." Just so, the word "appearance" means both shape and color in ordinary speech. In 3D computer graphics, it means only surface color.

Ultimately, a rendered image is just colors assigned to pixels. But from these colors the viewer interprets a great many things. The apparent texture or roughness of surface is suggested by intricate shadow patterns of light and dark. The apparent physical or chemical nature of an object is suggested by the way it seems to reflect light, which, in a rendering, is simply an illusion based on color gradients across an object. Even the shape of an object is revealed primarily by color gradients that suggest curvature or shadows. The VRML Appearance node contains all (or rather almost all) of the information that determines the surface colors of a rendered object.

The Appearance node is an area in which Shout has diverged from the VRML 2.0 Specification. The full VRML Appearance node in the VRML specification contains three fields:

```
Appearance {
   material
   texture
   textureTransform
}
```

For right now, experiment with the Material node within the `material` field. The Material node contains a `diffuseColor` field. This is the primary color of the object, and as is typical of digital graphics, it is defined by the combination of red, green, and blue (RGB), each measured from 0 to 100 percent. Thus, the current color of red is 1 0 0. Green would be 0 1 0. Try some values of your own. Save, reload or refresh your browser, and check out the new color.

Shout3D content exported from MAX makes use of Shout's own MultiAppearance node, which supports a wide range of MAX's material and texture features that are much more extensive than those in VRML export.

Object Hierarchies and the Scene Graph

Thus far, we've been working with a scene that contains only a single geometric object. A more complex scene might include many objects. These objects may be entirely independent of each other, or they may be components in larger structures that amount to integrated units.

To take the most obvious example, a character figure might be built out of separate geometric objects (Shape nodes) for head, torso, and the different sections of the arms and legs. These will all be subject to their own Transform nodes, so that each unit can be rotated independently. However, the entire body must form an integrated whole. In all 3D graphics, this is achieved by "parenting" objects into a transform hierarchy. The hierarchy itself (in this case, the body) becomes a sort of meta-object in the scene. All 3D animation packages have tools for parenting and unparenting objects to create hierarchies.

3D Studio MAX uses the term "linking" to describe the parenting of a child object to a parent. This term is unique to MAX, and is not standard 3D graphics terminology.

Parenting Transforms

When an object in a 3D animation program (the child object) is parented to another object (the parent object), the transforms of the child are made subject to the transforms of the parent. In a simple, practical sense, this means that any translation, rotation, or scaling of the parent object will also apply to the child object. But the opposite is not true. The child object can be transformed (translated, rotated, or scaled) independently of the parent. If you move the parent object, the child goes along for the ride. But if you move the child, the parent stays where it is.

Understanding transform hierarchies is absolutely essential for working in interactive 3D graphics. Work slowly and carefully through the following material to gain a strong introductory grasp of this subject.

When one object is parented to another in a VRML scene description, the transform of the child object is included within the transform of the parent. The simplest and most direct approach involves the direct parenting of one geometric object to another:

```
Transform (Parent) {

  Shape (Parent)

  Transform (Child){
      Shape (Child)
  }


}
```

The Transform node of the parent controls both its own Shape node and the Transform node of the child. The Transform node of the child contains its own Shape. Thus the child shape is effectively subject to two layers of transformation, while the parent shape is subject to only one.

Let's add a second cube to the scene we've been working with throughout this chapter. I did this by simply copying the entire scene and pasting the copy within the original Transform node. I did some indenting and a couple of minor edits to make things clearer, and I changed the diffuse color of the child object to blue. In particular, I set the translation of the child to 2.5 0 0. Notice something else new: In VRML, you can give a unique name to any node using the DEF (define) keyword. I named the two Transform nodes PARENT and CHILD, respectively. The use of node names is very important, as we shall see throughout this book.

Take some time to look over this code and see how it implements the nested transform structure I just described.

LISTING 3.2 PARENT AND CHILD HIERARCHY (*TWOBOXES.WRL*)

```
#VRML V2.0 utf8

DEF PARENT Transform {

  translation   0 0 0


  children [

    Shape {
      appearance  Appearance {
```

```
      material  Material {
        diffuseColor   1 0 0
      }
    }

    geometry  IndexedFaceSet {
      coord  Coordinate {
      point  [ -1 1 1,
               -1 -1 1,
                1 1 1,
                1 -1 1,
                1 1 -1,
                1 -1 -1,
               -1 1 -1,
               -1 -1 -1 ]
      }
      coordIndex  [ 0, 1, 3, 2, -1, 4, 5, 7,
                    6, -1, 6, 7, 1, 0, -1, 2,
                    -1, 1, 7, 5, 3, -1 ]


    } #end Parent IndexedFaceSet
  } #end of Parent Shape

DEF CHILD Transform {

  translation  2.5 0 0

  children  Shape {
    appearance  Appearance {
      material  Material {
        diffuseColor   0 0 1
      }
    }
    geometry  IndexedFaceSet {
      coord  Coordinate {
        point  [ -1 1 1,
                 -1 -1 1,
                  1 1 1,
                  1 -1 1,
                  1 1 -1,
```

```
                          1 -1 -1,
                         -1  1 -1,
                         -1 -1 -1 ]
                }
                coordIndex  [ 0, 1, 3, 2, -1, 4, 5, 7,
                              6, -1, 6, 7, 1, 0, -1, 2,
                              3, 5, 4, -1, 6, 0, 2, 4,
                              -1, 1, 7, 5, 3, -1 ]


            } #end Child IndexedFaceSet
          } #end of Child Shape
        } #end of Child Transform


      ]#End of Children of Parent Transform

    } #end of Parent Transform
```

Relative Translations

Let's play with the scene to learn some important things. Copy this VRML file (twoboxes.wrl) from the CD to the models folder of your Shout installation. Then copy the supporting HTML page (twoboxes.html) to the demos folder. When you load the HMTL page, you'll see the following scene: The red cube (the parent) is sitting in the middle of the screen at (0,0,0) in world space; the blue cube (the child) is 2.5 units (meters) to the right, at (2.5,0,0) in world space.

The values in any Transform node are always relative to its parent Transform. The PARENT Transform is this scene doesn't have a parent—it's a top-level Transform. That means its values are directly in world space. The CHILD Transform is relative to the PARENT Transform. Since the PARENT Transform's position is at (0,0,0) in world space, the CHILD's is at (2.5,0,0) in world space. But the moment we move the PARENT Transform from the world origin, the CHILD's values will no longer correspond to world space.

Open the .wrl file from the `models` folder and change the PARENT Transform translation to 0 1 0. Save the file and reload or refresh your browser. As you can see, both cubes have moved up one unit (one meter) in the *y* (vertical) direction.

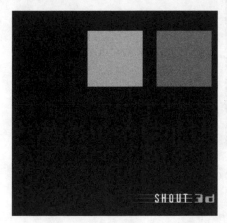

Let's make sure we understand precisely why both cubes moved up when we changed the position of the PARENT Transform. The red cube is the Shape node that is directly controlled by this Transform, so it's obvious why that cube moved to (0,2,0) in world space. The blue cube is a shape node subject to both Transforms. The PARENT Transform establishes a translation value of (0,2,0). The CHILD Transform is relative to this. Thus the CHILD is positioned at (2.5,2,0) in world space. Wherever the red cube is positioned, the blue cube will always remain in the same relative position. This is why moving a parent object causes its child to move along.

We can summarize the scene like this:

```
Transform (PARENT) {
position 0 2 0 in world space

  Transform (CHILD){
    position 2.5 0 0 relative to PARENT
```

```
    position 2.5 2 0 in world space
  }

}
```

Now change the CHILD's translation values to (2.5,–2,0), save and reload. The blue cube is now back where it began, but the red cube is still at (0,2,0) in world space.

We can summarize the current state of the scene like this:

```
Transform (PARENT) {
position 0 2 0 in world space

  Transform (CHILD){
    position 2.5 -2 0 relative to PARENT
    position 2.5 0 0 in world space
  }

}
```

Rotations and Pure Transforms

Reset the twoboxes.wrl file from Listing 3.2 to its original state, or just copy the original from the CD over the edited version in the models folder. The translation values will therefore be (0,0,0) for the PARENT Transform and (2.5,0,0) for the CHILD Transform, and the scene will look just as it did before you made any changes.

Now let's look at rotations. Rotate the PARENT Transform one radian around its *z* axis by typing in a rotation field just below the translation field. The relevant lines of code will read:

```
DEF PARENT Transform {

    translation   0 0 0
    rotation      0 0 1 1

...

    DEF CHILD Transform {

        translation   2.5 0 0
```

Save the file and load the demo. Your scene should look like this:

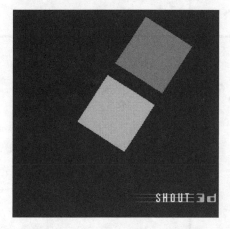

The entire hierarchy operates like a wheel. The PARENT Transform rotates both objects as a rigid unit, in this case around a center set at (0,0,0) in world space. Think this process through very carefully, because there is a very subtle idea involved. The blue cube is still located 2.5 meters in the *x* direction relative to the red cube. But the rotation of the PARENT Transform has changed the meaning of the *x* direction. After rotation, the x (and y) directions of the PARENT Transform are no longer aligned with the x and y directions in world space.

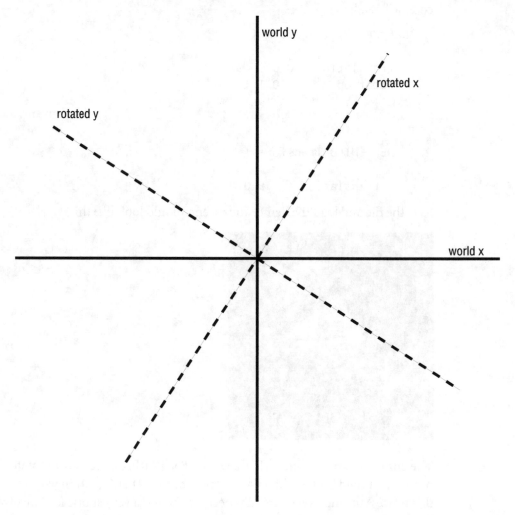

This should suggest a very important idea. Right now, the PARENT Transform is directly associated with a piece of geometry—the red cube. The red cube is rotating around a point in its own center. But what if that geometry (the Shape object) were omitted? What if the PARENT Transform contained only the CHILD Transform, like so:

```
Transform (Parent) {

    Transform (Child){
```

```
    Shape (Child)
  }


}
```

The red cube would disappear, and the blue cube would still rotate around the point defined by the translation value of the PARENT Transform—in this case, the center of world space. In other words, we could use a parent Transform to create a rotational axis in whatever position we wish.

Let's give this a try. Look over the .wrl file and identify the Shape node of the red cube (the parent shape). You'll find it in the following block of code.

```
Shape {
  appearance  Appearance {
    material  Material {
      diffuseColor 1 0 0
    }
  }

  geometry  IndexedFaceSet {
    coord  Coordinate {
      point  [ -1 1 1,
               -1 -1 1,
                1 1 1,
                1 -1 1,
                1 1 -1,
                1 -1 -1,
               -1 1 -1,
               -1 -1 -1 ]
    }
    coordIndex  [ 0, 1, 3, 2, -1, 4, 5, 7,
                  6, -1, 6, 7, 1, 0, -1, 2,
                  3, 5, 4, -1, 6, 0, 2, 4,
                  -1, 1, 7, 5, 3, -1 ]

  } #end Parent IndexedFaceSet
} #end of Parent Shape
```

Delete this code and save the file. Reload the scene, and you'll find that the red cube is gone, but the blue cube is still rotated as before. Go back to the .wrl file and change to rotational value of the PARENT Transform to 2 radians:

```
DEF PARENT Transform {

    translation  0 0 0
    rotation     0 0 1 2

...

DEF CHILD Transform {

    Translation   2.5 0 0
```

Save and reload. The scene will now show the blue cube rotated 2 radians (about 115 degrees) from its original position.

I can't recommend enough that you take some time to experiment on your own right here. Play with different translation and rotation values on both the PARENT and CHILD Transforms and see if you can figure out what is happening. You are developing the basic conceptual skills that underlie all work in interactive 3D graphics, and it takes some time for these ideas to sink to an intuitive level. And the opportunity to work directly with VRML code in a text editor is priceless. You'll never understand VRML unless you practice editing it by hand.

Paths and the Scene Graph

With all this background behind us, we are finally in a position to think about 3D scenes in a more sophisticated way. In the language of 3D graphics programming, a scene description file is more properly understood as a *scene graph*. Everything is connected to everything else in a tree-like structure. To continue with the botanical metaphor, the scene is tied together at the *root*.

You don't see the root explicitly in the VRML file, but one is created when the scene is loaded into memory. The root node of a scene is the parent of all other nodes. It is a Transform node, and all the top-level nodes in the scene are its direct children. These children may have their own children, and so on.

Each branch of the tree can be considered as a *path* through the scene graph. The concept of a path between a given node and the root node of the scene is extremely important. This path allows us to navigate from any node in the scene to any other, and it allows us to work through different levels of Transform space by collecting all the different Transform values up or down the path.

To take the simple example of our two-box scene, you can easily recognize that it would be impossible to figure out where the child (blue) box is in world space unless you had access to all the Transforms it is subject to. The Transform immediately above the specific Shape node would not be enough. To determine the location of the Shape node in world space, we need the complete path to this object, from the root on down. In this case the path would consist of

1. Root Transform
2. Parent Transform
3. Child Transform
4. Shape

The concept of a path can be continued into the individual Shape. For example, the path to the Material node of the Shape would read

1. Root Transform
2. Parent Transform
3. Child Transform
4. Shape
5. Appearance
6. Material

When working with Shout's Java API to build interactivity, you'll often find that you need to work with the path to a desired node in the scene graph, rather than with just the node itself. The path provides the context of the node within the entire scene.

The concept of a scene graph, and its description in a .wrl or .s3d, is the foundation for all we will learn about using Shout3D. In this chapter, we have considered only geometric objects, but lights and the camera (the Viewpoint) are also nodes in the scene graph, each with its own characteristic fields. There are also nodes that create and control animation and other nodes that implement different kinds of interactivity. These are a bit different because they don't have a location in the space of the scene, and they cannot be conceived of by reference to physical objects. Yet paths connect all of the nodes, of whatever species, and these paths create a tree structure representing the scene and all that it is capable of doing.

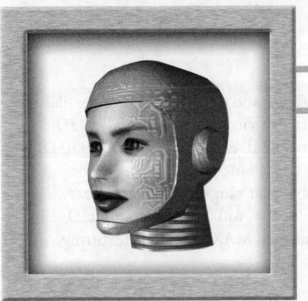

Exporting Shout3D
Content from
3D Studio MAX

SHOUT3D

Chapter 4

Shout3D is founded on VRML and can use VRML scene files created in VRML authoring environments or standard 3D packages that provide for VRML export. However, Shout3D content will be most effectively created in 3D Studio MAX. The Shout3D package provides an exporter plug-in that permits easy export of MAX content to .s3d format. You'll find that Shout3D supports a remarkably broad range of MAX modeling, texturing, and animation features.

Basic Export Issues

The vast majority of 3D Studio MAX users work entirely within that application. They rarely need to consider the consequences of exporting model or scene information for use in another context. By contrast, most MAX professionals who create graphical content for games must develop a strong understanding of how MAX works internally and therefore how it exports scene information for use outside the program.

In this section, we will work through some simple exercises that will help you to understand the way in which MAX creates scene data for export. Without this background, you will consistently be confused by much of the output generated by the Shout3D MAX exporter. It's important to realize that this confusion is not due to the Shout3D MAX exporter, but rather to the way in which MAX stores scene information internally. When you get a handle on how MAX works inside, you'll be able to solve most of your problems easily. These exercises assume that you have installed the exporter plug-in and know how to access it from File ➜ Export on the MAX menubar.

Pivot Points and Local Space

Create a Box object in MAX that is 100 units in all three dimensions and positioned at (0,0,0) in world space. This is most easily done using the Keyboard Entry rollout, but you can create it interactively if you wish.

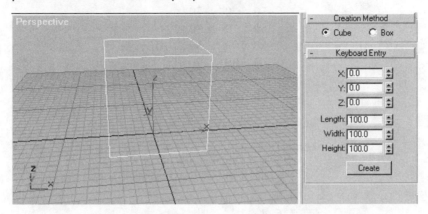

Note that the pivot point is at the center of the bottom face of the object, and that this point is located at (0,0,0). This is the center of the local space of the object, which, for the present, coincides with the center of world space. Collapse this object to an Editable Mesh (using the right-click menu) and export the scene to Shout3D. There's no animation here, so you can pass right through the animation dialog box in the export process. Save the .s3d file in the models directory of your Shout3D installation and give it whatever name you wish. When you open this file in a text editor, you'll find the information shown in Listing 4.1. (I've deleted the fields that are irrelevant to our purposes.)

LISTING 4.1 BASIC BOX EXPORTED FROM MAX (*TEST1.S3D*)

```
DEF Box01 Transform {
    translation 0 0 0
    children [
        Shape {
            appearance [
                MultiAppearance {
                    material Material {
                        diffuseColor 0.6039 0.6039 0.898
                    }
                }
            }
        ]
    ]
```

```
geometry MultiMesh {
    coord DEF Box01-COORD Coordinate {
        point [
            -50   0    50
             50   0    50
            -50   0   -50
             50   0   -50
            -50 100    50
             50 100    50
            -50 100   -50
             50 100   -50
        ]
    }
    coordIndex [
        0 2 3 -1
        3 1 0 -1
        4 5 7 -1
        7 6 4 -1
        0 1 5 -1
        5 4 0 -1
        1 3 7 -1
        7 5 1 -1
        3 2 6 -1
        6 7 3 -1
        2 0 4 -1
        4 6 2 -1
    ]
}
}
]
}
```

Consider this file very carefully. There is only a single Transform, and its position is set to (0,0,0). This means that the center of local space is at the center of world space. Now consider the positions of the eight vertices in the points list. These vertices are measured from the center of local space. Thus it makes sense that the lower four of them are in the plane $y=0$, and the upper four are in the plane $y=100$.

Back in MAX, move the pivot point to the center of the cube.

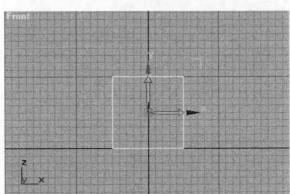

The box stays where it is. Check the Move Transform dialog box by right-clicking the Move button on the toolbar to confirm that the new position of the box is (0,0,50) in MAX's world space system. This corresponds to (0,50,0) in the more conventional system used by Shout (in which *y* is the vertical direction). In any case, it's clear that MAX treats the position of the object as the position of the pivot point.

There are two possibilities here. One is that MAX has actually changed the location of the center of local space from the bottom to the center of the cube. If so, all of the coordinate values of the vertices must change to reflect this. The other possibility is that the center of local space stays where it is, and MAX has created a hidden parent-child hierarchy in which the pivot point is made the parent of the box. If you export to .s3d and check out the file, you'll discover that the second of the two alternatives is Listing 4.2 here.

LISTING 4.2 PIVOT MOVED TO CENTER (*TEST2.S3D*)

```
DEF Box01 Transform {
    translation 0 50 0
    children [
        Transform {
            translation 0 -50 0
            children [
                Shape {
                    appearance [
                        MultiAppearance {
                            material Material {
                                diffuseColor 0.6039 0.6039 0.898
                            }
```

```
                    }
                  ]
                  geometry MultiMesh {
                    coord DEF Box01-COORD Coordinate {
                      point [
                              -50    0    50
                               50    0    50
                              -50    0   -50
                               50    0   -50
                              -50  100    50
                               50  100    50
                              -50  100   -50
                               50  100   -50
                      ]
                    }
                    coordIndex [
                        0 2 3 -1
                        3 1 0 -1
                        4 5 7 -1
                        7 6 4 -1
                        0 1 5 -1
                        5 4 0 -1
                        1 3 7 -1
                        7 5 1 -1
                        3 2 6 -1
                        6 7 3 -1
                        2 0 4 -1
                        4 6 2 -1
                    ]

                  }
                }
              ]
            }
          ]
        }
```

Take a moment to think this through. There are now two nested Transforms. The parent Transform represents the pivot point located at (0,50,0) in world space. This is the only Transform we will find in MAX. The child Transform gets us to the center of local space, which is 50 units below the pivot point. Note that the coordinates of the vertices have not changed because the center of local space has not changed. This approach treats the pivot point as though it were a hidden parent null object. It's confusing, but workable, at least in this simple situation, as long as we operate only on the parent Transform (the pivot point), and not the child.

The Reset Pivot button on in the MAX Hierarchy Panel returns the pivot point to the center local space. This demonstrates that MAX preserves that local origin even when the pivot is moved.

We can clean things up by moving the local origin to the current position of the pivot point. With the object selected in MAX, go to the Utilities Panel, select Reset XForm, and click the Reset Selected button. Within MAX, this places an XForm modifier on the stack above the Editable Mesh object, which you should confirm by going to the Modifier Panel. The XForm modifier is an adjustment Transform, and you can explore how its position values now differ from those of the object itself. For our purposes, however, it's the net effect that matters. You can collapse this modifier into the Editable Mesh before exporting if you wish, but it's not a requirement because the Shout exporter necessarily collapses the modifier stack. After exporting, you'll find only a single Transform, located appropriately at (0,50,0). All of the vertices are now measured from this location in the center of the box. The local origin now coincides with the location of the pivot point. Listing 4.3 shows this as a much more comprehensible structure.

LISTING 4.3 RESETTING XFORM (*TEST3.S3D*)

```
DEF Box01 Transform {
    translation 0 50 0
    children [
        Shape {
            appearance [
                MultiAppearance {
                    material Material {
                        diffuseColor 0.6039 0.6039 0.898
                    }
                }
            ]
            geometry MultiMesh {
                coord DEF Box01-COORD Coordinate {
                    point [
                        -50   -50   50
```

```
                           50   -50   50
                          -50   -50  -50
                           50   -50  -50
                          -50    50   50
                           50    50   50
                          -50    50  -50
                           50    50  -50
                        ]
                   }
                   coordIndex [
                        0 2 3 -1
                        3 1 0 -1
                        4 5 7 -1
                        7 6 4 -1
                        0 1 5 -1
                        5 4 0 -1
                        1 3 7 -1
                        7 5 1 -1
                        3 2 6 -1
                        6 7 3 -1
                        2 0 4 -1
                        4 6 2 -1
                   ]
              }
          }
       ]
    }
```

Rotations

Create the same basic Box object as in the previous section, positioned at the world origin. Collapse it to an Editable Mesh and rotate it 45 degrees around the vertical axis. Choose the local coordinate system on the MAX toolbar to see clearly that the local coordinate system of the box is rotated with respect to the world coordinate system represented by the grid.

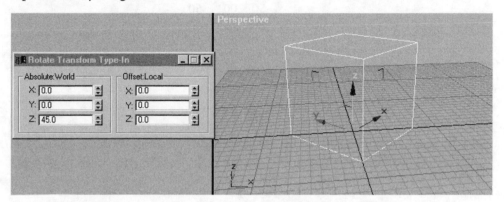

Export to .s3d format and you'll get a scene graph like Listing 4.4, with a single rotated Transform. The values 0 −1 0 −0.7854 indicate a rotation of −.7854 radians (−45 degrees) around the −y axis—the equivalent of 45 degrees around positive y.

LISTING 4.4 ROTATED BOX EXPORTED FROM MAX (*TEST4.S3D*)

```
DEF Box01 Transform {
    translation 0 0 0
    rotation 0 -1 0 -0.7854
    children [
        Shape {
            appearance [
                MultiAppearance {
                    material Material {
                        diffuseColor 0.03137 0.4314 0.5255
                    }
                }
            ]
            geometry MultiMesh {
                coord DEF Box01-COORD Coordinate {
                    point [
                        -50    0    50
                         50    0    50
```

```
                        -50    0   -50
                         50    0   -50
                        -50  100    50
                         50  100    50
                        -50  100   -50
                         50  100   -50
                ]
            }
            coordIndex [
                0  2  3  -1
                3  1  0  -1
                4  5  7  -1
                7  6  4  -1
                0  1  5  -1
                5  4  0  -1
                1  3  7  -1
                7  5  1  -1
                3  2  6  -1
                6  7  3  -1
                2  0  4  -1
                4  6  2  -1
            ]
        }
      }
    ]
  }
```

Go the Hierarchy Panel and click the Reset: Transform button. When you do, the local axis will snap into alignment with the world axis and rotation value of the object will become zero.

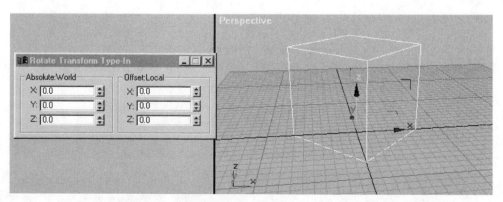

But what's happening internally? Export again and look at the scene graph. As with the pivot point in the previous section, MAX has created a hidden hierarchy. The parent Transform is unrotated, but its child remains rotated. This hierarchy is not visible within MAX, but becomes evident upon export, as you can see in Listing 4.5.

LISTING 4.5 ROTATED BOX WITH TRANSFORM RESET (*TEST5.S3D*)

```
DEF Box01 Transform {
    translation 0 0 0
    children [
        Transform {
            rotation 0 -1 0 -0.7854
            children [
                Shape {
                    appearance [
                        MultiAppearance {
                            material Material {
                                diffuseColor 0.03137 0.4314 0.5255
                            }
                        }
                    ]
                    geometry MultiMesh {
                        coord DEF Box01-COORD Coordinate {
                            point [
                                -50   0    50
                                 50   0    50
                                -50   0   -50
                                 50   0   -50
                                -50 100    50
                                 50 100    50
                                -50 100   -50
                                 50 100   -50
                            ]
                        }
                        coordIndex [
                            0 2 3 -1
                            3 1 0 -1
                            4 5 7 -1
                            7 6 4 -1
                            0 1 5 -1
```

```
                         5  4  0  -1
                         1  3  7  -1
                         7  5  1  -1
                         3  2  6  -1
                         6  7  3  -1
                         2  0  4  -1
                         4  6  2  -1
                     ]
                 }
             }
         ]
     }
   ]
}
```

You should be prepared for what comes next. Apply the Reset XForm command in the Utilities menu. Nothing changes on your MAX screen, but the exported file is fundamentally different. In Listing 4.6, the local coordinate system is now square to world space. There is only a single, unrotated Transform, but all of the vertices have been given new coordinates that correspond exactly with their positions in world space.

LISTING 4.6 ROTATED BOX AFTER RESET XFORM (*TEST6.S3D*)

```
DEF Box01 Transform {
    translation 0 0 0
    children [
        Shape {
            appearance [
                MultiAppearance {
                    material Material {
                        diffuseColor 0.03137 0.4314 0.5255
                    }
                }
            ]
            geometry MultiMesh {
                coord DEF Box01-COORD Coordinate {
                    point [
                         0        0    70.71
                         70.71    0     0
                        -70.71    0     0
                         0        0   -70.71
```

```
             0     100   70.71
           70.71   100     0
          -70.71   100     0
             0     100  -70.71
        ]
      }
      coordIndex [
         0 2 3 -1
         3 1 0 -1
         4 5 7 -1
         7 6 4 -1
         0 1 5 -1
         5 4 0 -1
         1 3 7 -1
         7 5 1 -1
         3 2 6 -1
         6 7 3 -1
         2 0 4 -1
         4 6 2 -1
      ]
    }
  }
 ]
}
```

It's easy to get confused between the Reset Transform command in the Heirarchy Panel and the Reset XForm utility in the Utility Panel. We have used both of these here to understand the difference. As a practical matter, you'll only need to use Reset XForm.

Scaling and Mirroring

Scaling is a troubling issue in MAX for many reasons that have nothing to do with export. As a general rule, it makes more sense to scale all of the vertices or faces at the sub-object level than to perform scaling at the object level. This keeps the adjustment out of the Transform and treats it merely as the translation of the vertices of the mesh. But object-level scaling necessarily arises in the context of mirroring—an extremely common and necessary practice in modeling. This is because mirroring in MAX is produced by negative scaling. These negative values may never generate problems within MAX, but require attention for export.

Create a new 100-unit cube, as in the previous sections, and collapse it to an Editable Mesh. Open Track View and confirm from the Transform tracks that the object is unrotated and the scale is 100 percent in all three dimensions. Make sure you are using local coordinates in the drop-down list on the Main toolbar.

Most mirroring involves making a reflected copy or instance of an object, but to keep it simple, just mirror the cube around itself on the *x* axis (using the No Clone option in the Mirror dialog box). You'll see the local *x* axis of the cube flip to the opposite direction. Open the Scale Transform dialog by right-clicking the Scale tool, and note that the object is scaled to –100 percent in all three directions.

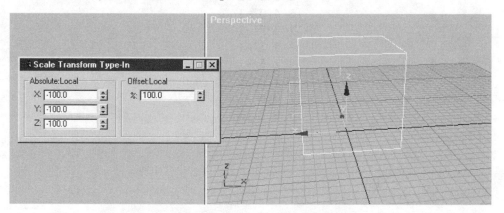

If you open the Rotate Transform dialog box, the object appears to be unrotated. If you look in Track View, however, it's clear that the object is rotated 180 degrees around the negative *x* axis. Experienced MAX users know that Track View always provides the most reliable information, as will be evident if you export the scene and examine the file. The Transform in Listing 4.7 and in the .s3d file contain both the negative scaling and a 180-degree (3.14 radians) rotation around the –*x* axis. (A negative 180-degree rotation is obviously equal to a positive 180-degree rotation).

LISTING 4.7 MIRRORED BOX (*TEST7.S3D*)

```
DEF Box01 Transform {
    translation 0 0 0
    rotation -1 0 0 -3.142
    scale -1 -1 -1
    children [
```

```
Shape {
  appearance [
    MultiAppearance {
      material Material {
        diffuseColor 0.3373 0.3373 0.3373
      }
    }
  ]
  geometry MultiMesh {
    coord DEF Box01-COORD Coordinate {
      point [
        -50   0   50
         50   0   50
        -50   0  -50
         50   0  -50
        -50 100   50
         50 100   50
        -50 100  -50
         50 100  -50
      ]
    }
    coordIndex [
      3 2 0 -1
      0 1 3 -1
      7 5 4 -1
      4 6 7 -1
      5 1 0 -1
      0 4 5 -1
      7 3 1 -1
      1 5 7 -1
      6 2 3 -1
      3 7 6 -1
      4 0 2 -1
      2 6 4 -1
    ]
  }
}
```

Compare the `coordIndex` field here with all of the previous ones. This list indicates how the vertices in the `point` field are connected to create triangles. These numbers are now in reverse order. This is very important because the order in which vertices are connected determines the direction of the normal. A triangle will face the opposite direction if the order of its vertices is reversed.

The model looks fine in MAX, but if you load the exported file into a Shout-ExamineApplet, you'll discover that the box is inside out. There are a couple of ways to deal with this problem. One way is to cover it up. By default, Shout and VRML meshes determine the direction of faces using a counter-clockwise (ccw) convention. We can therefore reserve all of the surface normals by adding the following field to the Multi-Mesh node.

```
geometry MultiMesh {
    ccw false
```

This method preserves the negative scaling and the peculiar rotation, and therefore only covers up the problem. To clean everything up completely, and to avoid the hassle of having to edit the .s3d file, you can use the Reset XForm utility (not Reset Trans-form). The negative scaling disappears, as does the rotation, but the normals are now reversed on the MAX screen, such that you are looking inside the box. To finish the job, select all the faces in the Editable Mesh panel and flip the normals (in the Surface Properties rollout). Export again, and behold a clean and comprehensible scene graph. The scaling and rotations are gone. The order of the vertices in the `coordIndex` array, although rearranged since the last test, is still in the wrong direction, but the vertices in the `point` field have been reordered to accommodate this. Compare this `point` field in Listing 4.8 with all previous versions of the file to understand.

LISTING 4.8 MIRRORED BOX AFTER RESET XFORM (*TEST8.S3D*)

```
DEF Box01 Transform {
    translation 0 0 0
    children [
        Shape {
            appearance [
                MultiAppearance {
                    material Material {
                        diffuseColor 0.3373 0.3373 0.3373
                    }
                }
            ]
```

```
geometry MultiMesh {
coord DEF Box01-COORD Coordinate {
point [
    50    0    50
   -50    0    50
    50    0   -50
   -50    0   -50
    50  100    50
   -50  100    50
    50  100   -50
   -50  100   -50
]
}
coordIndex [
2 0 3 -1
1 3 0 -1
5 4 7 -1
6 7 4 -1
1 0 5 -1
4 5 0 -1
3 1 7 -1
5 7 1 -1
2 3 6 -1
7 6 3 -1
0 2 4 -1
6 4 2 -1
]
}
}
]
}
```

The most important and typical form of mirror occurs when you have modeled one-half of a bilaterally symmetrical mesh and need to create the other half. In MAX, you must attach the two halves to create a single object before you will be allowed to weld points along the centerline. Life will be easier if you attach the mirrored half to the original, rather than the other way around, such that the finished object retains the positive scaling of original half. In any case, you can eliminate the effects of negative scaling using the techniques just described.

Materials and Textures

Shout3D's powers to create beautiful and realistic surfaces represent a breakthrough in Web 3D technologies. Most old-fashioned VRML scenes suffered from a stark and lifeless quality that represents the polar opposite of what a sophisticated audience expects from computer graphics today. With Shout, your results can rival pre-rendered 3D content in subtlety and richness.

From VRML to Shout3D

Shout3D, as we know, is built from VRML. Nowhere is this point more evident than in the subject of appearances (materials and textures). We need to understand the way in which Shout3D has extended VRML in this regard in order to make sense of the Shout3D approach. This is true whether you will be using MAX and exporting to .s3d or whether you will be using VRML export from other modeling and animation packages.

Appearance in VRML

As we learned in Chapter 3, a VRML Shape node (representing an object) contains an `appearance` and a `geometry` field. The `appearance` field contains an Appearance node, which contains a `material` and a `texture` field. These are some important limitations inherent in this structure:

- There can only be one Appearance node on a given Shape. The Shape must therefore have only a single material definition and a single texture map. To accommodate different appearances on a single mesh, you have to break the mesh up into separate Shapes.

- There can be only one image map associated with a Shape—a texture map that modulates the diffuse color of the surface. There is no provision for bump mapping or for mapping other material parameters.

- The entire Shape is subject to the single smoothing angle (called the `creaseAngle`). To create smoothing breaks, you must divide the mesh into separate Shape nodes.

These limitations are serious in themselves, but they are particularly restrictive for those who develop models in sophisticated packages, like 3D Studio MAX, which provide extremely flexible material and texture editing tools.

Appearance in Shout3D

Shout3D provides far more power over object appearance than traditional VRML. Multiple appearances can be assigned to a single, seamless mesh, with specific materials and textures delegated to specific surface regions. You can map a number of material parameters—not just diffuse color. And you can divide a contiguous mesh into different smoothing groups to provide precise smoothing breaks without dividing the geometry into separate Shape nodes.

In VRML, an `appearance` field contains only a single Appearance node. In Shout3D, the `appearance` field holds an array of BaseAppearance nodes. Look up the BaseAppearance class in your Shout online Javadocs documentation and note that two classes are derived from it—Appearance and MultiAppearance. The Appearance node class is simply the old VRML Appearance node, which is retained in Shout3D to remain compatible with .wrl files. Compare this node with the new MultiAppearance in your documentation.

Both the Appearance and MultiAppearance nodes contain a `material` field that holds a Material node. Look up the Material node to see how it defines the overall parameters of the surface, including diffuse color, specularity, emissive color, and transparency (opacity). Past this point, the MultiAppearance node provides many more features than its older brother. In addition to the standard diffuse color map, it offers environmental mapping, specular mapping, bump mapping, opacity mapping, wireframe, and an option to self-illuminate the entire appearance (including the maps).

The name MultiAppearance may seem a little confusing because there is nothing about these features that involves applying different appearances to different regions of a single mesh. To address this issue, Shout3D offers an alternative to the standard IndexedFaceSet geometry, called MultiMesh.

MultiMesh Geometry

As we saw in Chapter 3, the standard VRML IndexedFaceSet specifies the geometry of a mesh using a single list of vertices and single list of faces connecting these vertices. The IndexedFaceSet also contains other information, including colors to be assigned to vertices, texture coordinates for mapping images to the surface and a smoothing angle. It doesn't, however, provide a way of dividing the mesh into groups of faces that can be assigned different materials.

The new Shout MultiMesh node fills this gap. Look up the MultiMesh node class in the online Javadocs documentation and note the `appearanceIndex` field. This field contains a list of numbers that correspond to one or more MultiAppearance nodes in the `appearance` field array. Consider the scene file in Listing 4.9.

LISTING 4.9 MESH WITH TWO APPEARANCES (*TWOCOLORBOX.S3D*)

```
Transform {

   translation   0 0 0

   children   Shape {
      appearance [
        Appearance {
          material   Material {
             diffuseColor 0 1 0 #green


          }
        }
        MultiAppearance {
          material   Material {
             diffuseColor 1 0 0 #red
          }
          selfIlluminate true
        }

      ]
      geometry   MultiMesh {
        coord   Coordinate {
          point
            [ -1 1 1,
             -1 -1 1,
              1 1 1,
              1 -1 1,
              1 1 -1,
              1 -1 -1,
             -1 1 -1,
             -1 -1 -1 ]
        }

        coordIndex
            [ 0, 1, 3, 2, -1,
              4, 5, 7, 6, -1,
```

```
                    6, 7, 1, 0, -1,
                    2, 3, 5, 4, -1,
                    6, 0, 2, 4, -1,
                    1, 7, 5, 3, -1 ]

        appearanceIndex
                [ 0,
                  0,
                  0,
                  1,
                  1,
                  1, ]


            } #end of MultiMesh
          } #end of Shape
        } #end of Transform
```

This scene file was written completely by hand, and is just a modification of the simple onebox.wrl file from Chapter 3. Look first at the MultiMesh node that replaces the former IndexedFaceSet. Just as in the IndexedFaceSet, the six rows in the coordIndex field specify the six faces of the cube-shaped object. The appearanceIndex assigns each such face an appearance from the appearance array above. The first three faces are assigned the appearance with the green material. The second three faces are assigned the second appearance in the array, with the red material. Note that these two appearances are indexed as 0 and 1 (not 1 and 2).

You may already have noticed something peculiar. The appearance array contains both types of BaseAppearance nodes. The first is the old-fashioned VRML Appearance node and the second is a new Shout3D MultiAppearance node. The MultiAppearance node contains a selfIlluminate field (set to true) that is not in the regular Appearance node. You'll probably never create a file like this, but I did it to make a point. The MultiMesh node divides the mesh into different appearance regions, and each of these can be assigned its own BaseAppearance node in the appearance array. It doesn't matter whether that BaseAppearance node is an Appearance node or a MultiAppearance node.

MultiMesh geometry doesn't require multiple BaseAppearance nodes. Very often you will have only a single appearance on MultiMesh geometry exported from MAX.

Look over the scene file in Listing 4.10.

LISTING 4.10 MESH WITH ONE APPEARANCE (*ONECOLORBOX.S3D*)

```
Transform {

  translation   0 0 0


  children   Shape {
    appearance  MultiAppearance {
        material   Material {
          diffuseColor 0 0 1
        }
    }

    geometry   MultiMesh {
      coord   Coordinate {
        point
        [ -1 1 1,
          -1 -1 1,
           1 1 1,
           1 -1 1,
           1 1 -1,
           1 -1 -1,
          -1 1 -1,
          -1 -1 -1 ]
      }

    coordIndex
        [ 0, 1, 3, 2, -1,
          4, 5, 7, 6, -1,
          6, 7, 1, 0, -1,
          2, 3, 5, 4, -1,
          6, 0, 2, 4, -1,
          1, 7, 5, 3, -1 ]


    } #end of MultiMesh
  } #end of Shape
} #end of Transform
```

Here, the MultiMesh node has no **appearanceIndex** array, which is the same as if it had one with all values set to 0. In either case, all of the faces in the mesh are assigned to the first (and only) BaseAppearance in the appearance array. This turns out to be a MultiAppearance node, although it could have been a regular Appearance node. The point is that a MultiMesh geometry node need not be divided into multiple appearance regions. In such a case, it doesn't matter whether the geometry is a MultiMesh or an IndexedFaceSet. We can use a MultiAppearance node for either one.

Observant readers may have noticed that the appearance field in this example is lacking the square brackets that indicate an array. If there is only one appearance on the mesh, and therefore only one BaseAppearance in the array, you can dispense with the brackets. This accommodation allows the Shout viewer to be able to read standard VRML files, in which the appearance field is never an array. However, an array is actually created within Shout, and any Java code you write to interact with the appearance field must reflect this.

Those who create content in MAX and use the Shout3D plug-in will find that all of their mesh geometry is exported as MultiMesh nodes, regardless of whether an object has been divided into multiple Material ID or Smoothing Groups in MAX. All MAX materials will likewise be exported as MultiAppearance nodes, even if they only make use of features included in the older Appearance node.

On the other hand, those users who create content in other programs for VRML export will find only the older Appearance node and IndexedFaceSet geometry in their .wrl files. That doesn't prevent you from hand-editing the .wrl file to replace an Appearance node with a MultiAppearance one. That way, you can add mapping options that can't be exported directly. You can easily add environmental mapping (reflections or light maps) in this way. And, as Shout only supports only a single set of texture coordinates for a given region of mesh, you can add any other kinds of mapping that use these coordinates. If you have tried out a bump map or a transparency map in your 3D package using the same texture coordinates as your diffuse color (texture map), you can be assured that these maps will work correctly in Shout if added by hand to a MultiAppearance node. In short, there are many ways to take advantage of Shout's powerful appearance features even if you are not working with 3D Studio MAX.

Using the MAX Material Editor

The Shout3D MultiAppearance node was designed to capture much of the functionality of the 3D Studio MAX Material Editor. The ideal is to be able to preview materials and textures in MAX and just export to Shout's .s3d format.

As a practical matter, you'll often find that it makes more sense to test materials by editing the .s3d file directly. Shout's rendering quality is excellent, but materials and geometry do not respond to lighting in exactly the same way as they do in MAX. You'll always have to tweak values to get the desired result, and the best place to do this is in the .s3d file. Just edit, save, and reload into an applet to see the result.

Basic Materials Editing

Let's get rolling with a brief exercise that will introduce the use of the MAX Material Editor and hand editing of exported files.

Create a Sphere object in MAX with a radius of 100, and centered at the world origin. Collapse it to an Editable Mesh object. In the Editable Mesh panel, select all the faces north of the equator and set their Material ID to 1. The southern half will retain the default Material ID of 2. Open the Material Editor and select a slot. Change the Material type from Standard to Multi/Sub-Object and assign that Material to the selected Sphere.

Set the number of Materials in the Multi/Sub-Object Material to 2. Select contrasting diffuse colors for the two mesh regions. At this point, the entire mesh is still assigned to a single smoothing group. In the Editable Mesh panel, select all the faces north of about 30 degrees north. In the Smoothing Groups section of the Editable Mesh panel, remove these faces from group 1 and assign them to group 2. You should see a distinct crease between the two smoothing groups.

Leave the specular values on the lower Material at the defaults. For the Material on the upper half, increase the Specular Value to 90 and Glossiness to 50. Note that the default Specular Color is light gray. When you're done, the Sphere should look something like this in a shaded perspective view.

Export the file to .s3d format using the Shout3D Scene Export option under File ➔ Export. Save the file to the models directory of your Shout3D installation as sphere1.s3d. After saving, open sphere1.s3d in a text editor. You can also find a copy of this file on the CD.

Note the two MultiAppearance nodes representing the two Materials in the Multi/Sub-Object Material. Go down to the bottom of the MultiMesh geometry node to see how the faces in the mesh are equally divided between these two MultiAppearances in the appearanceIndex field (indexed as 0 and 1). Look at the smoothingIndex to see how the faces are divided between the two smoothing groups (1 and 2).

To test this out in the Shout player, create an HTML file with the following <APPLET> tag and save it to the demos directory of your Shout3D installation as spheretest.html. (You can copy a finished version of spheretest.html from the CD if you wish.)

```
<applet CODEBASE="../codebase" CODE="applets/ExamineApplet.class"
ARCHIVE="shout3dClasses.zip" WIDTH="300" HEIGHT="300">
  <param name="src" value="models/sphere1.s3d">
  <param name="backgroundColorR" value="1">
  <param name="backgroundColorG" value="1">
  <param name="backgroundColorB" value="1">
  <param name="headlightOn" value="true">
</applet>
```

Load the HTML file into a browser to check it out. The headlight is on, and therefore any specular highlights will face directly toward the viewer. You are using the Examine-Applet, so you can rotate the Viewpoint around the object by dragging the mouse, and zoom by dragging with the Ctrl key pressed. You'll see that the top half of the sphere has a strong specular highlight that will break noticeably over the line between the two smoothing groups. The lower half of the sphere has no meaningful specularity.

Let's consider only the appearance array by itself. Your diffuse colors will be different if you created this file yourself.

```
appearance [
        MultiAppearance {
          material Material {
            diffuseColor 0.9843 1 0.5255
            specularColor 0.8082 0.8082 0.8082
            shininess 0.5
            transparency 0
          }
        }
```

```
MultiAppearance {
    material Material {
        diffuseColor 0.2588 0.3922 0.2157
        specularColor 0.045 0.045 0.045
        shininess 0.25
        transparency 0
    }
  }
]
```

Notice the difference in the way specularity is handled as compared to the MAX Material editor. In the Material Editor, specularity is a function of three parameters— Specular Color, Specular Level and Glossiness. The Shout Material node contains only `specularColor` and `shininess` fields. Glossiness is the amount of "spread" in a specular highlight, and higher values produce a smaller, tighter hotspot. Note that the .5 value in the `shininess` field corresponds correctly to the Glossiness value of 50 in the MAX Material Editor.

On the other hand, the values in the `specularColor` field may not make obvious sense at first. The Shout3D exporter generates these values by multiplying the MAX Specular Color by the MAX Specular Level. We set the Specular Level to 90 percent and the default Specular Color is (.898,.898,.898), corresponding to (229,229,229) in the 0–255 system. If you multiply each of the red, green, and blue components of the Specular Color by 90 percent, you'll come up with the `specularColor` in the Shout3D Material node.

With this knowledge, we can adjust the specularity by editing the values directly in the scene file. To change the intensity of the highlight without changing its neutral color, set the `specularColor` field to any three equal values. These values can be greater that 1.0, if you wish. This may seem funny if you think of the field only as a color, but it reflects the fact that the Specular Level in the MAX Material Editor can be set above 100 percent. To create a colored highlight, the three values must be uneven. For example, a `specularColor` field of .5 .5 .8 will create a blue highlight.

Take some time here to experiment with different specularity values in the scene file, on both halves of the mesh. Just save the edited file and reload it to see the result. This will not only teach you a fair amount about the power of specularity in Shout3D, but also how easy it is to test material parameters by hand editing a scene file. While you're at it, experiment with the `transparency` field. Transparency is the inverse of Opacity in the MAX Material Editor. Thus typing the value of .3 in the `transparency` field produces the same result at as setting the Opacity to 70 percent in MAX and exporting. Test this out to confirm it for yourself.

There's one situation in which hand editing is especially important. The Shout3D Material node contains an `emissiveColor` field in which you can set a color that will render regardless of the amount of light cast on the surface. The MAX Material Editor provides a Self-Illumination parameter that functions in two different ways. If you use the Color option, you can set a Self-Illumination color that can be different than the Diffuse Color. If the Color option is off, you can set a percentage by which the current Diffuse Color will become self-illuminating. The most direct way to create a self-illuminating color is simply to type in an `emissiveColor` field in the Material node. If you don't want this color complicated by a diffuse color, edit the `diffuseColor` field to be black (0,0,0). The following code sets the `emissiveColor` to a bright red.

```
MultiAppearance {
    material Material {
        diffuseColor 0 0 0
        specularColor 0.045 0.045 0.045
        shininess 0.25
        transparency 0
        emissiveColor .8 0 0
    }
}
```

The Shout3D MAX exporter makes use of the Self-Illumination section of the MAX Material Editor in an interesting way. It does not export to the `emissiveColor` field, and thus setting a Self-Illumination color in the Material Editor has no effect on the resulting .s3d file. However, if you turn off the Color option and use the percentage slider, any value above 50 percent will generate a `true` value in the `selfIlluminate` field of the MultiAppearance node, like so:

```
MultiAppearance {
    material Material {
        diffuseColor 0.9843 1 0.5255
        specularColor 0.8082 0.8082 0.8082
        shininess 0.5
        transparency 0
    }
    selfIlluminate TRUE
}
```

The selfIlluminate field is set to false by default, and is therefore not generally printed out by the Shout3D MAX exporter. When it's set to true, it illuminates the diffuse color of the object, whether that diffuse color is from the Material node or whether it's from any diffuse color texture map applied to the surface. That's why selfIlluminate is a field of the MultiAppearance node and not a field of the Material node within MultiAppearance. It's probably just as easy to type the field into the MultiAppearance node by hand as it is to use the MAX interface. (The MAX Self-Illumination percentage spinner affects both the diffuse color material and any diffuse color texture maps when rendering within MAX itself.)

Texture Mapping

The term "texture map" is much abused. It is typically used to refer to the application of a bitmap image to control the diffuse color of a surface. We'll use it here in a broader sense to mean the image mapping of any material parameter and of bumps. The Shout3D MultiAppearance node provides for texture mapping of diffuse color, specular level, bump level, and opacity. Despite the fact that the MultiMesh node provides for an array of texture mappings (sets of texture coordinates), you can only use a single set of texture coordinates at present. In MAX terms, you can only make use of a single Map Channel with respect to any group of faces. This will not generally be much of an inconvenience.

A short exercise will be sufficient to get you started. I'll assume that you already understand the basics of texture mapping in 3D Studio MAX.

In an empty MAX scene, create a Box object 100 units in all dimensions and collapse it to an Editable Mesh object. Place a UVW Mapping modifier on the stack and use the default Planar projection. Select the Y Alignment option to project from the front, and click the Fit button to snap the projection gizmo squarely to the model. This process creates texture coordinates for all of the vertices of the model.

Open the Material Editor and select a slot. Place a bitmap in the Diffuse Color channel. A good choice for this test is Yellobrk.jpg from your MAX maps directory. Assign the material to the Box object and click the Show Map in Viewport button in the Material Editor to preview the image on the object. The image should be correctly aligned to the front and back of the Box, and smeared on all other sides. I've provided a copy of this MAX file as texture.MAX and have also included the image (reduced to a reasonable file size for Web use).

Export this file in .s3d format to the models directory in your Shout3D installation. Use the filename texture.s3d. Open this file in a text editor. It should look like Listing 4.11.

LISTING 4.11 BOX WITH DIFFUSE TEXTURE MAP (*TEXTURE.S3D*)

```
DEF Box01 Transform {
    translation 0 0 0
    children [
        Shape {
            appearance [
                MultiAppearance {
                    material Material {
                        diffuseColor 0.5373 0.1961 0.1961
                        specularColor 0.045 0.045 0.045
                        shininess 0.25
                        transparency 0
                    }
                    diffuseMap DiffuseMap {
                        texture ImageTexture {
                            url "Yellobrk.JPG"
                        }
                    }
                }
            ]
            geometry MultiMesh {
                coord DEF Box01-COORD Coordinate {
                    point [
                        -50 0 50 50 0 50 -50 0 -50
                        50 0 -50 -50 100 50 50 100 50
                        -50 100 -50 50 100 -50
                    ]
                }
                coordIndex [
                    0 2 3 -1 3 1 0 -1 4 5 7 -1 7 6 4 -1
                    0 1 5 -1 5 4 0 -1 1 3 7 -1 7 5 1 -1
                    3 2 6 -1 6 7 3 -1 2 0 4 -1 4 6 2 -1
                ]
                smoothingIndex [
                    2 -1 2 -1 3 -1 3 -1 4 -1 4 -1
                    5 -1 5 -1 6 -1 6 -1 7 -1 7 -1
                ]
                appearanceIndex [
                    1 1 0 0 4 4 3 3 5 5 2 2
                ]
```

```
          textureMappings [
            TextureMapping {
              texCoord TextureCoordinate {
                point [
                    0.0004995 0.0004995
                    0.9995 0.0004995
                    0.0004998 0.0004995
                    0.9995 0.0004995
                    0.0004995 0.9995
                    0.9995 0.9995
                    0.0004998 0.9995
                    0.9995 0.9995
                ]
              }
            }
          ]
        }
      }
    ]
  }
```

Notice the list of texture coordinates in the TextureCoodinate node. There are eight pairs of *(u,v)* coordinates corresponding to the eight vertices of the box. All of the values in these pairs are extremely close to 0.0 or 1.0, which makes sense because all of the vertices are mapped to the edges of the bitmap.

The `appearanceIndex` contains six different values even though there is only one MAX Material (MultiAppearance node) assigned to the entire object. MAX automatically creates separate Material IDs for the six faces of a parametric Box object, and these are preserved upon export. However, as there is only a single MultiAppearance node, this division into separate mesh regions is ultimately ignored.

Finally, note the `diffuseMap` field. The `url` field of the ImageTexture node contains only the name of the image, without any path information. This will be true regardless of the path of the bitmap used in MAX. This means that Shout player will not be able to load the image unless you put a copy of it in the same directory in which you place the .s3d file. Place a copy of `Yellobrk.jpg` in the `models` directory of your Shout3D installation. If you wish to place the image elsewhere, you must edit the path in the .s3d file. For example, if you choose to place the image in `models\images\shared`, you must change the `url` field to read as follows:

```
url "images/shared/Yellobrk.JPG"
```

Note the direction of the slashes in this path. Test it out by editing the `spheretest.html` file used in the previous section to reference `texture.s3d` and save it as `texture.html`— or copy `texture.html` from the CD to your `demos` directory. Load the HTML file into a browser. The textured result is pretty impressive.

A brick texture like this will often be tiled. If you set the tiling to 2.0 in the U direction in the Material Editor, the map will tile horizontally in your MAX preview. However, this tiling information does not export to .s3d. There's another way. Return to U tiling of 1.0 in the Material Editor. Set the U Tile parameter to 2.0 in the UVW Mapping modifier panel and export again. This time, the result will be tiled in the Shout player.

If you open up the .s3d file, you'll notice that the texture coordinates have changed to values of 0 and 2, instead of 0 and 1.

Even though you can't use the Tiling spinner in the Material Editor, you can still use the Offset spinner. Remove the tiling in the UVW Mapping modifier, and set the U Offset value in the Material Editor to .1. This will shift the map horizontally such that the top row of the image starts and ends with complete bricks. Export again and open the .s3d file in a text editor. Notice how the DiffuseMap node contains a new field.

```
offsetUV 0.1 0
```

Load the revised scene into a browser to see the result.

As is often the case, the brick image can serve as a bump map as well as a diffuse map. In the Maps rollout of the MAX Material Editor, drag a copy of the map down from the Diffuse Color channel to the Bump channel. Set the Bump amount to 100. Export to .s3d format and open the file in a text editor. You'll find a BumpLevelMap node added to the MultiAppearance node in its `bumpLevelMap` field. Load the file into your browser and notice the difference. You may have to zoom in a bit to appreciate it, but there is distinctly more contrast and relief.

The bump effect in the Shout player will generally look different than it does it MAX, so you'll often find it useful to edit the bumpLevel field by hand for rapid testing and adjustment. Since we used the default level of 100 when exporting from MAX, the bumpLevel field was not written out. Had we used any other value, for example, 50, it would have appeared in the .s3d code.

```
bumpLevelMap BumpLevelMap {
  amount 0.5
  texture ImageTexture {
    url "Yellobrk.JPG"
  }
  offsetUV 0.1 0
}
```

Take some time to experiment with different amount values by typing the field into your .s3d file.

Texture painting and mapping is an art of critical importance to the quality of the 3D rendering, particularly where one is seeking a photo-realistic effect. Shout3D has brought superb texturing to realtime Web 3D, opening up long-promised possibilities for e-commerce and entertainment content that require high graphical production values.

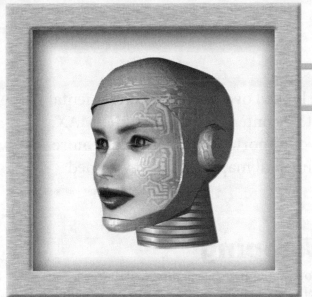

More MAX Export Issues

SHOUT3D

Chapter 5

In the previous chapter, we looked over the most fundamental aspects of exporting Shout3D content from 3D Studio MAX. Let's now turn to a couple of important, but somewhat more sophisticated, topics—environmental mapping and keyframed animation.

Environmental Mapping

Environmental mapping is the process of causing an image to surround the scene. The image can be made visible during rendering to create an environmental background, but it is often used solely for its effects on objects in the scene. A reflection map creates the sense of an environment surrounding the object by "reflecting" the mapped image on the object's surface. Reflection mapping is particularly important for convincing metallic surfaces. A light map, by contrast, is a way of using the intensity and color of surrounding bitmaps to "illuminate" the surface of an object in place of regular light sources.

Environmental maps in Shout3D can make use of an environmental sphere or an environmental cube. A spherical environment uses only a single image mapped to a sphere surrounding the scene. The cube applies six bitmaps to the six inside faces of a surrounding cube, although it's possible to gang the six images up in a single file. Only a cube map can be made into a renderable environmental background in the form of a Panorama node. It's possible to texture map an image to the inside of a true geometric spherical object that is made large enough to enclose the entire scene, and thereby create a spherically mapped renderable background. This, however, is texture mapping, not environmental mapping, and such a sphere could not be used for reflection mapping or light mapping of the objects inside it.

Environmental mapping does not use texture coordinates assigned to the geometry because the image is projected on scene geometry in real time. That's why reflections on an object will change as it is rotated against a surrounding reflection map. As no texture coordinates are required, the use of MAX (or any other 3D package) is unnecessary when adding environmental maps to a scene. It's easy to add environmental maps to .s3d files in a text editor, as we shall see. Creating new images for cubic environmental maps can be done in MAX.

EnvironmentMap Basics

Open the Shout3D online Javadocs documentation and look at the MultiAppearance node. You'll see that it contains an environmentMap field. This field holds an EnvironmentMap node. Look up the EnvironmentMap node and note its style and tintColor fields; its two subclasses, EnvironmentSphereMap and EnvironmentCube-Map, inherit these fields. Investigate further to see how the EnvironmentalSphereMap adds a texture field that contains a Texture node. By contrast, the EnvironmentCube-Map contains six texture fields for the six sides of the cube, plus a single texture field to be used where all six images have been arranged into a single bitmap.

This is a good moment to look into the Texture node. It has no fields and its only subclass is the PixelBasedTexture node. The PixelBasedTexture node introduces methods for getting and setting the red, green, blue, and alpha channels of a color bitmap. The only subclass of PixelBasedTexture is ImageTexture, which adds an url field that identifies the image file (in GIF or JPEG format) from which the bitmap data is to be loaded. The ImageTexture node will be the most commonly used occupant of the texture field in an EnviromentMap node. However, Shout3D provides a Gradient-Texture node in the Custom_nodes directory that creates a gradient bitmap from colors that you assign.

The process of working your way through the Shout3D class library, as you've just been doing, is extremely important. The new user is tempted to make do with a superficial understanding, but the sooner you come to understand Shout3D as a structured class library, the more useful it will become to you.

Spherical Environment Maps

A spherical environment map is easy to create and is generally used for reflection mapping. Spherical maps cannot be exported from MAX and must be added to a .s3d file by hand.

Spherical Reflection Maps

Create a Box object in MAX—the dimensions and color don't matter—and center it in world space. Export it in .s3d format to your models directory, and name it reflect.s3d. Open the file in a text editor and add an environmentMap field as follows:

```
MultiAppearance {
    material Material {
        diffuseColor 0 0 1
```

```
    }
    environmentMap  EnvironmentSphereMap {
      texture ImageTexture {
        url "images/shared/wooden_stage_bg.jpg"
      }
    }
  }
```

Take some time to understand the structure. The `texture` field contains an Image-Texture node, which in turn contains an `url` field. When this begins to make sense, try it out by loading it into an ExamineApplet. If you wish, you can copy the `reflect.s3d` and `reflect.html` files from the CD into your Shout3D installation. You'll see that the box is reflecting the `wooden_stage_bg.jpg` image that is used as the background image in the `modswing.html` Shout demo.

Rotate the camera by dragging the mouse. Note how the reflections change.

Spherical Light Maps

By default, the style of an EnvironmentMap generates a reflection map. By changing the style, you can produce a light map.

```
    MultiAppearance {
      material Material {
        diffuseColor 0 0 1
      }
      environmentMap  EnvironmentSphereMap {
        style LIGHT_MAP
```

```
        texture ImageTexture {
            url "matte.jpg"
        }
    }
}
```

A light map uses the intensity and color of the surrounding image to "illuminate" the surface to which it's applied. If light map is use, the surface will not be affected by regular light sources. Light maps are, in effect, a kind of self-illumination modulated by the image. It takes a fair amount of experimentation to get the results you want, especially when illuminating surfaces with diffuse texture maps.

The following is a typical example of a grayscale "lightball" image for a light map. This image, `lightball.gif`, is provided on the CD.

Cubic Environment Maps

The primary purpose of cubic environment maps is to provide renderable panoramic backgrounds. If all you need is a reflection map, a spherical environment map will do the job nicely and easily. However, if you are using a cubic environmental map as a panoramic background, you'll obviously want to make use of it for reflections, as well.

The best way to understand cubic maps is by looking at a demo provided in your Shout3D installation. Open the RenderTests folder of your demos directory, and run `multimesh_chrome_teapot.html`. This scene, running in an ExamineApplet, contains a teapot and a Panorama node. The EnvironmentCubeMap node used for the Panorama is also used as a reflection map for the teapot. The effect is extremely convincing.

Look at the source code of the HTML file to determine the scene file being used. It turns out to be multimesh_chrome.wrl, located in the RenderTests folder in the models directory. Open this scene file in a text editor. The following excerpt from this file isolates the use of the EnvironmentCubeMap.

```
DEF myPanorama Panorama {
  bilinearFilteringEnabled FALSE
  environmentCubeMap DEF envMap EnvironmentCubeMap {
frontTexture ImageTexture {
url "../images/envmap_haze/front.jpg"
 }
    rightTexture ImageTexture {
url "../images/envmap_haze/right.jpg"
 }
    backTexture ImageTexture {
url "../images/envmap_haze/back.jpg"
 }
    leftTexture ImageTexture {
url "../images/envmap_haze/left.jpg"
 }
    upTexture ImageTexture {
url "../images/envmap_haze/up.jpg"
 }
    downTexture ImageTexture {
url "../images/envmap_haze/down.jpg"
 }
 }

DEF Teapot01 Transform {
```

```
translation 0 0 0
children [
 Shape {
 appearance [
   MultiAppearance {
     environmentMap USE envMap
   }
 ]
]
```

The Panorama node contains an environmentCubeMap field that holds an Environment-CubeMap node. This node, in turn, holds the six ImageTexture nodes constituting the six faces of the cube. Note how the EnvironmentCubeMap is DEF named envMap. This permits the node to be used (instanced) as a reflection map in the teapot's MultiAppearance node with a simple USE statement.

Look at the six bitmaps in the models\images\envmap_haze directory in Photoshop or another bitmap editor. (You can load them directly into a Web browser, if necessary.) They connect seamlessly to create a complete panorama.

Panorama nodes yield impressive results, but there are important practical limitations to consider. A high-quality background means six high-quality images—a significant cost in download time. A Panorama node also slows the user's frame rate, which may be an important issue in games and other applications demanding rapid rendering. The use of bilinear filtering disguises the jagged quality of lower resolution images, but comes at its own cost in frame rate. Change the `bilinearFilteringEnabled` field to `true` in `multimesh_chrome.wrl`. Save it, reload the demo, and compare the background quality. The images are slightly blurred, which is no advantage with these high-resolution images, but might be necessary with lower-resolution bitmaps that might otherwise look "pixilated." Compare rendering speeds by pressing the 'f' key to display the frame rate.

The six images of an EnvironmentCubeMap can be consolidated in a single strip and saved as a single file. Look at `miniblur_all.jpg` *in the* `envmap_redrock` *folder for an example. Compare it with the six separate images in the same directory. Such a reduced and low-resolution image does not make a satisfactory panoramic background, but is good enough for reflection mapping. Also, the small, blurred images can be used for a brushed-metal effect since they do not produce sharp reflections.*

You can produce your own images for EnvironmentCubeMaps within 3D Studio MAX. Create a small Box object and place it at the world origin. Arrange a number of simple objects all around the Box to serve as the contents of the panoramic background. Place them in all directions relative to the central Box. When you're satisfied, open the Material Editor and assign a material in a slot to the Box.

MAX provides a valuable method for rendering the environment around a selected object into six images. Place a Reflect/Refract map type in the Reflection channel of the Maps rollout in the Material Editor. Set the Source to "From File." The default image size in the Size spinner is 100. Change it to 256 to create bitmaps with 256×256 dimensions. At the bottom of the panel, click the To File button. Browse to the directory you want to store the images in and give the file a name. Finally, click the Pick Object and Render Maps button. Click the Box object in your scene and watch the six images render. You'll find them in the directory you designated, ready for use in an EnvironmentCubeMap node.

Exporting Keyframe Animation

Traditional VRML keyframed animation is limited to linear interpolation. MAX, like all 3D animation packages, offers spline interpolation. To approximate the smooth curvature and subtle speed changes of spline interpolated function curves, the MAX VRML exporter provides a sampling mechanism. The greater the number of frame samples, the closer the linear interpolated result approximates the spline interpolated original. This method can never be very accurate, especially for the demanding purposes of character animation, but it tends to generate large scene files that capture animation data at small frame intervals.

Shout3D has extended VRML's standard linear Interpolator nodes to support Bezier and TCB (Tension-Continuity-Bias) spline interpolation. Thus MAX animation created with spline interpolated controllers can be accurately exported to Shout3D without sampling. Whenever you export from MAX, a small dialog box offers the choice between using the keys set in MAX and sampling the animation at a given frame rate. When you use the former choice, your spline interpolation is preserved.

Controllers govern animation in 3D Studio MAX. There is always a default controller for a specific animatable parameter, but knowledgeable MAX animators will often select a more appropriate one for the task. Thus the most important consideration when animating for Shout3D export is determining how the various animation controllers survive the conversion process into Shout3D interpolators.

Animating Transforms

Most animation involves keyframing the transforms—position, rotation, and scale. MAX offers many controller choices for each of these, but the consequences for Shout3D export must be factored into the decision.

Position Controllers

The default controller for position (translation) animation in MAX is called Bezier Position. It uses three Bezier splines as function curves in Track View for the x, y, and z dimensions. This information is contained in only a single animation channel, and there are thus x, y, and z values for every keyframe. In other words, if you move an object only the x direction and set a key, you'll find keys created in the y and z function curves as well.

Shout3D export of Bezier Position animation is flawless. To test it, create a very simple animation of a Box object translating from $x=-100$ to $x=100$ over 100 frames, using the Bezier Position controller. Keep the function curve straight between the two key frames. Export to .s3d format and open the file. You'll find a BezierVecInterpolator node with two keys at the start and end of the animation (0 and 1), and a set of key values.

```
DEF Box01-BEZPOS-INTERP BezierVecInterpolator {
    key [ 0 1 ]
    keyValue [ -100 0 0 -33.34 0 0 33.33 0 0 100 0 0 ]
}
```

The keyValue field is a little difficult to understand at first, but you can identify the (x,y,z) values of the two keyframes at the beginning and the end of the list. The second three values (−33.34,0,0) represent the positions of the Bezier handles following the first key. The handle for the x direction curve is at −33.34. The handles for the y and z curves are at 0. You can see this by opening up a function curve view of the Position track in Track View. (The flat y and z curves lay on top of each other.)

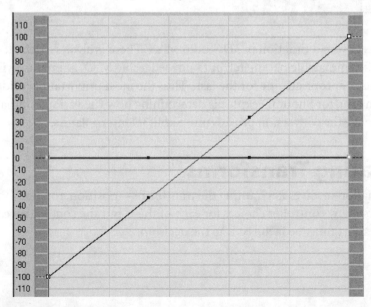

The next group of three values indicates the position of the next group of Bezier handles—those entering the second key. If you adjust the Bezier handles in Track View to create a typical pair of "ease-in" and "ease-out" accelerations and decelerations, the exported values will reflect the new positions of the Bezier tangent handles for the x direction function curve.

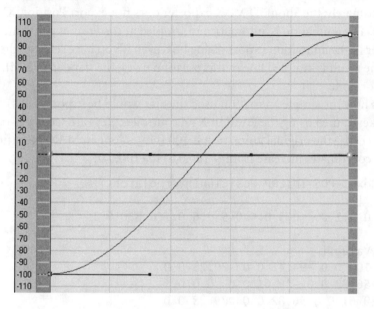

```
DEF Box01-BEZPOS-INTERP BezierVecInterpolator {
    key [ 0 1 ]
    keyValue [ -100 0 0 -100 0 0 100 0 0 100 0 0 ]
}
```

The keys can only make sense in the context of the TimeSensor node. The exported TimeSensor sets the length of the animation to 3.33 seconds, corresponding to 100 frames at 30 frames per second. Note how keys in VRML and Shout3D are set as percentages of the total time length of the animation, and not as specific frames.

```
DEF world-TIMER TimeSensor {
    loop TRUE
    cycleInterval 3.333
}
```

The most important translational controller in MAX, after Bezier Position, is Position XYX. This controller uses Bezier spline interpolation just like Bezier Position, but divides the three function curves for the *x, y* and *z* dimensions into three separate tracks. Thus, a key placed on one track does not appear on another. For example, if we create the same animation as before, but using Position XYZ, only the *x* direction function curve will have key frames. This structure can be easier to edit in many cases because changes made in one dimension have no impact on the other two.

Unfortunately, the Shout3D MAX exporter does not export Position XYZ keyframes. The animation is automatically sampled at the Frames per Sample rate on the spinner in the animation export dialog box, even if you have selected the Use Keys option. The result is sampled linear interpolation using the standard VRML Position-Interpolator node.

Here's how the simple animation used thus far would be exported at 10 frames per sample if keyframed using the Position XYZ controller. Keys are set at ten-percent intervals because the original animation is 100 frames long in MAX. Note how the keyValue coordinates increase from (−100,0,0) to (100,0,0).

```
DEF Box01-POS-INTERP PositionInterpolator {
  key [
     0 0.1 0.2 0.3 0.4 0.5 0.6 0.7 0.8 0.9 1
  ]
  keyValue [
    -100 0 0 -94.42 0 0 -79.23 0 0
    -56.82 0 0 -29.61 0 0  0 0 0
    29.61 0 0 56.82 0 0  79.23 0 0
    94.42 0 0 100 0 0
  ]
}
```

This kind of sampling and linear interpolation is obviously inferior to using the true Bezier function curves from MAX, and it argues for using the Bezier Position controller in lieu of the Position XYZ. This will generally be possible without major inconvenience. Note that converting existing animation from Position XYZ to Bezier Position within MAX can damage it in ways that require tedious editing to restore. If you intend to export to Shout3D, it makes sense to animate with the Bezier Position controller from the start.

Path animation, using the Path controller, is another important approach to translational animation. The Path controller causes an object to follow a spline that the animator draws in the scene. Path controller keyframes represent percentages of the total distance along the path, and not (*x,y,z*) coordinates in space. Once again, the exporter will sample values and export with linear interpolation. MAX, however, allows you to sample Bezier Position keyframes along a spline, and thus create a sampled "path" animation within MAX. This approach will be far preferable to using the Path controller if you intend to export to Shout3D. Because Bezier interpolation is used, the sampled animation can follow the path more accurately than can linear interpolated samples. To perform this sampling, use the Bezier Position controller and open the Trajectories rollout in the Motion Panel in MAX with the object selected. Set the Sample Range spinners as desired and activate the Convert From button. Click the spline and watch keys appear along the "path." Experiment with different sample rates to get the best result.

Relatively few MAX users are familiar with the TCB Position controller. This controller uses Tension-Continuity-Bias spinners to shape interpolation along a spline, instead of Bezier tangent handles. Most of animators who choose to use TCB interpolation instead of Bezier interpolation have honed their skills in the old 3D Studio, the DOS ancestor to MAX, or in another package (such as the older versions of Lightwave) that lacked Bezier function curves. Shout3D MAX exporter can export Position TCB keyframes using the TCBVecInterpolator node.

Rotation Controllers

Rotational animation in MAX nearly always comes down to a choice between the default TCB Rotation controller and the EulerXYZ controller. This is not the place to engage in a full-scale discussion of this difficult subject. It's enough to note that, quite apart from its use of Tension-Continuity-Bias interpolation, the main feature of TCB Rotation is the use of axis-angle rotational values that cannot be graphed (and edited) as function curves. As no other 3D-animation package uses this approach to rotations, many MAX animators use the EulerXYZ controller for all rotational animation. Most people who use TCB animation do so either because they don't know any better or because they have become especially skillful with this controller.

The Shout3D MAX exporter can export TCB Rotation keys using the TCB-OrientationInterpolator node. This node preserves all of the values that you set for each TCB key, although the ranges are defined differently. The tension, continuity, and bias values that vary between 0 and 50 in MAX are mapped to a range from –1.0 to 1.0 in the TCBOrientationInterpolator. The ease-in and ease-out values that vary between 0 and 50 in MAX are mapped to a range from 0.0 to 1.0 in the Shout3D node. Angles that are measured in degrees in MAX are converted to radians, as in all VRML or Shout3D nodes.

The EulerXYZ controller in MAX uses Bezier interpolation, but is more significantly distinguished from the TCB Rotation controller by its use of composite rotations around the x, y, and z axes—each with its own editable function curve in Track

View. This is the most comprehensible and useful method of animating rotations for general purposes. The Shout3D MAX exporter correctly exports EulerXYZ keys, preserving the separate tracks of this controller as separate scalar interpolators within the larger EulerXYZInterpolator.

The following example shows the exported result of a simple animation involving separately keyed rotations around two axes. The values in the keyValue fields match the values you would find in Track View function curves, as we have discussed with regard to the Bezier Position controller; however, all of the exported values have been converted from degrees to radians.

```
DEF Box01-EULER-INTERP EulerXYZInterpolator {
    yInterpolator BezierScalarInterpolator {
      key [ 0 1 ]
      keyValue [ 0 0.5236 1.047 1.571 ]
    }
    zInterpolator BezierScalarInterpolator {
      key [ 0 0.49 ]
      keyValue [ 0 -0.1353 -0.2705 -0.4058 ]
    }
}
```

Scale Controllers

There will rarely be a need to use a scale controller in MAX other than the default Bezier Scale. Like Bezier Position, all three function curves are combined in a single track, and thus all keys have three values. As you might suspect, the Shout3D MAX exporter exports Bezier Scale animation to a BezierVecInterpolator node in the same manner as Bezier Position animation. Those who have a reason to use the TCB Scale controller in MAX will be able to export these function curves as well.

Morphing

Morphing is, at bottom, translating the vertices of a mesh. In traditional VRML, morphing is accomplished with a CoordinateInterpolator node. This node is notoriously inefficient. It stores the coordinates for every vertex and for every key. This means that vertices are listed regardless of whether they actually move, and the vertices of a given state (representing a morph target) are fully repeated each time it is used for a keyframe. The CoordinateInterpolator node supports only linear interpolation. All these weaknesses contributed to unreasonably large .wrl files.

CoordinateNodeInterpolator

Shout3D has improved the CoordinateInterpolator node in an important way. The new CoordinateNodeInterpolator can interpolate between named point lists, making it easy to create simple, linear interpolated morphs by hand-editing .s3d files.

Create your morph targets in the normal way, by editing the "anchor" object. Morph targets can be reliably constructed only as edited copies of a single, original object. The following image shows a typical setup, with two targets created by moving vertices on copies of the original box-shaped mesh on the right.

When exporting to .s3d format, check the Export Animation Keys box, even though you don't have any animation, as this will write out a TimeSensor node for you to use.

Within MAX (and every other animation package) the anchor object itself is available as a morph target. However, when using the CoordinateNodeInterpolator, you'll need two copies of your anchor object—one to use as the object being morphed and another to use as a morph target (a shape state). Thus you'll need to duplicate the entire Transform of the anchor object to elsewhere in the file.

You must DEF name all of the Coordinate nodes for each piece of geometry. Having done so, you can use these names in the CoordinateNodeInterpolator and route the output to the Coordinate node of the object being morphed.

```
DEF CNI CoordinateNodeInterpolator {
    key [ 0.0 .25 .5 .75 1.0]
    keyValue [
      USE ANCHOR
```

```
        USE UP
        USE ANCHOR
        USE ANCHOR
        USE DOWN
    ]
}

    ROUTE world-TIMER.fraction TO CNI.fraction
    ROUTE CNI.value TO MESH.point
```

The entire example file can be found on the CD as `cni.s3d`. Note in that file how all of the morph targets are made invisible by setting the `hidden` fields of their Transform nodes to `true`.

Exporting from MAX

Any kind of sophisticated morphing must be animated in MAX. MAX provides two morphing tools. The older Morph Compound Object is simple to use, but limited. The Shout3D MAX exporter does not export any animation created with this tool, even by sampling.

The Morpher modifier was introduced in MAX 3, and is extremely powerful and flexible. It implements weighted, additive morphing. Weighted morphing permits you to set the percentage by which a morph target will deform the anchor object. Additive morphing allows two or more targets to affect the anchor at any given time. The following image shows the anchor object (at right) morphed by the both targets (to the left) at the same time. The bottom of the anchor is fully morphed to the shape of its target, but the top is only partially morphed.

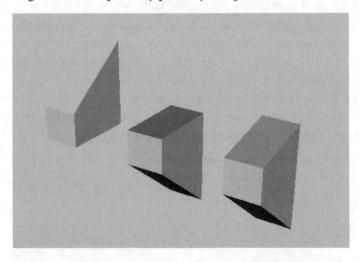

Animations produced with the Morpher modifier export perfectly. By default the animated channels use Bezier interpolation, which is exported correctly. And if you change the governing controllers in Track View to TCB interpolation, Shout will preserve the TCB interpolation on export and will export this correctly, as well. If you hide your morph targets in MAX, they will conveniently be dropped from the exported file, saving you the trouble of having to delete them.

The more serious and inquisitive reader will want to take some time to see how the ChannelDeformer node implements this kind of morphing. This node reflects the channels in the MAX Morpher modifier, and identifies the specific vertices affected by each channel. Make a quick test by creating a simple morphing animation of your own and look over the exported .s3d file.

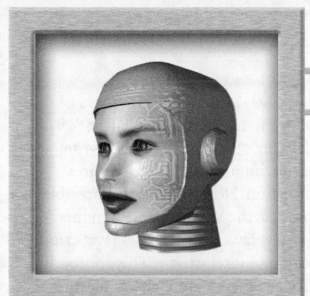

Java Basics for
Shout3D

SHOUT3D

Chapter 6

Most interactivity in Shout3D is achieved through Java or JavaScript programming. High-end commercial work is best done entirely in Java, in which the developer writes custom applets and/or nodes that augment the standard features that come with the Shout3D installation. However, it is also possible to use the JavaScript language to access the Shout Java API. In this case, the developer does not write new Java code and uses JavaScript on the HTML page to provide logic and interactivity. This approach is more limited and is not effective on all Web browsers. Thus, this book focuses primarily on writing Java classes for Shout, and it will address the use of JavaScript in only a cursory way.

Many readers will approach this book with some knowledge of programming and perhaps of Java programming in particular. But Shout3D will often be a 3D artist's or a Web developer's first exposure to Java or to programming generally. This chapter is designed to get such readers off the ground.

Treated abstractly, Java programming is a monumental subject. Our goals here are quite specific. We are concerned with Java only for the purpose of creating custom interactivity in Shout3D. Everything you can learn about Java will certainly help you, but it is definitely possible for the motivated newbie to learn a set of Java skills that are tailored precisely to the task of Shout3D development. Use this chapter to get started, and find some other books about Java to help you out and give you a broader perspective. You can never learn too much.

One of the great powers and premises of object-oriented programming languages like Java is the concept of encapsulation. Tools can be treated as "black boxes." You can learn how to use them in a practical way without understand their internal working. Of course, the inquiring mind will always want to understand how things operate, but for practical purposes it will often be enough to know that writing a certain line of code produces a certain result without worrying about why. You can go a long way in Shout3D by using the toolset at face value.

This chapter is limited to the bare minimum needed to start working with the examples and projects in the chapters that follow. We will further develop our understanding of Java as we deal with concrete problems throughout the remainder of this book. Don't worry if you don't understand everything covered in this chapter. Seek a basic familiarity now, and then come back and review when we turn to real Shout3D examples.

You will find that this chapter stresses the large and often challenging concepts upon which your Shout3D programming work must rest. Many of the mechanical and more detailed elements of Java programming will be addressed as we write and compile code in subsequent chapters. Java's greatest strengths come from its clear and uncompromising application of object-oriented programming principles, and it is precisely these principles that I hope to inculcate in the reader through the course of this chapter.

Although this chapter is divided into discrete topic headings, it is designed as a single continuous tutorial. Many important issues will be introduced and addressed as they arise in context. You will gain the greatest value by following the development of ideas through the entire chapter, as divergent threads intertwine. Programming languages, like standard human languages, are interdependent systems that are far more than the sum of their parts.

Writing and Compiling Java

To create a project in Shout3D, you will be writing two kinds of classes—an applet and a panel. (You'll also write node classes later in the book, but for now we'll focus on just these two.) The applet class can be considered the container of the panel, which is the actual 3D viewing window. You will create text files to contain the code (called "source code") for these two classes. These source files are always saved with the.java extension. Thus your project may have files named `MyProjectApplet.java` and `MyProjectPanel.java`. Notice the capitalization. Conventions regarding capitalization are very important in Java. The first letter of every word in the names of classes should be capitalized.

Web browsers can't just open textual .java files and run them as a program; browsers require the program to be in a different form—a *compiled* form. To create an operating program, you must compile the .java files. A compiler is a program that converts source code written in ASCII text into whatever form is necessary to create a working program. The compiler will produce files with the same names as the source files, but with the .class extension. Thus, after successful compilation, you will find files named `MyProjectApplet.class` and `MyProjectPanel.class`. These are the files that will be used by the Web browser to run your Shout content. They will no longer be human-readable, and they will appear as gibberish if you open them in a text editor.

There are many Java compilers out there, but this book will assume that you are using Sun Microsystems's Java JDK (Java Development Kit). The JDK is free and, as it's produced directly by Sun (the inventor of Java), is an absolute standard. On the downside, the JDK interface is about as crude as it gets. It runs only from a command line and lacks any graphical tools whatever. When writing large Java applications, this can be a big problem, but Shout applet and panel classes are generally pretty small and therefore manageable for development using only the JDK.

Different Versions of Java

Java has been around since 1996 and has passed through a number of generations as of the time of this writing. The first generation, Java 1.0, is also called Java 1.02, as it went through a couple of development cycles in the form we now have it. The next generation, Java 1.1, introduced very significant advancements. The next version, Java 1.2, was so much more sophisticated that Sun has marketed it as Java 2. The current version, Java 1.3, continues to be called Java 2.

The different versions of Java mean, above all, an expansion of the class libraries in a user's standard installation. A computer with a 1.1 version of the JVM will run Java applets and applications that use either the 1.1 version class library or the older 1.02 version. Thus applets and applications written under prior versions are always supported and will continue to run on all present and future JVMs.

However, the advancements in Java have not all passed through to the Web browsers. The 1.02 version of Java was implemented in Netscape 3 and Internet Explorer 3 many years ago. The 1.1 version was implemented in the 4.0 and all later versions of these browsers. None of the browsers has implemented Java 2 (Java 1.2 or Java 1.3), even though it has been available for some time. Even if Java 2 were to appear in the very next generation of browsers, the vast majority of users would still require time to migrate.

The current version of Shout3D uses Java 1.1. That means Shout content will not be available to users with the very oldest browsers. There are few such users today, and their numbers are declining rapidly. The Java performance of the version 3 browsers is largely inadequate for the demands of Shout3D, and there are many features of Java 1.1 that are essential to its current and future development.

Readers who are new to Java must learn to take care when purchasing or consulting books on the subject to be sure that they address the desired version of Java. Java 1.1 has not been the most recent version for a long time, and most texts today are devoted to later versions.

Installing the JDK

The Java Development Kit (JDK) is offered for free by Sun Microsystems and can be downloaded from the Sun Web site (www.java.sun.com). The main package at present is the Java 2 SDK (Software Development Kit), which is designed for Java 1.3, but also contains a Java 1.1 JDK. I recommend downloading only the standalone 1.1 version of the JDK so as to avoid all issues concerning Java 2 (which is not available with any current Web browsers). At the time of this writing, the latest version using 1.1 is currently 1.1.8, but you should use a later version if one is available because Sun continues to debug and improve the older JDKs.

Installation of the JDK is very straightforward, but make sure you follow the instructions. Once you have installed it, take a look through the various folders in the JDK directory that is created on your hard drive. The most important of these is /bin. This is where all the software is, including javac, the Java compiler.

Like all of the programs in the JDK, javac has no graphical interface and is run from the command line. That means you have to bring up a Command prompt (also called "MS-DOS prompt") in Windows from the Start menu to compile. If you are like the vast majority of sophisticated computer users today, you have either forgotten or never learned how to use DOS commands. Don't be embarrassed. The little you need to know to use the Java compiler can be mastered in a few minutes.

In order to compile your Java source code, you have to have access to both the compiler and to the Java class libraries that the compiler needs. The javac program is in (assuming you installed in the C: drive) C:\jdk1.1.8\bin\. This is the complete path through the directory structure. At any given moment when you use a Command prompt, you are located in a current directory. Of course, if you are already in C:\jdk1.1.8\bin, you can run javac from the Command prompt without a problem. But you will generally be in an entirely different directory when you seek to run javac, and need to be sure that the operating system can find it. To do this, you need to add the location of javac to the system's path. The system path is an environmental variable that contains a list of paths through the directory structure of your hard drive. Whenever you call a program from the Command prompt, the operating system will look for that program in all of the directories specified in the path variable if it can't find it in the current directory. By adding C:\jdk1.1.8\bin to your path variable, you will always be able to run javac, regardless of your current directory.

In Windows NT and Windows 2000, the path variable is easily set in the System Properties dialog (System) of the Control Panel. You'll need to log on with administrator privileges to set the path. Select Path from the System Variables (under the Environment tab), and add `;C:\jdk1.1.8\bin` to the end of the current list in the Value box at the bottom of the dialog. (Remember to include the semicolon to separate it from the preceding entry.) Set the path and close the dialog. That should do it.

In Windows 95 and 98, the path variable is set in the `autoexec.bat` file, a textual script that is run whenever you boot the system. Open that file in a text editor and add the path to your current path variable. The result will be something like:

```
PATH C:\WINDOWS;C:\WINDOWS\COMMAND;C:\JDK1.1.8\BIN
```

When you restart the system, the new path will take effect.

However you set the path variable, you can test it by bringing up the Command prompt and, using whatever directory you currently find yourself in, type **javac** after the prompt and press the Enter key. If the path is set correctly, javac will be found and the Command prompt window will print out some usage information. If javac was not found, you will be told that the name is not recognized. A successful result looks like this (exact text will vary depending on your version of the JDK):

```
C:\users\rob>javac

use: javac [-g] [-O] [-debug] [-depend] [-nowarn] [verbose]
[-classpath path] [-nowrite] [-deprecation] [-d dir]
[-J<runtime flag>] file.java…
```

If the path variable is not working, try closing the Command prompt window (if it is open) and opening a new one.

The second issue is whether the compiler, once running, can find all the Java classes it needs. This should require no attention on your part. The Classpath variable determines where the compiler looks for classes. If you don't bother with it, a default Classpath is used that can find the Java classes in your JDK installation. You will quickly understand how the Shout3D classes are integrated with the standard Java classes when we begin compiling in Chapter 7.

Java Primer

The basic unit of thought in Java is the *class*. All classes are related in a single genealogical tree. There is an Adam, a first progenitor, at the root of this tree—a class called Object. From this point, the tree branches out in myriad directions in a process called *extension*. The Object class is a base class that contains certain very fundamental features. All other classes are extended from Object and thus incorporate these features, plus such additional features as distinguish them from other classes.

The class provides the rules for the creation of *objects*. When we use a class to create an object, we are creating an *instance* of a class. All this is speaking very precisely. In practice, the terms "class" and "object" are often used loosely and interchangeably. We can think of a class as a template for creating objects of that class (instances of that class). An instance of a class is often called a *class object*. You will often find yourself creating multiple instances of the same class—producing multiple objects of the same class.

The difference between a class, which describes a type of object, and an instance, which is an actual created object of that type, may be better understood by this example: The definition of a sphere class may state that all spheres contain a radius variable. So all instances of the sphere class will contain a radius. But once created, one instance of a sphere may be assigned a radius of 2, while another instance is set to have a different radius of 4. Both instances are still members of the sphere class, but each is a separate entity.

The Concept of Extension

The concept of *extension* is absolutely central in Java and must be tackled from the start. The applet class produces a type of object that implements a program in a window within a Web browser. Needless to say, this is a very sophisticated object. The applet class is built on the shoulders of many ancestor classes, with each one providing additional refinements of functionality to its own parent. The idea is like this:

Object   The base class in the Java system

Component (extends Object)   A graphical unit on the user's screen

Container (extends Component)   A Component that may contain other graphical Components inside its window space

Panel (extends Container)   An empty space for drawing

Applet (extends panel)   A panel designed especially to run inside a Web browser

This is highly simplified, but it illustrates the core concept of building by extension. For example, because applet is extended from panel, you can draw in an applet object just as you can in a panel. Because applet is extended from the container class, you can place all kinds of graphical components within it, such a buttons or text boxes. We often speak of an extended class as if it were the base class. For example, we might say that an applet *is* a container. The concept of shared identity is more than a convention. For many purposes in Java, as we will often see when working with Shout3D, an instance of a derived class can be treated as an instance of any of its base classes. This makes sense because the derived class has, by definition, all of the features of the base class.

Fields and Methods

We have been speaking loosely of the "features" of a class. In the most general sense, we can consider the process of programming as working with data. The data—the information—must be stored. In Java, classes hold data in storage that is referred to as *fields*. Working with the data means using it and changing it. In the traditional language of programming, we speak of *functions* as the activities that a program performs.

In Java (as an object-oriented language), we organize data and functions into units. These units are what we have been calling classes. A class contains both data and functions. In the language of object-oriented programming, the functions of a class are called *methods*. The methods of a class are the kinds of actions it can perform. To give a concrete example, the applet class contains a paint method. This method draws the contents of the window whenever it is called. To "call" a method means to cause it to execute. In the applet class, the paint method might be called automatically to refresh the window if it had been obscured by another window, or called explicitly by another method in the class, as where an animation is being run and the window must redraw with every new frame.

A method may or may not take an *argument*. An argument is input data required by the method and is placed in parentheses after the method name. For example, a method that adds two numbers obviously needs arguments—the two numbers to be summed.

```
addUm(int a, int b)
```

But many methods do not require arguments, and empty parentheses are required when calling these methods to assure they are recognized as methods and not as data.

```
doIt();
```

Methods may also *return* values when they complete their execution. For example, the adding functions should probably return the sum of its two arguments.

```
int addUm(int a, int b)
```

This method might be called in a program like this:

```
int x = addUm(3, 2);
```

The answer, 5, would be stored in the variable *x*.

Data Types

A class, as we have said, may (and generally does) contain both methods and data. Data is stored in *variables*. A variable is a location in memory that holds the data. The word "variable" suggests the value held in that location can change. This is usually what we want, but you can direct the program not to change a value placed in a location in memory.

The variables used by a class are called *fields*. They are created when a class is instantiated to create a class object, and they exist for as long as the class object exists. By contrast, the individual methods of a class can have their own *local* variables. These apply only to the specific method and not to the class object as a whole. They are created when the method is executed and disappear when it is finished.

The most important aspect of a variable is its type. When it comes right down to it, we can only store certain very limited forms of information in memory. Above all, we can store numbers. There are two basic kinds of numerical values, and these must be clearly distinguished. An integer, specified as `int` in program code, is a counting number like 5 or 3576 or −27. A floating-point value, or `float` in program code, is a number with a decimal point like .478 or −5786.91. These are fundamentally different data types.

Another important data type is called *Boolean*. A Boolean value is either true or false. Some 3D artists approach the word Boolean with certain assumptions that are completely irrelevant to the use of this word in programming. In programming, a `boolean` variable is just a place to store the values `true` or `false`, which has nothing to do with geometry.

Arrays

The `int`, `float`, and `boolean` variables are what we call *primitive data types*. They can be used by themselves, or they can be collected into more complex types. Arrays and class objects are more complex data types built out of primitive types.

An array is simply a list of primitive types. To take a practical example, the (*x,y,z*) position of an object in space would be stored in an array of three `float`s. (Consider why these must be `float`s and not `int`s.) It takes a while for the new programmer to become accustomed to working with arrays. This is partly because there are many overlapping conventions for creating and working with arrays that Java inherited from the C programming language, and that only make sense in practice. As arrays are lists, you need a means for specifying individual members, and this is done by an *index*. Here is some simple code that will introduce you to arrays. We are trying to store the position of an object as (3.5,10.2,4.0)

```
float [] pos;
pos = new float[3];
pos[0] = 3.5f;
pos[1] = 10.2f;
pos[2] = 4.0f;
```

I've written this in the longest possible manner to teach a great number of important points, so consider this material slowly.

The first line of the code creates a variable to hold the array. I named the variable pos, to stand for "position," but the name was entirely up to me. I could have called it p or position or here, or anything I wanted. The statement float [] in the first line declares the type of the variable pos. It tells us that pos is an array of floating point numbers. But what, exactly, is this variable named pos? It is not the array itself. It is a *reference* to an array—an array that has not yet been created.

The next line actually creates the array. The statement new float[3] will set aside a place in memory to hold three floating-point numbers. The equals sign is an *assignment operator*. It takes the value generated by the expression on the right side of the equals sign and places it in the variable on the left side. After creating the space in memory to hold the array, the statement new float[3] returns a reference to that array. That reference is then stored in the variable pos by the assignment operator.

What is a reference? We don't really need to understand this concept precisely, even though we'll be using references constantly. References are often called *handles* and sometimes *pointers*, although the true pointer in the C language is somewhat different. In any case, a reference is simply a way of accessing data that is stored somewhere in memory. Now that we have stored a reference to the array in pos, we can use pos to access the array.

This is what occurs in the next three lines of code. The statement pos[0] = 3.5f will copy the value 3.5 into the first element of the array. A couple of issues are worth noting here. The elements of the array are indexed as 0, 1, and 2 and not as 1, 2, and 3. This is a basic programming convention. Numbering starts with zero and not with one. The element pos[3] would be the fourth element in the array, and doesn't exist. Note also the f after the 3.5. This indicates that 3.5 is a float variable, and can therefore be properly placed in a float array. This seems funny. Didn't we say that a floating-point variable is a number with a decimal point? Shouldn't this line of code work without the specifying f?

This is an important question that points toward a broader issue. The float is not the only kind of floating-point variable. There is a data type called double, which is a higher-precision version of a float. If you simply type in a number with a decimal point (like 3.5), the compiler treats it as a double so as to assure the highest degree of precision. We don't need this much precision, so we must *cast* the number to float. The concept of *casting* comes up so often that it is worth understanding in this context. If we have a high-precision double and want to place it in an array that can contain only floats, the value will lose precision when converted from a double to a float. The compiler will not let us do this automatically. We must explicitly cast the value to the coarser data type to tell the compiler that it is OK to lose precision. The requirement of casting, which can often seem tedious, is a protection against losing data.

If you can understand all that happened in our coding example, you may choose to compress all these operations into shorthand versions. The first two lines could be fitted into one as:

```
float [] pos = new float[3];
```

This *allocates* the memory to hold the array and stuffs a reference to that array in the variable pos. We can go even further and perform all five steps in a single line.

```
float [] pos = {3.5f, 10.2f, 4.0f};
```

This line both allocates the memory for the array and *initializes* it with the three values. Then it assigns a reference to the array to the variable pos. This kind of shorthand, as important as it is in practice, can be difficult for the beginner who fails to understand how many independent operations are involved.

Throughout this book, I will tend to provide code examples in a way that may appear simplistic to the experienced programmer. The primary purpose of this book is to teach principles by making logical steps as obvious and clear as possible. Thus, you will often find code that could be written more tersely, but which is easier to understand for those who are new to programming.

Classes as Data Types

We previously distinguished between arrays and classes as two kinds of complex data types. This is not entirely correct because, in Java, arrays are actually classes themselves, a subject that we will have some opportunity to explore at different points. But the distinction between arrays and (other) classes is useful for most practical purposes.

A class can be a data type—a variable—within another class. This idea sounds so abstract that it's best to get right to a concrete example.

Let's say we are building a basic Shout3D application in which we have a model that we want to be able to move around in space using the mouse. This application will be built by extending the Shout3DPanel class to create a new class named MoveObject-Panel. In order to operate, the MoveObjectPanel class will need to store and manipulate certain data. At bare minimum, it will need to store the position of the model in the world space of the scene and the position of the cursor on the screen. The model's position must be an array of three floats and the cursor position on the screen must be stored as two ints. Think through this second element for a moment. The cursor position is defined as a pixel location, measured horizontally (x) and vertically (y) from the top-left corner. Pixels must be stored as integers. They are counted in whole numbers—there's no such thing as a fraction of a pixel. The only question here is whether it's better to store the x and y pixel values as separate variables or as two elements in a single array. Both methods would work, but let's use the first. So the fields defined at the top of the MoveObjectPanel class would start with:

```
int x;
int y;
float [] pos = new float[3];
```

This pos array is just a place to hold values. It doesn't directly control the position of the model in the scene. To actually communicate with the model in the scene, we need to access its top-level Transform node. When the scene was loaded into memory, a Java Transform class object was created reflecting the top-level Transform in the scene file. We will need to get a reference to this Transform class object, and store it in our MoveObjectPanel. Just as we previously named the reference to an array whatever we wanted, we can name the reference to the Transform class object whatever we choose.

```
int x;
int y;
float [] pos = new float[3];
Transform mover;
```

Take a moment to think through this list of fields for the MoveObjectPanel. The two int fields are primitive data types. There is only one memory location for each variable, and that location contains the integer value. By contrast, both pos and mover are references to complex data types. pos does not itself contain the array, which is actually allocated elsewhere in memory. In the same way, mover does not contain the Transform class object, but merely provides access to it. At this point, mover is just an empty reference, holding a *null* value (*null* means that the reference does not refer to anything yet. It is the default initial value for any variable that stores an object reference). We will have to include code in the MoveObjectPanel that finds the Transform object and stores its reference in mover. Let's ignore precisely how this is done for the present and assume that we have been able to make this assignment. Thus, mover is now a functioning reference to the Transform object.

We have already seen how to assign values into an array. Assume that, based on the location of our mouse cursor on the screen, the desired position of the model is computed to be (14.3,3.7,–5.0). These values are directly assigned to each of the three elements of the array, in a manner like this:

```
pos[0] = 14.3f;
pos[1] = 3.7f;
pos[2] = -5.0f;
```

But how would these values get from this array into the translation field of the Transform so the model actually moves to this position? First, we refer to the Shout3D API and look up the Transform class. We find that it has a field named translation, which makes sense because it follows the structure of a VRML Transform node. To access the fields of a class from within another class, we use "dot" notation. Thus the translation field can be accessed through the reference as:

```
mover.translation
```

At this point, we would probably think to make the assignments like this:

```
mover.translation[0] = pos[0];
mover.translation[1] = pos[1];
mover.translation[2] = pos[2];
```

After all, the translation field of the Transform must be an array of three floats, so one would think to simply copy each of the elements from one array to the other. But the situation is a bit more complex than this and brings us into contact with an important aspect of object-oriented programming as reflected in Shout.

If you look at the online Javadocs documentation, you'll see that the translation field of the Transform is not a basic float array, but rather a class object of its own, named FloatArrayField. Look up the FloatArrayField in the online Javadocs documentation, and you'll see no fields listed at all. There's got to be an actual float array somewhere. How do we access it?

One of the most important practices of object-oriented programming is called "data hiding." The FloatArrayField class does contain a float array, but this array cannot be addressed directly. That's why the array is not named as a field in the online Javadocs documentation. The array is *private* and can only be addressed by methods within the FloatArrayField class. These are called *accessor* methods, or *getter* and *setter* methods.

To set the values in the translation field of the Transform to those in the pos array, we have a number of options. The most obvious is to use the setValue method:

```
mover.translation.setValue(pos);
```

This is a basic operation that you'll be performing constantly in Shout, so take the time to understand it carefully. mover is a reference to the Transform class object we want to control. mover.translation points to the translation field of that Transform. This field, as it turns out, is not itself an array of floats, but is rather a class object itself, named FloatArrayField. That object has a method for setting its value called (obviously enough) setValue(). That method takes as its argument a reference to an array. Thus, the entire statement mover.translation.setValue(pos) sets the value of the hidden array that controls the translation of the Transform to that of the pos array. Moreover, the values in the array are not actually copied. Rather, the translation field of the Transform node simply contains the same reference to the array that pos holds. Any time you change a value in the array using the pos reference, the change is necessarily reflected in the position field of the Transform object. An example will further serve to introduce the *getter* method and the use of print statements. Ponder the following lines of code:

```
pos[0] = -1.0f;
System.out.println(pos[0]);
System.out.println(mover.translation.getValue()[0]);
```

Recall that the original pos[0] (the *x* position) was set to 14.3. Now we change it to −1. We test the result using print statements. The statement System.out.println() will print out whatever value is contained in the variable named within the parentheses to the Java Console. If we were to open the Java Console after this code had run, we would find a line reading "−1.0." This makes sense and confirms that the assignment statement in the first line actually changed the value of the first element of the array.

The next line asks to print out the *x* value of the translation field. Once again, take time to carefully understand the structure of this statement. Remember that the translation field of the Transform object contains a FloatArrayField object. Just as we set the value of the FloatArrayField using the setValue() method, here we get the value using the getValue() method. The FloatArrayField contains only a reference to the array. Thus getValue() returns that same reference. To get the first element of the array, we must write getValue()[0].

This kind of thinking is, in my experience, the most difficult aspect of Java for the novice programmer. After a while, it begins to make perfect sense, but it is undoubtedly confusing at the start. It takes time for these concepts to sink in. See if you can hold on the basic ideas and let your understanding develop as you go along.

The entire statement thus prints the *x* value of the translation field of the Transform node to the Java Console. It should come as no surprise that this will also be −1.0. It can hardly be anything else. Both the pos variable and the position field of the Transform are references to only a single array. In fact, if we were to see this scene in the applet window, we would find that the model had moved in the *x* direction to −1.0.

Print statements are an extremely important part of programming that you will use constantly when working with Shout. These statements can be used, as we have here, to test the current value in a variable. They are also valuable simply to determine whether a line of code is actually executing. For example, a questionable line of code can be bracketed above and below with the statements System.out .println("before") *and* System.out.println("after"). *If two lines containing the words* before *and* after *appear in the Java Console, you can be certain that the line of code between has executed.*

Character Strings (and Method Overriding)

Text is stored in String objects. Typing text in your code within double quotation marks creates a *string literal*, which is stored in a String class object.

```
"This is String 1.";
```

To store a reference to a String object created in this way, you must declare a String variable and assign the string literal to it.

```
String myString = "This is String 1.";
```

These ideas are, hopefully, beginning to sink in to the novice. Just as with the arrays and other class objects, memory has been allocated to hold the text. We cannot access the memory directly, but rather only through a reference that is held elsewhere in memory—

in the variable myString. (Note how variable names are properly written in lowercase, with the first letter of each word after the first capitalized. This makes it easier to read long variable names without confusing them with class names.)

We can create another string literal and pass its reference to our existing String variable.

```
myString = "This is String 2.";
```

Now myString references the new text, and the old text will be lost unless a reference to it had previously been preserved in another String variable.

The most important concept for the newbie to grasp follows from the fact that Strings, like all class objects, are accessed through references. Look at the following code:

```
String stringA = "This is a good string.";
String stringB = stringA;
```

In the first line, a String object is created from a literal and a reference to that object is stored in the variable stringA. In the second line, we create a variable named stringB, and assign it the value in stringA. The variable stringA contains only a reference to the actual String object, so after assignment, both stringA and stringB contain references to the same object.

We often need to determine whether two variables contain the same string. We might use the following test:

```
if (stringA == stringB) {do a bunch of things}
```

Note the form of this if statement. The keyword if is followed by a test in parentheses. If the test is passed—the result of the test is "true"—any code contained in the following curly braces will be executed. Note especially the double equals sign. A single equals sign is, as we have seen, an assignment statement. A double equals sign is a test. It asks, "Does the value in the variable stringA equal the value in the variable stringB?" In our case, this will be true because they both contain the same value—a reference to a single String object.

Using a single equals sign instead of a double one in an if statement is one of the most common coding errors you will make. After a while, you will get used to checking to make sure you've done it right.

But what if we create two separate String objects that contain the same text?

```
String textA = "Stop the world!";
String textB = "Stop the world!";
```

Now there are two objects (two independent instances of the String class) and therefore `textA` and `textB` do not contain the same reference. In this case, the following `if` statement will not be true.

```
if (textA == textB) {do some other things}
```

In this case, we probably want to know whether the two String objects contain the same text. We'd have to do it this way:

```
if(textA.equals(textB)) {do some other things}
```

Once again, take it slowly here because there is a significant amount to learn. We have said that a String is a Java class object. It therefore comes with some handy methods. One of these methods is the `equals()` method. To call the `equals()` method for a given String object, use the same dot notation we used for accessing the fields of a class object. Thus the `equals()` method for the String object referenced by `textA` is called as `textA.equals()`. The reference to the String object for comparison is passed as an argument to this method within the parentheses.

To tie things into the larger picture, you might be interested to discover that the `equals()` method is inherited from the object class. Recall that the object class is the root of the entire Java class library, and that all Java classes are derived from it. Thus every Java class contains an `equals()` method. Yet this method operates differently in each class because the meaning of equality is inherently different for different kinds of objects. This means that, like all other classes, the String class needs its own custom version of the `equals()` method. This customization is achieved through *method overriding*, another central concept in object-oriented programming.

All classes are derived by extension from other classes. Thus, all classes inherit methods from their ancestor classes. By default, a class inherits the exact functionality of the methods of its parent class. But a class may change the functionality of an inherited method by simply rewriting the code under the name of that method. Doing so overrides the method of the parent class with a new version in the extended class. The name of the method is preserved, but the functionality is changed.

Method overriding is basic to the use of Shout3D and to Java Applet programming generally. We previously noted the `paint()` method of the applet class. In the applet class, the `paint()` method does nothing. It is called when it's time to draw the applet window but contains no functionality. To create a working applet, a developer must extend the applet class to create a derived class. The derived class inherits the `paint()` method from the applet class, but overrides it with code to create the precise functionality desired by the developer. For example, the `paint()` method might be overridden to draw a picture and some text in the applet window. Still more to the point, every time we create a Shout3D application, we extend the Shout3DPanel class. This class contains a method named `customInitialize()`, which is called immediately after the scene is loaded. Once again, this method contains no functionality in the Shout3DPanel class, and we must override it when creating the derived class to make it perform useful work.

 We can see that the idea of extending classes in Java may involve both adding new methods and over-riding existing ones. When classes such as applet and Shout3DPanel contain empty methods that must be overridden to create functionality, they are a providing an application framework for developers to build on. It is as though slots were provided for developers to fill in.

Interfaces and Abstract Classes

We are now in a position to consider the uniquely Java concept of *interfaces*.

We have seen that both Shout and the standard Java class library often provide us with empty methods—methods that exist in name only. The purpose of such methods is to provide a place to add custom functionality by overriding them when extending the class.

Interfaces are classes in which every method is empty. Why would we need such classes? There are many reasons, but for now we will focus on only one. Interfaces provide the structure for custom functionality to be added to classes.

Thus far we have considered only the extension of classes. A class is extended from only a single parent. To take a practical example, any custom Shout3DPanel class that we may want to create will be extended from Shout3DPanel. Let's say we want to add user interactivity. In other words, we want the program to respond to user input in the form of mouse and keyboard events. The basic Shout3DPanel class does not provide this functionality, and it doesn't even provide empty methods to override as a place to include this functionality.

The Shout3D class library contains an interface named DeviceObserver. Look up this interface in the online Javadocs documentation and you'll see that it contains only a single method named `onDeviceInput()`. This is an empty method without any func-tionality—simply a placeholder. After we actually code it, it will be used to *handle* user-generated events. That is, it will determine how the program responds to mouse clicks or keystrokes. We fold this functionality into our extended Shout3DPanel class by *implementing* the DeviceObserver interface. This means two things. First, we state at the top of the definition of the class that we are implementing this interface. Second, we include all the methods of that interface in our class. As there is only one method in this particular interface, this means no more than including the `onDeviceInput()` method in the extended Shout3DPanel class and writing some contents to this method to provide the functionality we want.

Methods, like variables, are most properly written in lowercase. If there is more than one word in the name, the first letter of each word after the first one should be capitalized. This makes it possible to compose readable and descriptive names for methods and variables.

You may wonder why it should be necessary to do this. Why can't we just write a method to handle user input and call it whatever we want? The reason is that this event-handling method must be called automatically by other classes in the Shout3D class library whenever a user input event occurs. Those other classes can call this method only if they know its name, and by implementing the interface, you are agreeing to use a method name that is already known to the rest of the package. If you made up your own name for the method and added it as a simple extension of the Shout3DPanel class, the event-handling method would never be called.

This raises a second point about interfaces. Implementing an interface is similar to extending a class. You may remember that an extended class can be treated as though it were the base class wherever this may be necessary, because the extended class has, by definition, all of the fields and methods of the base class. In the same way, when we implement an interface, we can treat the class that implements the interface as though it were the interface itself because it contains the same methods as the interface.

An interface is an abstract class. It has no functionality and is only used as a framework for implementation in other classes. You cannot instantiate an interface object directly. But the idea of abstract classes is even more general. An abstract class is a class that cannot itself be instantiated and is used only for deriving other classes. It provides structure to a hierarchy of classes.

For example, when we implement the DeviceObserver interface in an extended Shout3DPanel class, we must *register* the class to receive user-generated events. Only after we have done so will the `onDeviceInput()` method in our class be called when a user performs any input activity. The method of the Shout3DPanel class (and inherited by our extended class) that registers the class in this way accepts only a DeviceObserver object as an argument. Because we have implemented the DeviceObserver interface in our class, we can treat the class itself as a DeviceObserver object and can pass it as an argument to the registration method. This makes sense because the registration method wants to make sure it is registering a class that contains a method named onDeviceInput(). These are subtle ideas for the newcomer to grasp, but they become very clear and valuable with a little practice.

Readers with a background in C++ programming will be familiar with the concept of multiple inheritance, in which a class is derived from two or more classes and thus contains all of the fields and methods of its parents. Java does not permit multiple inheritance, and each class is extended from only a single parent. However, the use of interfaces permits something similar to multiple inheritance.

The node class in the Shout3D API is an excellent example. All of the different kinds of nodes in the scene graph—such as Transform, Appearance, and IndexedFace-Set—are derived from the node class. The node class contains all of the methods that all of the different kinds of nodes share in common, and which are necessarily inherited by every derived class. For example, the node class contains a method named get-DEFName() that returns the DEF name of that node in the scene graph. All the specific kinds of nodes can make use of this method, and we can call it for any class that has been derived from node. The node class itself is an abstract class. You cannot instantiate a node class object, but only nonabstract classes derived from Node.

The Light class is also an abstract class. You cannot create an instance of Light class object, but rather only an instance of class derived from Light. At this point, there is only one class derived from Light in the Shout3D library, the DirectionalLight. Take a look at the Light class in the online Javadocs documentation, and you'll note that this class has no methods. But it does have a number of fields:

```
affectedGroups
color
defaultColor
intensity
on
```

These are features desirable in any kind of Light. A Light must have given color and intensity. There must be a way of turning it on and off, and (unlike real lights in the physical world) there can a way of determining what geometry in the scene is "lit" by the Light.

A DirectionalLight is a light that shines only in a specific direction. The fields added by the DirectionalLight class address this issue:

```
direction
defaultDirection
isHeadlight
```

Yet, because a DirectionalLight is also a Light—that is, because it is derived from the Light class—it contains all of the underlying fields. When determining the fields (and methods) of the DirectionalLight class, we must look both at the class itself, and at its abstract ancestor classes, Light and Node. In the language of object-oriented programming, a DirectionalLight is both a Light and a Node. Using an abstract class for Light permits the addition of new and different kinds of LCDights to the Shout3D library as they are developed. Like the DirectionalLight, these will have all of the fields derived from Light and will have only such additional fields as distinguish them from other kinds of Lights. For example, a bulb or "omni" Light would not require a direction field, but would need a location field.

Abstract classes introduce us to notions concerning the *design* of a class library. The strength of a powerful class library such as Shout3D derives not only from the number of classes and their individual features, but also from the way the entire network of classes functions as an integrated unit capable of organic expansion. The library is a whole that is more than the sum of its parts.

To learn Java programming, you must become comfortable with some big ideas that necessarily take time to digest. The better you understand the underlying concepts, the more comfortable and productive you will be. But you can start right away in Shout with just the basics presented in this chapter and build your understanding in a practical context. As you work through the following chapters, return to this chapter as necessary to refresh your memory and strengthen your grasp on the fundamentals.

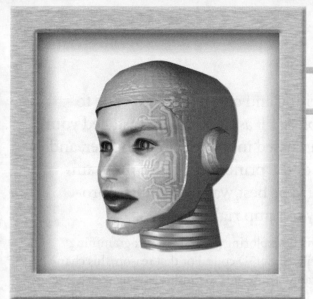

Getting Started with Shout3D Applets and Panels

SHOUT3D

Chapter 7

In this chapter, we'll start writing and compiling Java code to create custom Shout3D applets. I'll assume you've installed your Java Development Kit, as discussed in the previous chapter, and you have also assimilated some of the principles of Java programming introduced in that chapter. The best way to learn Java programming in Shout3D is simply to jump right in.

Just as in the previous chapter, we will be exploring general Java programming issues as they arise in the context of specific Shout3D code. For that reason, this chapter is (once again) intended for consideration from start to finish, allowing concepts to build cumulatively. Take your time with ideas that are new to you, and think about how they fit into the bigger picture. This is exciting stuff, which (unless you are already an object-oriented programmer) is not likely to slip into pre-existing slots.

Elements of a Shout3D Project

Every Shout3D project consists of these four elements:

- An applet class (stored in the `applets` folder of your Shout3D installation)

- A panel class (stored in the same place)

- A scene file in .wrl, .s3d, or the corresponding compressed formats (stored in the `models` folder)

- An HTML file of the Web page that is to contain the Shout3D applet (stored, for present purposes, in the `demos` folder)

A project may also include additional resources such as:

- Image files (stored in the `images` folder)

- Audio files (stored in the `sounds` folder)

Take a moment to look through your Shout3D installation to make sure you understand the organization of these files. You'll find them all in the `codebase` directory.

The scene file and any image or audio files are obviously created outside Shout3D. The HTML files can be generated automatically using the Shout3D Wizard; however, in this chapter's exercises we will modify a template HTML file in a text editor.

The HTML File

Listing 7.1 is the HTML template we will use. Copy `template.html` from the CD into the `demos` folder in your Shout installation.

LISTING 7.1 TEMPLATE HTML FILE (*TEMPLATE.HTML*)

```
<HTML>

<HEAD>
<TITLE>template</TITLE>
</HEAD>

<BODY>


<APPLET CODEBASE="../codebase" CODE="applets/???Applet.class"
➥ARCHIVE="shout3dClasses.zip" WIDTH=320 HEIGHT=240>
<param name="src" value="models/???.wrl">
<param name="headlightOn" value="true">
</APPLET>


</BODY>

</HTML>
```

For those who are not familiar with basic HTML, a short explanation will suffice. HTML elements are typically enclosed between opening and closing tags. The entire page is enclosed between <HTML> (opening) and </HTML> (closing) tags. The head includes only a title that will appear in the title bar at the top of the Web browser.

The body contains only an applet. Let's understand the structure of the applet tags. Unlike all of the other tags on this page, the applet tags do not enclose other elements. The opening tag, <APPLET (....)>, is followed immediately by the closing tag, </APPLET>. All the information about the applet is contained within the opening tag.

The CODEBASE attribute of the tag indicates where to look for the necessary Shout3D Java classes. These are all in the `codebase` directory. Note the use of the two dots in `../codebase`. The HTML file is in the `demos` directory, and the CODEBASE is determined relative to that directory. As the `codebase` and `demos` directories are both children of the `Shout3d_runtime` directory, the path from `demos` to `codebase` passes up to `Shout3d_runtime`, and then down into `codebase`. The two dots indicate the parent directory of the current directory.

Now that we have determined the `CODEBASE`, we need to indicate the specific applet we wish to run. This is the function of the `CODE` attribute. The applet class file specified in this attribute is relative to the `codebase`. The applet files are stored in the `applets` folder in the `codebase` directory. The template uses `???Applet.class` as a placeholder. You'll replace the question marks with the name of the applet you create.

Only custom applets are stored in the `applets` *folder. The standard* `Shout3DApplet.class` *is located in the* `Shout3D` *folder. Thus the Shout demo* `modswing.html`, *which contains no interactivity, uses the* `CODE` *attribute* `CODE="shout3d/Shout3DApplet.class"`.

The `ARCHIVE` attribute indicates where a .zip file is available that contains Shout3D Java classes that will be needed in support of the applet. This .zip file contains the classes that are most likely to be needed, but not the entire Shout3D library. Packaging these files in a .zip file saves time because they can all be downloaded in a single transaction. If your project requires class files that are not included in this .zip file, it must grab them individually out of the various folders in the `shout3d` directory under `codebase`. Take a moment to open up the .zip file in WinZip and check out the contents. Then look through the full library of class files in the `shout3d` directory. Classes used less often, like IndexedLineSet, will be found in the full library, but not in the zipped archive.

The `WIDTH` and `HEIGHT` attributes of the `<APPLET>` tag define the dimension of the applet window, in pixels. These allow the size of the applet on the page to be determined by the manager of the Web page, rather than the applet developer.

All the attributes we have considered thus far are standard for all applets. The final attributes of our `<APPLET>` tag are the custom parameters of the specific applet. They consist of pairs that associate a name with a value. The applet developer writes code within the applet to extract the values and use them. In this case, the standard Shout3DApplet needs to know the name of the scene file to load. Other parameters are optional. If you failed to pass a headlight parameter as true, there would be no headlight. The standard applet parameters were discussed in Chapter 2.

All the custom applets you write will be extended from Shout3DApplet, and will therefore be prepared to receive all the standard parameters. However, custom applets can add new parameters. For example, the WalkPanel, which implements "walk-through" navigation, accepts parameters for the height and radius of the avatar so that you can override the default values on the HTML page without having to edit and recompile the Java code. This kind of planning can make your Shout3D projects flexible and reusable. As we will see, due to the close connection between the related applet and panel classes, the custom parameters in an <APPLET> tag can be handled by either class.

The Applet Class File

Shout3D applets are containers for Shout3D panels. Every Shout3D project involves a pair of applet and panel classes. In most cases, the applet is completely filled by the panel, which is the actual 3D rendering space. Thus the only purpose of the code in the applet class is to create the applet, and then create the panel to fill it. This can be achieved in only a few lines of code that can be easily edited from a template.

More sophisticated projects may involve a panel that is smaller than its containing applet, leaving space around the panel for interface components (like buttons or text). In this situation, the applet must be coded to do more than simply create the panel.

For the present, we'll stick to the simple case of an applet that is filled completely filled by a panel. Thus the entire space is devoted to a camera view of the 3D scene.

Here is the source code for a template applet. Copy the file `TemplateApplet.java` from the CD to the **applets** folder in your Shout installation. (Note that, as a Java class name, the first letter in each word in the name is capitalized.)

```
package applets;
import  shout3d.*;

public class TemplateApplet extends Shout3DApplet {


   public void initShout3DPanel(){
      panel = new TemplatePanel(this);
   }

}//end of class
```

This class is extremely short. To create a basic applet, all you need to do is replace the word "Template" with a name of your choice. Let's spend a moment, however, to get oriented to reading Java source code.

Two lines at the top precede the actual class definition. The class definition begins with the statement:

```
public class TemplateApplet extends Shout3DApplet
```

This informs us that a class named TemplateApplet is to be derived from the existing class, Shout3DApplet. Because TemplateApplet is extended from Shout3DApplet, it automatically contains all the methods and fields of Shout3DApplet.

The class definition begins with the opening curly brace and ends with the final closing curly brace at the end of the file. Note how, in this properly written code, the closing brace lines up precisely below the first letter in the declaration of the class (the "p" in public). This practice helps to match up opening and closing braces and parentheses. This may not seem so important in a tiny block of code like this one, but once things get more complex, you'll need all the help you can get.

To help us understand our code, we add comments. Comments are ignored by the compiler and provided solely for the use of human readers of the source code. One important way of adding a comment is by using two slashes. This works only for single-line comments, and if you have more than one line, you'll have to repeat the comment sign at the start of each new line. In the applet code we just looked at, I used a comment to make clear that the closing curly brace closes the entire class definition.

 The comment sign is commonly used to deactivate code. Placing double slashes before a line of code "comments it out," causing the compiler to ignore it as if it were a comment.

Our class definition contains no fields and only a single method.

```
public void initShout3DPanel(){
   panel = new TemplatePanel(this);
}
```

The method is named `initShout3DPanel()`. The empty parentheses after the name tell us that this method takes no arguments. The word `void` before it tells us that it returns no value. The method contains only a single statement and ends with the closing curly brace.

The name of the method indicates that its purpose is to create a Shout3DPanel to fit within the applet. For the present, let's ignore exactly how it does this and think about class extension. If we define a method in an extended class, it either overrides an existing method of the same name or constitutes a completely new method that we are adding from scratch. To get used to thinking in Java and using the Shout Java documentation, look up the Shout3DPanel class in the Javadocs in your Shout3D installation. You'll see from the Method Summary that `initShout3DPanel()` is a method of the Shout3DPanel class. That means we are overriding this method in our extended class.

Without getting deeper into the code, we should at least be able to recognize from the **new** keyword that a class object is being instantiated, in this case a TemplatePanel object. A reference to this object is being assigned to (stored in) the variable named panel. Where did this variable come from? Once again, look at the documentation for the Shout3DPanel class.

You'll find that class contains a field named panel, and our extended class necessarily inherits this field. Note further that this field is defined to be of type Shout3DPanel. We are passing it a reference to a TemplatePanel object. Because the TemplatePanel is (as we will soon see) extended from Shout3DPanel, we can store a reference to a TemplatePanel in a reference that will accept a Shout3DPanel. In other words, a TemplatePanel *is* a Shout3DPanel.

To create a proper pair of applet and panel classes, use the same names for both, and make sure that both are reflected in the applet code. For example, if you wanted to create an applet named FunApplet, you'll need a FunPanel as well. When using the template, you'll change both names (from Template) before you save, like so:

```
package applets;
import  shout3d.*;

public class FunApplet extends Shout3DApplet {


  public void initShout3DPanel(){
    panel = new FunPanel(this);
  }

}//end of class
```

The Panel Class File

The panel class is where all the action is. Unless you intend to build an applet frame around your 3D window, coding the applet class will be as simple as changing a couple of names in a template. But the panel class will typically be the home of all of the interactivity that you design and fashion in a Shout3D project.

The Big Picture

When you build a panel class, you operate within a framework. There are three elements to the framework:

1. Overriding methods that are inherited from Shout3DPanel

2. Implementing an interface to provide for user input

3. Implementing an interface that engages the render loop

You will always perform the first of these. The second two are theoretically optional, but as a practical matter, one or both of these interfaces will generally be necessary. Let's get everything into perspective.

An interactive 3D application will typically require some "setup" before it's ready to run and receive user input. In other words, it must be *initialized*. This will become clear the moment we begin. Actions that need to be performed at the very start must be included in an initializing method that is automatically called right after the scene is loaded, but before anything is displayed to the viewer. In the Shout3DPanel class, this method is named `customInitialize()`, but it is an empty method that does nothing. To give it substance, we must override it when we extend a class from Shout3DPanel, writing the code for whatever actions we wish to perform on initialization. There is also an empty method named `finalize()`, which will be automatically called when the user closes the applet. It will sometimes be necessary to override this method to perform certain cleanup activities.

Once the initializing method has run, the scene is visible and prepared for action. Likely as not, you will want the scene to respond to mouse and keyboard input from the user. To do this, you must implement the deviceObserver interface, which essentially means including a method in your class named `onDeviceInput()` to respond to (*handle*) user input.

Finally, you must decide whether you need to engage the render loop. The concept of a *render loop* is central to realtime graphics, as was discussed at the start of this book. A realtime rendering engine, like that implemented in the Shout3DPanel class, runs as fast as it can. It renders the scene again and again in a continuous loop. Animation occurs when the scene is changed in some way between render cycles, so the current rendered frame looks different from the preceding one. Keyframed animation that is created directly in a 3D animation program, and is exported in VRML format using VRML interpolator nodes, is handled automatically and transparently. This kind of animation involves changing values between render cycles just as much as any other kind of animation, but the Shout3D developer does not have to write any Java code to implement it.

However, a great deal on animation for realtime 3D is best handled procedurally. Instead of keyframing the animation in a 3D animation package for export in VRML form, the animation is programmed directly in Java code. You'll have plenty of opportunity to see how procedural animation is used, but for the present, it's enough to note that this kind of animation cannot be achieved unless the panel class is signaled every time a render cycle is completed and the Renderer is prepared to start the next frame. To engage the render loop in this way, you must implement the RenderObserver interface, which means including two methods in your panel class—onPreRender() and onPostRender(). These methods will be automatically called immediately before and after each frame is rendered so that values in the scene can be changed. But procedural animation is not the only reason you may need to engage the render loop. It will often be necessary to perform tests between frames. For example, in a game, you may need to determine the current position of an object after every frame in order to determine whether it has hit a target or passed a boundary.

The basic structure of a panel class that includes all the elements we have discussed might be represented as shown below. Make sure you understand this abbreviated version before you go on to the real code to be used as a template.

```
TemplatePanel  extends Shout3DPanel

(implements DeviceObserver and RenderObserver interfaces)
{


customInitialize() // overridden from parent class

finalize() // overridden from parent class

onDeviceInput() // from DeviceObserver interface

onPreRender() // from RenderObserver interface

onPostRender() //from RenderObserver interface
}
```

The Panel Template

You can find Listing 7.2 (TemplatePanel.java) on the CD. Copy it into the applets directory of your Shout3D installation. Take some time to see how the structure of this class definition follows that of the abbreviated version above.

LISTING 7.2 TEMPLATEPANEL (*TEMPLATEPANEL.JAVA*)

```java
package applets;

import shout3d.*;
import shout3d.core.*;
import shout3d.math.*;


public class TemplatePanel extends Shout3DPanel implements
➥DeviceObserver, RenderObserver{

  //fields to be placed here


  //the constructor

  public TemplatePanel (Shout3DApplet applet){
    super(applet);
  }


  //called immediately after scene is loaded

  public void customInitialize() {
    addDeviceObserver(this,"MouseInput", null);
    getRenderer().addRenderObserver(this, null);
  }



  //cleanup actions performed when viewer closes applet

  protected void finalize() {
    removeDeviceObserver(this,"MouseInput");
    getRenderer().removeRenderObserver(this);
  }
```

```
//method from DeviceObserver interface
//to handle user input-
//will only receive mouse input as registered

public boolean onDeviceInput(DeviceInput di, Object userData) {

  return false;

}


//method from RenderObserver interface,
// called before each frame is rendered

public void onPreRender (Renderer r, Object o) {

}


//method from RenderObserver interface,
// called after each frame is rendered

public void onPostRender (Renderer r, Object o) {

}


} //end of class
```

We're going to go over this template carefully because it provides the foundation for most of your development work and because it offers an excellent opportunity to learn some important Java programming concepts.

Package and Import Statements

Let's start by noting that, just as with the TemplateApplet, there is heading material above the class definition. We passed over these lines before, but they are worth considering now. Just as with the TemplateApplet source code, there is a package statement that defines the package as applets. Packages are a way of organizing classes, and the full name of a class includes its package. Thus the full name of the TemplateApplet is actually `applets.TemplateApplet`.

This point leads easily into an understanding of the import statements directly below the package statement. In order to compile a class source file like this one, the compiler needs access to classes that are used by the current class. For example, this TemplatePanel class extends Shout3DPanel and implements the two interfaces. The compiler must be able to find the compiled Shout3DPanel and the interfaces in the Shout3D class libraries in order to use them in this context. The import statement informs the compiler of which classes it can use when compiling the current class. To make things easier, you can import entire packages and thereby give the compiler access to all of the classes in them. The entire Shout3D class library is divided into five packages:

```
shout3d

shout3d.core

shout3d.hanim

shout3d.math

shout3d.sound
```

These package names correspond to the directories in which you'll find the class files in your Shout3D installation. (This should give you a clue as to why the custom applet and panel classes are placed in the applets package.) The use of the asterisk in the import statement allows the compiler to use any classes in that package. In our TemplatePanel, we are ignoring classes in the rarely needed `shout3d.sound` and `shout3d.hanim` packages. If you need to use any of these classes, you'll need to add another import statement. It makes sense to always include the three main Shout packages so that you are free to use all of their classes when building your panel class.

 Note how the TemplateApplet class imported only from the Shout3d package. This simple class needed access only to the Shout3DApplet and Shout3dPanel classes, which are in the Shout3d package.

Now we can get into the class definition itself. The line that declares the new class as an extension of Shout3DPanel is similar to that in our TemplateApplet, with the addition of some words stating that TemplateApplet implements the two interfaces. I have made extensive use of comments in the code. The first comment indicates that you will declare any fields you need for the class at the top, before the methods.

The Constructor

The next comment introduces the *constructor*. The constructor is a special method that uses the name of the class. It is the method that is called when an instance of the class is created. Remember how the TemplateApplet's `initShout3DPanel()` method created a TemplatePanel object using the new keyword? That statement calls the constructor of the TemplatePanel to perform any desired actions when the new object is first allocated.

Our constructor is doing nothing more than calling the constructor of the Shout3DPanel_class from which our TemplatePanel class is derived. The keyword super always refers to the parent of the current class.

When you create a custom panel, you'll need to change the name of the method from TemplatePanel to the name of your panel. You'll probably never need to edit the constructor in any other way.

The Overridden Methods (Registering Observers)

Beneath the constructor are the `customInitialize()` and `finalize()` methods that we inherited from Shout3DPanel. These are, as we have said, empty in the parent class, and so we override them here with some necessary code. You'll use the `customInitialize()` method for lots of things, but for the purposes of this template, you'll use it only to register your observers.

The concept of registering objects to receive *callbacks* is basic in Java. You open communication links by registering objects that implement an interface with other objects that will "call them back" at well-established times. Think of it like a mailing list: You register your e-mail address with a mailing list server to automatically receive messages from that server. This is accomplished by adding your address to a list kept by the server. When you wish to stop receiving messages, you remove your address from the list.

In the same way, certain objects keep a list of other objects that want to hear from them. The other objects register by invoking a method of the calling object that adds them to the list. Every time the calling object needs to send out a message, it goes down the list and calls the appropriate method for every object on the list, passing the message as an argument. The calling object can be assured that every receiving object has the necessary method to call because it will only register objects that have implemented the proper interface.

Let's understand this process in action. The code in our `customInitialize()` method registers the TemplatePanel to receive callbacks on each render cycle and when the user performs any action with the mouse. Take the render cycle first, even though the registration method is listed second. Shout3D will create a Renderer class object to perform the rendering tasks each time a Shout3D applet is run. This Renderer class object is an object that implements the Renderer interface, as described in the API documentation. That means that the Renderer class object created at runtime will have all of the methods listed in that interface.

We want to make sure that the Renderer object notifies our TemplatePanel immediately before and immediately after each frame is rendered. In other words, we want the Renderer to call the onPreRender() and onPostRender() methods in TemplatePanel at the appropriate times so that TemplatePanel can perform any tasks we put into these methods. The Renderer is designed to call these methods, at the correct times, for any object on its list. We therefore wish to add TemplatePanel to this list by registering it with the Renderer. Take a look at the Renderer interface in the online Javadocs, and you'll see that it contains a method named addRenderObserver(). This is the method that adds objects to the list. These objects must be RenderObservers, meaning they must be objects that implement the RenderObserver interface. In this way, the Renderer can be certain that they contain the necessary onPreRender and onPostRender methods. To register a RenderObserver object (like TemplatePanel) with the Renderer, you must call the Renderer's addRenderObserver method and pass it a reference to the object you are registering as an argument. You can also pass a second argument, one that we will consider later on.

We are writing code within the TemplatePanel. To call methods of the Renderer, we have to get a reference to the Renderer. TemplatePanel is extended from Shout3DPanel, and therefore inherits all its methods. Look up the Shout3DPanel methods in the API documentation, and you'll find a getter method called getRenderer() that returns a reference to the Renderer. Using this method, we can use dot notation to call the Renderer's addRenderObserver method in our customInitialize() method. Here is this statement, copied from the TemplatePanel.

```
getRenderer().addRenderObserver(this, null);
```

You've probably noticed the keyword this before now and wondered about it. We use it to designate the object that is executing the code. We are currently inside the TemplatePanel's class customInitialize() method, so within this context, this refers to the particular instance of TemplatePanel upon which customInitialize() is being invoked. Therefore we pass the argument this to inform addRenderObserver() that we are registering this TemplatePanel object as the RenderObserver that wishes to receive callbacks. The use of this is always a bit confusing to newbies, but it begins to make sense very quickly.

Now that we're registered with the Renderer to receive callbacks during the render loop, let's see how we register to receive mouse input from the user. Given what you've learned, the method call in customInitialize() should make some sense to you.

```
addDeviceObserver(this,"MouseInput", null);
```

Notice that there isn't any dot notation here. What object contains this method? Since there is no object reference before the name of the method, addDeviceObserver() must be a method of the current class, TemplatePanel, inherited from Shout3DPanel. Look up Shout3DPanel in the online Javadocs, and you'll find that it does indeed contain the addDeviceObserver() method. Apparently the TemplatePanel is registering to receive messages from itself!

As strange as this may first appear, it makes perfect sense. Think about mouse input. We want the TemplatePanel class to respond to mouse clicks and drags only within the 3D window, not elsewhere on the user's screen. Mouse events are channeled though the Java component over which the cursor is located. Thus the TemplatePanel is always notified when mouse events occur in its territory. By registering our Device-Observer, we are telling the TemplatePanel to pass along the mouse event information to its own onDeviceInput() method.

 The same logic applies, surprisingly enough, to keyboard input as well. You must click within a panel or any other Java component to establish the keyboard focus. Once you have, keyboard input is processed through that component. This is obvious in components like text boxes in which you type in text, but is true of all components.

Passing the this argument once again indicates our desire to register the class we are in, TemplatePanel. The second argument is new—a string that indicates the type of user input we wish to receive. Here, as is most common, we wish to receive mouse input only. If we wished to receive both mouse and keyboard input, we would pass the string "DeviceInput" as the second argument.

If we register our observers when the panel is initialized, we must unregister them when the user closes down. The two methods in the finalize() method perform these functions, and are self-evident.

DeviceObserver Method

The TemplatePanel is registered (with itself) to receive notification of any mouse events occurring in its pixel space. When the user clicks or drags, or simply moves the mouse within the 3D rendering region, information about this action will find its way to the

TemplatePanel (by processes we need not consider) and the onDeviceInput() method will be called. The onDeviceInput() method in TemplatePanel is empty, so we will have to write code if we want to respond to mouse events. But a few points are worth noting here.

First, onDeviceInput() will be called in response to any kind of user action with the mouse. Generally, you will want to program responses only to some kinds of input (such as clicks) and will wish to ignore others (such as moving the cursor). Thus, the first step in coding this method is to sort out the kinds of possible inputs and figure out which will produce a response. Further, note the two arguments that onDeviceInput() receives when it is called. Only the first is important right now. When onDeviceInput() is called, it receives information about precisely what happened. This information is stored in a DeviceInput object. The method can then use this information to determine how to respond.

DeviceInput is an abstract class. In practice, onDeviceInput() will receive one of three more specialized objects derived from DeviceInput: MouseInput, Keyboard-Input, or (much more rarely) WindowInput. Take a look at the online Javadocs to get a feel for the kind of information stored in these class objects. We have registered TemplatePanel only to receive MouseInput objects. However, if we had registered to receive any kind of DeviceInput, we would need to provide code at the start of onDeviceInput() to determine what kind of input is being sent in the current method call.

Finally, note from that onDeviceInput() returns a Boolean value. This is extremely common in methods that handle user input. You must structure your code so the method returns true if it responded to the input, and false if it ignored it. (When you return a value of true, this indicates that you have "used up the input" and so other DeviceObservers will not get a chance to examine it. The onDeviceInput()calls to other DeviceObservers in the list will not be made once any DeviceObserver returns a value of true.) For example, assume you were interested only in mouse clicks and wrote code to respond to them. The code that executes in response to mouse clicks must end (one way or another) with the statement return true. Other events, such as moving the mouse, must be funneled toward the statement return false. Our template includes a statement to return false as a placeholder because the compiler will reject the code without a return statement.

RenderObserver Methods

The methods that implement the RenderObserver interface are onPreRender() and onPostRender(). We have already registered the TemplatePanel object with the Renderer, and thus these methods will be called just prior to rendering and immediately after rendering, respectively. You will rarely need to use both of them. Typically, you will choose to provide all of your functionality in only one, leaving the other empty. However, just because you choose not to use one of the two methods, you cannot remove it from the class. In implementing the RenderObserver interface, you are committing to make available all the methods required by that interface, even if one or both are empty. If you remove one of them, javac will complain when you compile the class.

Both of the methods receive the same two arguments, but you will rarely make use of them. The DeviceInput argument to onDeviceInput() is very important because it contains information about the nature of the user's action. By contrast, onPreRender() and onPostRender() don't generally require any information from the Renderer—they only need to be triggered. However, both of these methods are passed references to the Renderer that called them. And they are also passed an *object*, meaning an instance of any kind of Java class. The contents of this argument are specified when you register as a RenderObserver in customInitialize(). The final argument in our addRenderObserver() method was null, indicating that we did not wish to have any object passed to the RenderObserver methods. (The same rules apply when registering as a DeviceObserver.)

Testing Things Out

You now have more than enough knowledge to try some hands-on testing. You'll find that the moment you start writing and compiling your own projects, things start coming together quickly. We'll begin by using only the Java Console in your Web browser.

We'll create a test project composed of the following four elements:

```
testing.html
```

```
testing.wrl
```

```
TestingApplet.java
```

```
TestingPanel.java
```

To create testing.html, open template.html in a text editor. You should have already placed a copy of template.html in the demos directory of your Shout installation, so open it from there. Edit the <APPLET> tag to enter the correct names in the two spots where question marks are used as placeholders. Your <APPLET> tag should now read

```
<APPLET CODEBASE="../codebase" CODE="applets/TestingApplet.class"
➥ARCHIVE="shout3dClasses.zip" WIDTH=320 HEIGHT=240>
<param name="src" value="models/testing.wrl">
<param name="headlightOn" value="true">
</APPLET>
```

Save this edited file in the demos directory under the name testing.html.

Make sure you capitalized the applet name correctly, as TestingApplet.class. *If you fail to do so, the browser won't be able to find the file. This is a common error that's easy to overlook. Correct capitalization is important throughout Java.*

Copy testing.wrl from the CD to the models directory of your Shout installation. This is just a copy of the very simple scene file we used when exploring VRML, consisting of only a single red cube positioned at the center of world space.

To create TestingApplet.java, open the TemplateApplet.java file in a text editor. Once again, you should have already copied this file from the CD to the applets folder in your Shout installation. Replace the word Template with the word Testing in both locations in which it occurs, and save the file to the applets folder as Testing-Applets.java. Make sure that everything is correctly capitalized, and that the file is saved under the correct name (and without an extra extension—like .txt—at the end). New programmers will soon learn to be careful about all these little details. Your applet should read as follows:

```
package applets;
import  shout3d.*;

public class TestingApplet extends Shout3DApplet {


  public void initShout3DPanel(){
    panel = new TestingPanel(this);
  }

}//end of class
```

Testing Initialization

Let's test the initialization process by printing out a string of text to the Java Console of the user's Web browser.

Open up `TemplatePanel.java` in a text editor. You should have already copied this file from the CD to the `applets` folder of your Shout installation. You'll need to make three changes to the template.

1. Change the name of the class to `TestingPanel`.

2. Change the name of the constructor to `TestingPanel`.

3. Add a println statement to the `customInitialize()` method.

Here is the entire class with the changes in boldface. You can put any text you want in the println statement—just make sure it's between double quotation marks to indicate that it's a text string.

```
package applets;

import shout3d.*;
import shout3d.core.*;
import shout3d.math.*;


public class TestingPanel extends Shout3DPanel implements
➡DeviceObserver, RenderObserver{


  //fields to be placed here



  //the constructor

  public TestingPanel (Shout3DApplet applet){
    super(applet);
  }


  //called immediately after scene is loaded
```

```
public void customInitialize() {
  addDeviceObserver(this,"MouseInput", null);
  getRenderer().addRenderObserver(this, null);

  System.out.println("Initialized!");
}




//cleanup actions performed when viewer closes applet

protected void finalize()  {
  removeDeviceObserver(this,"MouseInput");
  getRenderer().removeRenderObserver(this);
}




//method from DeviceObserver interface
//to handle user input-
//will only receive mouse input as registered

public boolean onDeviceInput(DeviceInput di, Object userData) {

  return false;

}




//method from RenderObserver interface,
// called before each frame is rendered

public void onPreRender (Renderer r, Object o) {

}




//method from RenderObserver interface,
// called after each frame is rendered
```

```
    public void onPostRender (Renderer r, Object o) {

    }
```

```
} //end of class
```

Save this file as `TestingPanel.java` in the `applets` folder of your Shout3D installation. Now you are ready to compile.

To compile, bring up the Command prompt and change the current directory to `Shout3d_2.0\Shout3d_runtime\codebase`. If the current directory is not at the root level of the C: drive, bring it up to the root before you start by typing the **cd** (change directory) command at the prompt, followed by a space and then a backslash.

```
cd \
```

After you have done this, the Command prompt will indicate the root of the C: drive as follows:

```
C:\>
```

Now move down from the root into the proper directory. You can do this in three steps:

```
C:\>cd Shout3d_2.0
C:\Shout3d_2.0>cd Shout3d_runtime
C:\Shout3d_2.0\Shout3d_runtime>cd codebase
```

Or, if you trust your typing skills, you can do it in one blow:

```
C:\>cd Shout3d_2.0\Shout3d_runtime\codebase
```

However you get there, your Command prompt should now read as follows:

```
C:\Shout3d_2.0\Shout3d_runtime\codebase>
```

We need to compile the applet and the panel classes. As it turns out, the applet class will always make reference to a corresponding panel class—in our case TestingApplet contains code to create an instance of TestingPanel. Thus you must compile the panel before you compile the applet. If you try to compile the applet first, the compiler will look for the compiled panel and won't be able to find it.

To compile the panel, type the following at the Command prompt:

```
javac applets\TestingPanel.java
```

Before you hit the Enter key to run the compiler, stop to consider what you're doing. The command `javac` will run the compiler. We have already set up the correct path variable to find javac in its location in your JDK. The text after the `javac` command tells the compiler what you want to compile. Think this through carefully. You are presently in the `codebase` directory, but `TestingPanel.java` is in the `applets` folder within `codebase`. So you must specify the path to the file. If you type only the filename, without the directory `applets`, the compiler will tell you that it can't find the file because it will look for it only in the current `codebase` directory.

This raises an interesting question. Why not just move directly into the `applets` folder as the current directory? Why not set the Command prompt to `applets`?

```
C:\Shout3d_2.0\Shout3d_runtime\codebase\applets>
```

The answer is that `javac` needs access to the Shout3D class library, which is contained in the `codebase\shout3d`. The compiler can find classes it needs in any directory beneath the current directory, and thus can find classes in both `shout3d` and `applets` from the current directory `codebase`. If the current directory were set directly to `applets`, `javac` would not be able to find the necessary classes in `shout3d`.

Another important issue is capitalization. You may have noticed that the Command prompt ignored cases when you changed directories. For example, all three of the following commands work equally well:

```
cd shout3d_2.0
cd SHOUT3D_2.0
cd Shout3d_2.0
```

However, Java is completely case sensitive. The Java compiler will only accept class names with the proper capitalization. Thus, the command

```
javac applets\TestingPanel.java
```

will work, but the command

```
javac applets\testingpanel.java
```

will not.

Web developers are used to using forward slashes (/ or //) in paths. Remember to use only backslashes when entering paths at the Command prompt. This is a very easy error to make. If the compiler is rejecting your file, check to make sure that you are typing `javac applets\TestingPanel.java` *and not* `javac applets/TestingPanel.java`. *I guarantee you will make this simple error more than once.*

Check your entry at the command line to make sure that you've done everything correctly. Then press the Enter key to run the compiler. If you did everything correctly, you will receive no error messages and you'll get a new Command prompt awaiting the next command. If you get error messages, start getting used to it right now. Learning to program is learning to respond to error messages. This takes practice and patience, but you can become skilled in this area after a remarkably short time.

There are two general reasons for error messages. One is that there is something fundamentally wrong with the file. The compiler may not have been able to find the file. Did you type the correct name, with the correct path and the correct capitalization? Is there actually a file with this name in the `applets` directory? It's easy to make simple mistakes like this.

The other reason for messages, which is far more common, is coding errors within your source files. These will sometimes be logical errors or errors based on a misunderstanding of Java. These are "good errors" and you can learn a lot from trying to solve them. But more often, especially at the beginning, most of your errors will be "dumb errors"—simple typing mistakes that you failed to notice. The most common one is probably failing to put a semicolon at the end of a statement. For example, your file will kick back an error if you added

```
System.out.println("Initialized!")
```

instead of

```
System.out.println("Initialized!");
```

If you made any mistakes like this, correct them in the source code, resave the file `TestingPanel.java`, and recompile. You don't need to retype the command at the prompt. Just use the up (and down) arrow keys to find prior commands, and press Enter.

If you are still getting errors, copy the `TestingPanel.java` file from the CD on top of your version and try to compile it. This is tested code, so if you are getting error messages, you are facing a more basic problem, probably in how you are specifying the file in the command line.

When `TestingPanel.java` has been successfully compiled, you'll find a file named `TestingPanel.class` in your `applets` folder. Now its time to compile `TestingApplet.java`. Give it a try, using the following command:

```
javac applets\TestingApplet.java
```

Make corrections if there are any error messages, and use the tested copy on the CD for reference if you run into problems you can't figure out. Once you have compiled versions of the applet and panel, run `testing.html` (in the `demos` folder) in a Web browser. The scene with the red box should load. Open the Java Console for your Web browser. You'll find it in the View menu in Microsoft Internet Explorer and in the Communicator ➜ Tools menu in Netscape. If you don't find it on the View menu in Internet Explorer, you'll need to add it as an Advanced Option under Tools ➜ Internet Options. The Java Console should display a line reading `Initialized!` Congratulations! You've created your first Shout3D project and proven that the `customInitialize()` method automatically executes whatever code you write in it.

You may find other messages in the Java Console. Ignore them for the time being if they occur. As you work with the Java Console on the two major browsers, you'll find that they can offer many messages you can safely ignore.

It goes without saying that a Shout3D practitioner must work with the most recent versions of the Netscape and Microsoft browsers during the development process. You can safely work with only one of these two, as long as you are sure to test your content on both before it is released to the public.

Testing the Render Loop

Let's continue with the panel class we have and test the RenderObserver methods in the same way we tested the initialization process. Edit your current `TestingPanel .java` file to add println statements to `onPreRender()` and `onPostRender()`. Leave the rest of the code alone, including the println statement that you previously added to `customInitialize()`. Your RenderObserver methods should read as follows:

```
public void onPreRender (Renderer r, Object o) {

    System.out.println("Before");

}


public void onPostRender (Renderer r, Object o) {

    System.out.println("After");
}
```

Save the file and recompile it. Use the up and down arrow keys as necessary to get the correct command at the prompt without retyping. Remember to recompile the panel class and not the applet class. `TestingApplet.java` does not need to be recompiled because you didn't change it. Work through any error messages you get until you get a properly compiled version.

Now run `testing.html` again with the Java Console open. You'll see alternating messages printing out many times a second.

```
Before
After
Before
After
Before
After
...
```

This demonstrates that `onPreRender()` is executing before the start of each render cycle and `onPostRender()` is executing at the end of each cycle. If your eye was fast enough, and the Java Console was open at the start, you would have see that the `Initialized!` message was printed out once before the render loop messages began printing.

When you recompile an applet or panel that you have been testing in a Web browser, you generally can't get by with a mere Refresh command to review the update. These commands reload the scene, but they typically do not reload the updated version of the applet. You can use Ctrl+Refresh in Internet Explorer to force it to reload the Java classes, but you'll often need to close your Web browser and reopen it to get it to load your new classes. If you cannot understand why changes you've made are not in evidence, the answer is sometimes because you failed to save your updated source code before you recompiled. But the answer may also be that the browser is mysteriously continuing to use the previous versions of the classes, which it has stored in a cache. Netscape is particularly persistent in preserving a cached version, which is an important argument for using Internet Explorer as your primary testing platform.

Now that we see how the RenderObserver methods operate, let's try out a couple of ideas. The RenderObserver methods will often be used for procedural animation—animation driven by program code. In a realtime rendering environment, the user's frame rate cannot be determined in advance. A realtime renderer simply renders as quickly as it can, and the frame rate depends on the complexity of the scene and the user's processing power. The frame rate will often change from frame to frame. One of the most important uses of the RenderObserver methods is to determine the current frame rate. Let's use the onPreRender() to print out the current frame rate to the Java Console.

We'll only use onPreRender(), so delete the contents of onPostRender(). To get the current frame rate, we'll use a method named getFramesPerSecond(). Look up the Shout3DPanel class in your Javadocs, and glance over all the various getter methods until you find getFramesPerSecond(). Note that this method returns a float value. We can therefore get the Java Console to print out this float value by passing the method name as the argument to System.out.println().

Your RenderObserver methods should read as follows:

```
public void onPreRender (Renderer r, Object o) {
   System.out.println(getFramesPerSecond());
}


public void onPostRender (Renderer r, Object o) {

}
```

You can call getFramesPerSecond() directly from your panel class because this method is a member method of Shout3DPanel and is therefore inherited by TestingPanel. Pay careful attention to the way a method can be passed as an argument to another method. This is the same as passing the return value of getFramesPerSecond() as the argument to the println method. Note how we don't use quotation marks here because we are not passing a string to System.out.println().

Make sure that you have typed all of the parentheses correctly—there are two pairs—and that you remembered the semicolon at the end of the statement. Save TestingPanel.java as edited and recompile. Reload the Web page and check your Java Console. You should see the current frame rate flying by, updated with each frame.

```
12.3
12.4
12.3
12.3
12.0
...
```

Procedural animation will involve both monitoring the current frame rate and changing values (for example, the translation field of a Transform) with each frame. Let's experiment with getting a value to increment with each frame. To do this, we need to create an int variable to hold the value. With each render cycle, onPreRender() will increase the value by one and print it out.

We'll name the variable counter and initialize its value to 0. But what kind of variable should it be? Should it be a local variable within the onPreRender() method, or should it be a field—a variable for the entire class? This is an important distinction that must be understood as soon as possible. A local variable disappears at the end of the method in which it is created. But we need to preserve the variable between method calls so that onPreRender() can also increment the most recent updated value. Thus counter must be a field of the TestingPanel class.

Here is a full version of TestingPanel.java as properly edited. The changes are highlighted. Note the declaration of counter at the top, as an int initialized to a value of 0. In onPreRender(), the current value of counter is incremented by 1, and the result stored back in counter. A comment indicates that this statement can be more succinctly written as counter++. The next line prints out the current value of counter, which will necessarily always be one greater than the last time it was printed.

```
package applets;

import shout3d.*;
import shout3d.core.*;
import shout3d.math.*;


public class TestingPanel extends Shout3DPanel implements
➡DeviceObserver, RenderObserver{


  //fields to be placed here
  int counter = 0;


  //the constructor

  public TestingPanel (Shout3DApplet applet){
    super(applet);
  }


  //called immediately after scene is loaded
```

```java
public void customInitialize() {
  addDeviceObserver(this,"MouseInput", null);
  getRenderer().addRenderObserver(this, null);

  System.out.println("Initialized!");
}



//cleanup actions performed when viewer closes applet

protected void finalize() {
  removeDeviceObserver(this,"MouseInput");
  getRenderer().removeRenderObserver(this);
}



//method from DeviceObserver interface
//to handle user input-
//will only receive mouse input as registered

public boolean onDeviceInput(DeviceInput di, Object userData) {

  return false;

}



//method from RenderObserver interface,
// called before each frame is rendered

public void onPreRender (Renderer r, Object o) {
  counter = counter + 1;   //same as counter++;
  System.out.println(counter);
}



//method from RenderObserver interface,
```

```
    // called after each frame is rendered

    public void onPostRender (Renderer r, Object o) {

    }


  } //end of class
```

Edit `TestingPanel.java` as indicated by the highlighted code and save it. Recompile and reload the HTML demo. Check out the Java Console to see a list of integers printing out, with values increasing each render cycle.

```
1
2
3
4
...
```

Testing Mouse Input

Now let's see if we can get our project to respond to mouse input. Remember that we have registered TestingPanel to receive mouse input. Thus, every time a user takes any action with the mouse, the `onDeviceInput()` method will be called. That method will receive a MouseInput class object that contains information about the event, and we'll use this information to determine how to respond.

Mouse Event Basics

Let's start with the smallest ambitions. Assume that we want to print out a message when the user presses the mouse button down. All other actions taken with the mouse will be ignored. To achieve to goal, we must examine each MouseInput object we receive to determine whether the event was produced by pressing the button down. If so, we will call the println method. If not, we will do nothing and return out of the `onDeviceInput()` method.

There is a fair amount to learn here, so let's take some time to consider the following code:

```
    public boolean onDeviceInput(DeviceInput di, Object userData) {

        MouseInput mi = (MouseInput) di;
```

```
switch (mi.which){

  case MouseInput.DOWN:
    System.out.println("Pressed Down!");
    return true;

}//end of switch


return false;

}
```

Let's start with the first line of code within the method. We create a local MouseInput variable to hold a reference to the MouseInput object that was received by onDevice-Input(). This is a good example of where we would use a local variable rather than a field. There is no reason to preserve the MouseInput information between calls to onDeviceInput() because new values will be received with each new method call. So we create a local MouseInput variable and name it mi. We then assign it the DeviceInput object di that was passed as an argument to the method. We have already discussed the idea that DeviceInput is an abstract class from which MouseInput and KeyboardInput are derived. The onDeviceInput() method must be prepared to receive any kind of DeviceInput, but in customInitialize() we have specifically registered only to receive MouseInput. Thus we can be certain the DeviceInput object di that onDevice-Input() receives is specifically a MouseInput object. Because we are certain of this, we can assign di to our new MouseInput variable mi. However, we must cast di to MouseInput before assigning it to mi by placing the name MouseInput in parentheses before di. Casting is a signal to the compiler that we understand we are assigning a value of one type or class to a variable of another type or class. It may seem strange to require such a cast here, because di is actually a MouseInput object, but the compiler cannot know this.

If you understood the preceding paragraph completely, you have an excellent command of some subtle principles of Java programming. If you did not, don't worry. It takes a little time for these ideas to sink in. In a short time, they will make perfect sense to you. In the meanwhile, you can simply use the code at face value.

Once we have our input information properly stored as MouseInput, we can examine the MouseInput_ to see what we've got. We use a `switch` statement to choose between different alternatives. Look up MouseInput in the online Javadocs. You won't find any methods, but you'll find a number of important fields. These fields can be divided into two classes—variables and constants.

The variables are *x*, *y*, `which`, and `button`. These may change with each new event. For each mouse event, the integer values in these variables report the *x* and *y* cursor location in the panel window, which kind of mouse action occurred, and whether the left or right button was involved. Note that these are all stored as `int` values. The left and right buttons are distinguished as 0 and 1. The different kinds of input that can be stored in the `which` field are also integers, but to make for more readable code, the appropriate integers has been assigned to *constants*. A constant is a variable that cannot be changed. By declaring a variable to be `final`, we permanently associate its initialized value with a variable name. We can then use the variable name instead of the value. In this case, we can use the field names DOWN, UP, MOVE, DRAG, ENTER, and EXIT instead of having to remember integer values. Note how constants are always capitalized to distinguish them from ordinary variables.

Look at the `switch` statement in the code. This `switch` takes different actions depending on the current value in `mi.which`. The alternatives are listed in the `switch` block, which is bounded by opening and closing curly braces. Each alternative is listed as a `case`. We need only one of the four possible alternatives, so our only case is `MouseInput.DOWN`. (I'll explain why we write `MouseInput.DOWN` rather than `mi.DOWN` in just a minute.) For this alternative, we print out a message (`"Pressed Down!"`) and then return out of the entire method with the Boolean value `true`. The `true` value indicates that `onDeviceInput()` handled the mouse event. By returning at this point in the method, we bypass all of the lines of code beneath. Thus we never execute the line that reads `return false`. However, if the mouse event were not a button press, the `case` would not execute, and the method would continue through to the end and would return a Boolean `false` value. This would properly indicate that `onDeviceInput()` did not respond to the kind of mouse event that called it. Note how the `return false` statement sits beneath the end of the `switch` block. It therefore serves as a catch basin for all events that are not handled in the `switch` block.

Let's test this out. Add the new code to onDeviceInput() in TestingPanel.java. Type it carefully, and make sure to remember the colon used at the end of the case statement. Remove the counter field and the code that you placed in onPreRender().

```
package applets;

import shout3d.*;
import shout3d.core.*;
import shout3d.math.*;

public class TestingPanel extends Shout3DPanel implements
➡DeviceObserver, RenderObserver{


    //fields to be placed here


    //the constructor

    public TestingPanel (Shout3DApplet applet){
    super(applet);
    }



    //called immediately after scene is loaded

        public void customInitialize() {
          addDeviceObserver(this,"MouseInput", null);
          getRenderer().addRenderObserver(this, null);

          System.out.println("Initialized!");
        }



    //cleanup actions performed when viewer closes applet

    protected void finalize()  {
      removeDeviceObserver(this,"MouseInput");
```

```
        getRenderer().removeRenderObserver(this);
    }



    //method from DeviceObserver interface
    //to handle user input-
    //will only receive mouse input as registered

    public boolean onDeviceInput(DeviceInput di, Object userData) {

        MouseInput mi = (MouseInput) di;

        switch (mi.which){

        case MouseInput.DOWN:
            System.out.println("Pressed Down!");
            return true;

        }//end of switch

        return false;

    }

    //method from RenderObserver interface,
    // called before each frame is rendered

    public void onPreRender (Renderer r, Object o) {

    }

    //method from RenderObserver interface,
    // called after each frame is rendered

    public void onPostRender (Renderer r, Object o) {
```

```
        }


    } //end of class
```

Save `TestingPanel.java` and recompile. Correct your errors, if any, until you've got a clean result, and then reload or refresh the scene in your Web browser. Open the Java Console and adjust your windows so the Java Console and Web browser do not overlap. This will allow you to see both at the same time. Now click the mouse while your cursor is over the panel. The message will print out every time you click. Like so.

```
Initialized!
Pressed Down!
Pressed Down!
Pressed Down!
```

Try some experiments. Press the mouse button down, but don't release it. The message appears because it is driven by a simple mousedown event as opposed to what we normally think of as a "click," which is a press followed by a release. Try pressing the right mouse button, and you'll see that this works as well. The event does not distinguish between left and right buttons. Finally, click in the Web browser window, but with the cursor outside the panel. Nothing happens because `onDeviceInput()` is only receiving events generated within `TestingPanel` pixel space.

Using MouseInput Fields

Let's print out some more detailed information for each click. The following statement will print out the current x and y cursor location, taken from `mi.x` and `mi.y` fields.

```
System.out.println("Cursor at x=" + mi.x + " y=" + mi.y);
```

Look it over carefully because it introduces the concept of *concatenation*. The different elements are concatenated with the + sign. This is way of mixing text strings with numerical values. The text strings are set in double quotation marks. Notice how a space is used at the start of the second string to separate it from the `mi.x` value. Replace the current println statement in `onDeviceInput()` with this new one. Save, recompile, correct errors, and reload in your Web browser. Try pressing the mouse button again and note how the Java Console prints out the current cursor location.

```
Cursor at x=57 y=53
Cursor at x=246 y=112
```

Note how the *x* value increases from left to right across the panel, and the *y* value increases from top to bottom. This can be a little confusing because we are often used to vertical values increasing from bottom to top. We set the panel to fill the applet, and the applet was set in the <APPLET> tag on the HTML page to WIDTH=320 HEIGHT=240. By clicking in the panel, you can test these dimensions. The lower right corner is at x=320 y=240.

Next, we'll ask onDeviceInput() to inform the user of which mouse button was used. This gives us a chance to look at a simple if statement. We need to test the value in mi.button. If the value is 0, the left button was pressed. If the value is 1, the right button was pressed. There are a number of ways to code this. The following is the least elegant, but the simplest to understand.

```
if (mi.button == 0) {System.out.println("Left Button");}
if (mi.button == 1) {System.out.println("Right Button");}
```

Each if statement is immediately followed by a test in parentheses. Note how the double equals sign is used to test equality. If the answer is true, the block of code in the following curly braces is executed. In this case, there is only one line of code in each set of curly braces. These kinds of structures are called *conditionals* because code is executed subject to specific conditions.

Our two conditionals are alternatives. If mi.button is not equal to 0, then it must be equal to 1. Either the first or the second message will be printed out. Thus we might prefer using an if-else conditional structure.

```
if (mi.button == 0) {System.out.println("Left Button");}
else {System.out.println("Right Button");}
```

Either of these will work, but edit your source code to add the second one. Leave the existing println statement as is. Your onDeviceInput() method should now look like this:

```
public boolean onDeviceInput(DeviceInput di, Object userData) {

    MouseInput mi = (MouseInput) di;

    switch (mi.which){

      case MouseInput.DOWN:

        System.out.println("Cursor at x=" + mi.x + " y=" + mi.y);

        if (mi.button == 0)
```

```
                    {System.out.println("Left Button");}

              else
                 {System.out.println("Right Button");}

              return true;

         }//end of switch


       return false;
     }
```

Give this a try by saving and recompiling. Check it out in the Java Console. You'll get messages like these:

```
Cursor at x=270 y=101
Left Button
Cursor at x=35 y=76
Right Button
```

I promised to explain why the case *statement refers to* MouseInput.DOWN *instead of* mi.DOWN. *Actually, we could have used* mi.DOWN *in this statement, with the same result, but the other form is more correct, and it's important to understand why. If you look up* MouseInput *in the online Javadocs, you'll notice that the four constant fields are designated as* static *and* final. *The final designation is what makes them constants, as this keyword indicates that the initial values stored in these variables can never be changed. The* static *designation means that these constants are associated with the* MouseInput *class, and not any particular instance of the class. For this reason, it's more logical to specify them as* MouseInput.DOWN *or* MouseInput.MOVE, *rather than* mi.DOWN *or* mi.MOVE. *The constants are not really associated with the specific instance of* MouseInput *referenced in* mi, *and to treat them so is misleading.*

Tracking Drag Distances

Let's put some pieces together to do something practical. Dragging the mouse is an extremely useful tool for interactivity. The user presses the mouse button down with the cursor within the panel. He or she then drags the mouse with the button depressed. The application tracks the number of pixels the user has dragged in both the horizontal and vertical directions, and then does something with this information. For example,

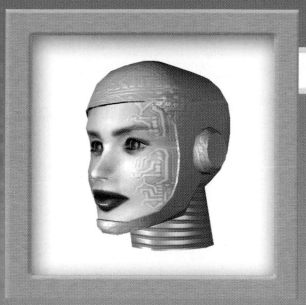

I n the following pages, you'll find color images reflecting the range of possibilities in Shout3D. Many of them are taken from the bonus projects on the accompanying CD. I think you'll find these bonus projects useful in developing your own methods of 3D content preparation and interactivity design.

SHOUT3D

Shout Out Loud

Mod Characters

Jo and Oscar, the ShoutInteractive dynamic duo, battle with evil in a 60-second character animation that can be found in your Shout3D installation. Check out the demos titled `BeatMonkBash` and `BeatMonkBash_with_sound`. Note the outstanding camera work and solid storyboarding characteristic of Randall Ho, lead creative talent at ShoutInteractive. ShoutInteractive, LLC, is the content production house associated with Eyematic Interfaces, Inc., the developer of Shout3D.

Bill Clinton

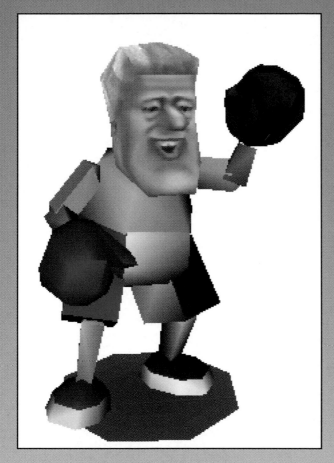

Clinton as boxer

This animated U.S. president is made subject to the closest scrutiny in the Examine_demo in your Shout3D installation. Rotate him by dragging the mouse, and zoom in and out by holding down the Control key while dragging. This piece was originally part of a game—Wundah in the Rotundah—in which the leader of the Free World takes on Saddam Hussein in the boxing ring. Almost all of the geometry is allocated to the textured head. When the character is in motion, the viewer doesn't notice that the limbs are little more than simple boxes.

Android

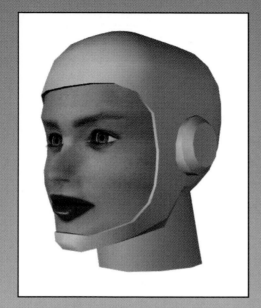

Android

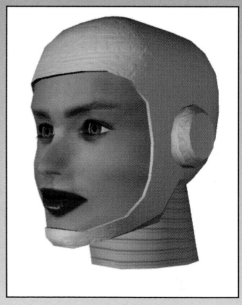

Android with bump mapping applied

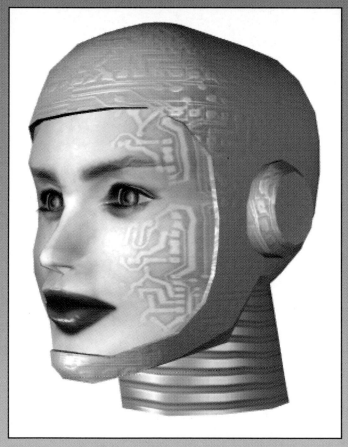

Android with bump mapping and specularity

Shout3D sets a new standard in realtime rendering quality for Web 3D. Here, we look at three versions of the Android model found in your Shout3D installation. The simplest version is impressive enough, but bump mapping adds detail and a sense of relief that would be impossible or costly if worked into the mesh geometry. The finished version adds specularity. Here the specularity is mapped to provide a pattern of highlights for a surreal effect. The image quality of this screen shot from a Shout3D applet is almost indistinguishable from a render in 3D Studio MAX.

Shout3D Sign

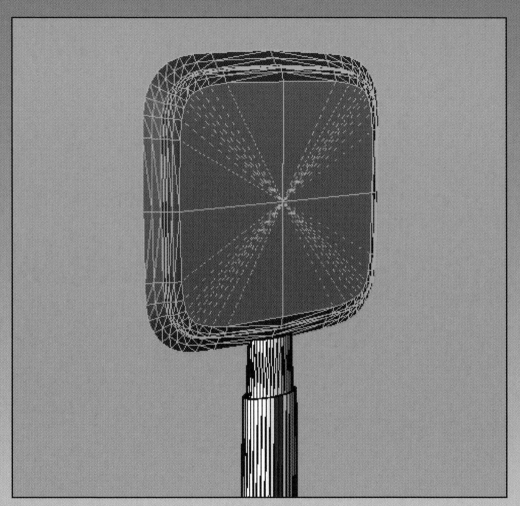

Sign—3D Studio MAX

Daylight   *Sunset*

In this bonus project on the accompanying CD, we try an interactive visualization, which is very important when communicating design ideas. The original model, as seen in a 3D Studio MAX screen shot, is 1596 triangles—enough to appear completely smooth on close inspection from all views. The user can rotate and zoom using three separate cameras, and can compare daytime and evening environments. Note the impact of reflection mapping on the chrome portion of the sign.

Piston

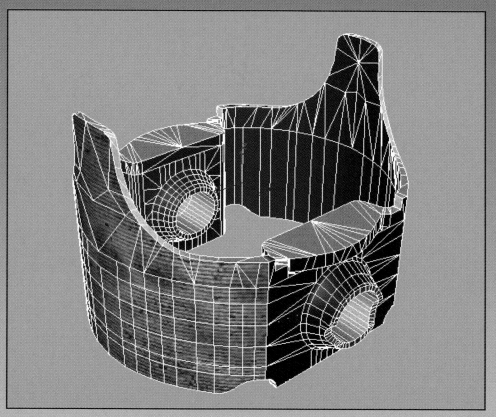

Piston—3D Studio MAX

In another bonus project on the CD, we use Shout to communicate the complex contours of machined products—in this case, a piston head for an automobile engine. This model maintains its resolution on extreme close-ups. In fact, packing this much resolution into 4,200 triangles took some skilled modeling by Dino Giannini. Examine the screen shot from MAX to see the difficult balance sought between a regular mesh and the lowest possible polygon count. The Shout3D applet designed for this project allows the user to switch between a fully textured view and a colored-surface view that makes it easier to understand the precise shape.

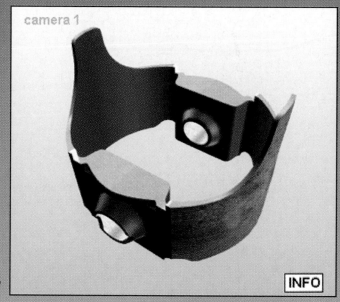

camera 1

Piston textured

INFO

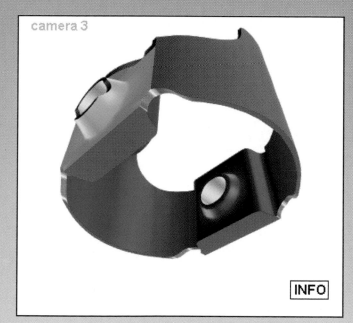

camera 3

Piston with colors

INFO

Sink

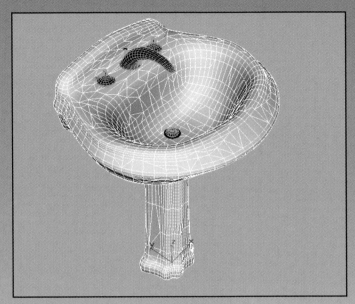

Sink—3D Studio MAX

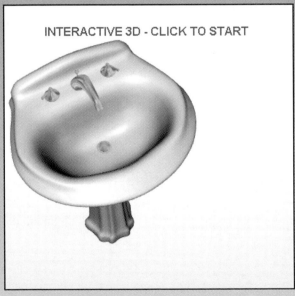

INTERACTIVE 3D - CLICK TO START

Sink—click to start

MUSK ROSE

SKYLIGHT BLUE

Rose sink

Blue sink

This bonus project from the CD illustrates an approach to showcasing products using interactive 3D. The model is composed of 7200 triangles, the minimum required to preserve the subtle curvature of this object on close examination. The screen shot from MAX reveals mesh irregularities due to polygon reduction using the Optimize modifier. This kind of reduction must be used carefully because the resulting mesh irregularities can generate irritating rendering anomalies, especially with specular highlights. The user is first invited to click on the Shout3D applet to bring up an instructional menu. You can rotate, zoom, change camera views, and select from a 2D color palette that overlays the 3D image. Color labels change in the upper left corner.

Floorplan

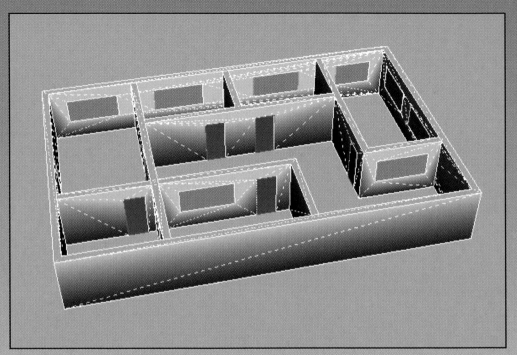

Floorplan—3D Studio MAX

This final bonus project was developed with the help of architects looking for a way to communicate a floor plan—in this case, a section of a floor of an office building. A "walk-through" approach to navigation tends to confuse clients, who lose track of where they are. This project uses a view pointer that is positioned in the floor plan and rotated with arrow keys. The adjustable field of view angle is indicated by the red guidelines. I developed a "pen and colored pencil" look typical of architectural illustration using IndexedLineSets and vertex colors. Compare the screen shot of the model in MAX with the rendering in the Shout3D panel. The Shout3D rendering of the vertex color gradients is actually more pleasing.

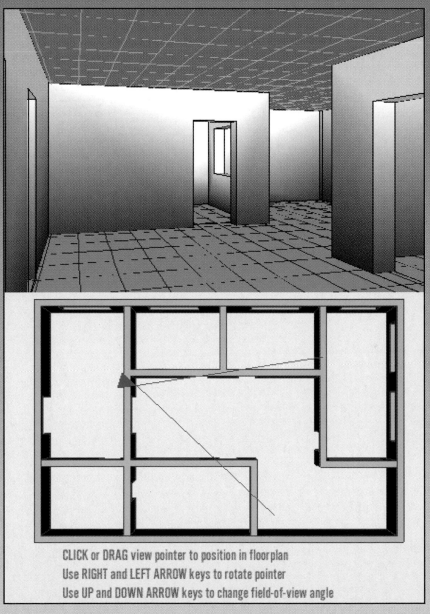

CLICK or DRAG view pointer to position in floorplan
Use RIGHT and LEFT ARROW keys to rotate pointer
Use UP and DOWN ARROW keys to change field-of-view angle

Floorplan rendering

Sydney Games

Triathlon map view

Triathlon sky view

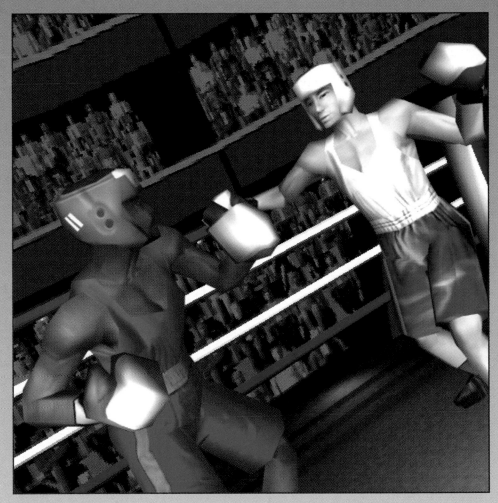

Boxing

ShoutInteractive produced some outstanding projects for the Sydney 2000 Summer Games. Web visitors could keep track of the Triathlon from different views that indicate the current position of the leader. Above, this image from 3D Studio MAX shows the models and backgrounds created for interactive boxing games that were developed for Shout3D delivery over the Web. Note the subtle texture mapping that conceals the low-poly structure of the models.

FortuneTeller

Fortuneteller

Fortuneteller talking

These images announce the arrival of miraculous technology developed by Eyematic Interfaces, Inc., the owner of Shout3D, that completely automates facial animation. Jim Stewartson, Co-CTO of Eyematic and President of ShoutInteractive, LLC, animated this model simply by speaking into a standard web cam. Eyematic facial sensing technology, soon to be released, animated the model to follow every movement of his face. The animation was then delivered in a Shout3D applet, complete with sound, and I made this screen shot directly from my browser while on the Internet. It's impossible to underestimate the significance of this breakthrough in 3D animation.

the horizontal drag distance might control the rotation of the viewpoint, as if the user were turning his or her head. The vertical drag distance might control the up-down tilt of the viewpoint, or it might move the viewpoint forward or backward in the scene. The possibilities are endless.

We'll edit TestingPanel to print out information that demonstrates it is correctly tracking drag information. To do this, we must start with a correct understanding of how mouse events get fed into the panel.

A mouse event is generated when the user first presses the mouse button down with the cursor within the panel's pixel space. The user then moves the mouse with the button depressed. At this point, the number of events generated depends upon the user's system. At an extreme, a new event is generated for each pixel the user drags over. If you drag over ten pixels in a single swipe, you get ten consecutive calls to onDevice-Input(). This, however, is unlikely to happen. Rather, individual drag events will be generated for movements over small numbers of pixels. This will become clear as we test it out.

To track distances, we will need fields to hold pixel values. We will need fields to hold the x and y values of the pixel where the user first pressed down the mouse. This is the start point from which the first drag distance is measured. Then we will need fields to hold the current location of the cursor so we can measure the distance back to the start point.

Look over the following code:

```
package applets;

import shout3d.*;
import shout3d.core.*;
import shout3d.math.*;


public class TestingPanel extends Shout3DPanel implements
➥DeviceObserver, RenderObserver{


    //fields to be placed here
    int startX;
    int startY;
    int currentX;
    int currentY;
```

```
//the constructor

public TestingPanel (Shout3DApplet applet){
  super(applet);
}


//called immediately after scene is loaded

public void customInitialize() {
  addDeviceObserver(this,"MouseInput", null);
  getRenderer().addRenderObserver(this, null);

  System.out.println("Initialized!");
}



//cleanup actions performed when viewer closes applet

protected void finalize()  {
  removeDeviceObserver(this,"MouseInput");
  getRenderer().removeRenderObserver(this);
}



//method from DeviceObserver interface
//to handle user input—
//will only receive mouse input as registered

public boolean onDeviceInput(DeviceInput di, Object userData) {

  MouseInput mi = (MouseInput) di;

  switch (mi.which){

    case MouseInput.DOWN:
      startX = mi.x;
```

```
        startY = mi.y;
        System.out.println("Down at x=" + mi.x + " y=" + mi.y);
        return true;

    case MouseInput.DRAG:
        currentX = mi.x;
        currentY = mi.y;
        System.out.println("x distance is "+(currentX - startX));
        System.out.println("y distance is "+(currentY - startY));
        return true;

    }//end of switch

    return false;  ;

}


//method from RenderObserver interface,
// called before each frame is rendered

public void onPreRender (Renderer r, Object o) {

}


//method from RenderObserver interface,
// called after each frame is rendered

public void onPostRender (Renderer r, Object o) {

}


} //end of class
```

We now have two `case` alternatives within the `switch` block in `onDeviceInput()`. When the user presses the mouse button down, the `DOWN` alternative stores the current cursor location in the two fields `startX` and `startY`, declared at the top of the class. These two values are then printed out to the Java Console. The `DRAG` alternative stores the current cursor location in `currentX` and `currentY` and then prints out the distance between the current and start values. Edit `TestingPanel.java` to reflect this new code, taking special care with the println statements. It's easy to make typing errors on these. Save, recompile, debug if necessary, and then reload into your Web browser.

Bring up the Java Console before you do anything and make sure it is not obstructing the browser window. Now click the mouse button in different locations within the panel to print out the cursor location. You should get messages like:

```
Down at x=255 y=101
Down at x=55 y=55
Down at x=267 y=152
```

Next, press down the mouse button and hold it. Drag slowly and carefully (to the best of your ability) in the horizontal direction only. The distance measures will print out with every DRAG event. Notice how many DRAG events occur within a single dragging movement of the mouse. You should see messages like

```
x distance is 2
y distance is 0
x distance is 3
y distance is 0
x distance is 7
y distance is 0
x distance is 9
```

Note how, depending on the precise speed of the drag, DRAG events were generated at 1, 2, and 4 pixel intervals. Try again, this time moving the mouse somewhat faster. The *x* distance will increase in much larger units with each event.

This gives us a good idea of how DRAG events are generated, but there is something else to observe about the code. The DRAG alternative measures the distance between the current cursor location and the original start point—where we originally pressed the mouse. What we will typically need is the distance from the last DRAG event. That's because the DRAG code will typically do something in the scene—like rotate the viewpoint—and we need to update only the change since the previous action. In other words, we typically need to use only the incremental drag distance since the previous DRAG event was processed. To achieve this, we need to reset the start values to the current values at the end of the DRAG alternative. This assures that the next time the DRAG code is executed, it uses the previous cursor location as the start point. Here is the `onDeviceInput()` method with the additional code in boldface.

```java
public boolean onDeviceInput(DeviceInput di, Object userData) {
    MouseInput mi = (MouseInput) di;
```

```
    switch (mi.which){

        case MouseInput.DOWN:
            startX = mi.x;
            startY = mi.y;
            System.out.println("Down at x=" + mi.x + " y=" + mi.y);
            return true;

        case MouseInput.DRAG:
            currentX = mi.x;
            currentY = mi.y;
            System.out.println("x distance is "+(currentX - startX));
            System.out.println("y distance is "+(currentY - startY));
            startX = currentX;
            startY = currentY;
            return true;

    }//end of switch

    return false;
}
```

Edit your source code to add the new lines, save it, and recompile. Reload (not just refresh) your browser and try dragging slowly as before. The Java Console should now track only the incremental distances—not the total distance from the original mouse press.

```
x distance is 2
y distance is 0
x distance is 6
y distance is 0
x distance is 2
y distance is 0
x distance is 8
y distance is 0
```

The only remaining problem with our code is that it responds to both left and right mouse buttons. We'd prefer it to respond only to the left button. To correct this, make the DOWN and DRAG code conditional on the use of the left button. Each block executes only if (mi.button == 0). Try out the following:

```
case MouseInput.DOWN:
  if (mi.button == 0) {

    startX = mi.x;
    startY = mi.y;
    System.out.println("Down at x=" + mi.x + " y=" + mi.y);
    return true;
  }
  break;


case MouseInput.DRAG:
  if (mi.button == 0) {

    currentX = mi.x;
    currentY = mi.y;
    System.out.println("x distance is "+(currentX - startX));
    System.out.println("y distance is "+(currentY - startY));
    startX = currentX;
    startY = currentY;
    return true;

  } break;
```

The break; *statements, while not strictly necessary in this particular example, are standard practice. They assure that execution leaves the* switch *immediately after completing a* case *and resumes after the end of the* switch.

Even though we've been working only with println statements, we've already learned an enormous amount. We've demonstrated that a Shout3D applet can respond to user input and to the render loop. Now we're in a position to use these powers to control the 3D scene itself.

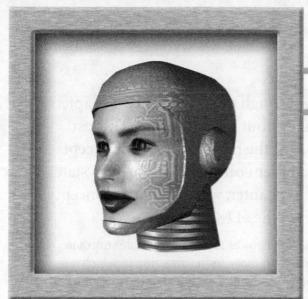

Interactively Moving
and Rotating Objects

SHOUT3D

Chapter 8

I f you have worked your way through the previous two chapters,
you are well prepared to make Shout3D come alive. The last
chapter introduced a number of the most important concepts
that you'll need, but implemented them only through println statements for the Java Console. In this chapter, we bring these concepts,
and many more, to bear directly on the 3D scene.

The best place to start is by giving users the power to move (translate) or rotate
objects in the scene. If the object can be made to move in the direction in which it is
rotated, you have created basic navigation—which can be applied to the camera
(Viewpoint) as well as to any geometric object. In every case, we must find a way to
convert information obtained from mouse inputs into changes in the Transform node
of the object being affected.

Interactive Translation

To create this project, we'll use (once again) the simplest possible scene with only a single
green cube located at the world origin. Copy the file named translate.wrl from the
CD to the models folder of your Shout installation. The file reads as in Listing 8.1:

LISTING 8.1 SCENE WITH BOX (*TRANSLATE.WRL*)

```
#VRML V2.0 utf8

DEF mytrans Transform {

   translation   0 0 0


   children   Shape {
     appearance   Appearance {
       material   Material {
       diffuseColor 0 1 0

       }
     }

     geometry   IndexedFaceSet {
```

```
         coord   Coordinate {
         point   [ -1 1 1,
             -1 -1 1,
              1 1 1,
              1 -1 1,
              1 1 -1,
              1 -1 -1,
             -1 1 -1,
             -1 -1 -1 ]
         }

         coordIndex  [ 0, 1, 3, 2, -1, 4, 5, 7,
              6, -1, 6, 7, 1, 0, -1, 2,
              3, 5, 4, -1, 6, 0, 2, 4,
              -1, 1, 7, 5, 3, -1 ]


      } #end IndexedFaceSet
    } #end of Shape
  } #end of Transform
```

Note how the Transform node that contains the Shape—the only Shape in the entire scene—has been given the DEF name "mytrans". This name was entirely up to me and was typed directly into the file. If you export from MAX, the .s3d file will assign DEF names to each Transform using the name of the object in MAX. As these names can often be cryptic, it may make sense to edit these DEF names directly in the .s3d file. In any case, the DEF name allows us to uniquely identify a node in the scene.

We'll create a pair of classes named TranslateApplet and TranslatePanel. The applet will be easy. Just edit TemplateApplet as follows, and save it as `TranslateApplet.java`.

```java
package applets;
import  shout3d.*;

public class TranslateApplet extends Shout3DApplet {


  public void initShout3DPanel(){
    panel = new TranslatePanel(this);
  }

}//end of class
```

Dragging in One Dimension

The panel class will require some planning. Let's start by translating the object only in the world *x* direction, which will be horizontally across the screen if the camera (Viewpoint) is facing in the default –*z* direction. We'll measure horizontal drag distances in pixels and convert them into world *x* distances in the scene. Then we will change the translation values in the affected Transform node to reposition the object in world space. This approach makes no use of the render loop at all. Thus, when editing Template-Panel to create our TranslatePanel, we can eliminate every aspect of the template code that pertains to the RenderObserver interface. There's no harm in keeping it in, but for clarity, we'll cut it out. As you examine the code in Listing 8.2, note carefully where the RenderObserver code has been removed.

LISTING 8.2 TRANSLATEPANEL (*TRANSLATEPANEL.JAVA*)

```java
package applets;

import shout3d.*;
import shout3d.core.*;
import shout3d.math.*;


public class TranslatePanel extends Shout3DPanel implements
➡DeviceObserver{

    Transform boxTrans;
    float worldPosX;
    int pixelStartX;
    int pixelEndX;


    public TranslatePanel (Shout3DApplet applet){
      super(applet);
    }

    public void customInitialize() {

      addDeviceObserver(this,"MouseInput", null);
```

```
    //get reference to the Transform node you need
    boxTrans = (Transform) getNodeByName("mytrans");

    //get the x position value from the transform
    //and store it in the worldPosX variable
    worldPosX = boxTrans.translation.getValue()[0];

    //print out the value in worldPosX
    //to confirm that starting x value is 0
    System.out.println("Box's x position is " + worldPosX);


}


protected void finalize() {
  removeDeviceObserver(this,"MouseInput");

}


public boolean onDeviceInput(DeviceInput di, Object userData) {
  MouseInput mi = (MouseInput) di;

  switch (mi.which){
    case MouseInput.DOWN:
      pixelStartX = mi.x;
      return true;

    case MouseInput.DRAG:
      pixelEndX = mi.x;

      //get pixel distance dragged
      int dragDistance = pixelEndX - pixelStartX;

      //convert pixel distance to meters
      // at 100 pixels/1 meter
      float deltaX = dragDistance/100f;
```

```
            //add delta to current X position
            //to get new position
            worldPosX = worldPosX + deltaX;

            //put the new X position
            //in the transform node.
            boxTrans.translation.set1Value(0, worldPosX);

            //reset the starting pixel for next drag
            pixelStartX = pixelEndX;

            return true;

        }//end of switch

        return false;
    }


} //end of class
```

This panel class contains so much fundamental material that it deserves a long and leisurely inspection. The concepts illustrated here, in the simplest possible way, will reappear again and again in your Shout projects.

Let's start with the fields—the variables declared at the top of the class. We are only tracking the mouse cursor horizontally, and thus we need integer fields only to hold the start and end pixels in the *x* direction. Note that `pixelStartX` and `pixelEndX` are locations on the surface of the screen, not in the 3D world space "behind" the screen. By contrast, the *x* position of the cube *is* in 3D space. The value to be stored in the floating point variable `worldPosX` is the current *x* position of the object in (*x,y,z*) world space. It's important to understand as quickly as possible the distinction between pixel locations on the screen (which are inherently pairs of `int` values) and locations in 3D space (which must be arrays of three `float` values).

Perhaps the most important thing you can learn from this code is the necessity of obtaining a reference to any node in the scene that you wish to query or manipulate. When the scene in `translate.wrl` is loaded into the Shout3D player at runtime, a scene graph is constructed out of Shout3D Node classes. The information in each of these Shout nodes is the same as in the VRML (or .s3d) nodes in the scene file. Thus, for example, the Shout player creates a Shout Transform node (a Java class object) with the DEF name "mytrans". In order to interact with this node, your panel class must obtain a reference to it. We therefore create a Transform node reference variable to hold this reference.

Notice that I named this Transform reference boxTrans. *But I DEF named the Transform in the .wrl file* mytrans. *I did this to make a point. The Java field you create to hold a reference to a Shout node need not have the same name as the DEF name contained in that node (and taken from the .wrl file). It might arguably make sense to use one name for both purposes, but the DEF name within the node and the name of a reference to that node are independent. This distinction can confuse beginners, but it will make good sense to you as you go along.*

Move down to the customInitialize() method. I've commented every significant line of code separately, and highlighted these comments to make the process as clear as possible. We've created a field to hold the Transform node, and now we need to actually fill that variable with the reference to the proper object. We find the object by its DEF name. The statement

```
boxTrans = (Transform) getNodeByName("mytrans");
```

uses the getNodeByName() method of the Shout3DPanel class. It takes a character string as an argument—thus the necessary double quotation marks. Using this string, it finds the requested object and returns a reference to it, which we assign to boxTrans. Now boxTrans can be used to access this Transform.

Take a moment to look up the getNodeByName() method in the Javadocs documentation. You'll find it in the Shout3DPanel class. Note how the return type for this method is node, which makes sense because it must be able to return any kind of node. This explains the need to cast the return value to Transform (in the parentheses) before assigning it to boxTrans. The compiler cannot know that the node being returned by the method is specifically a Transform and will not let us make the assignment unless we approve it. By casting the return value, we let the compiler know that the reference being assigned to boxTrans is a Transform. You'll often get error messages from the compiler that are due to the failure to make explicit casts like this. These problems are generally easy to solve.

Now that we have a reference to the Transform, we can access it to determine its current *x* position value. The statement

```
worldPosX = boxTrans.translation.getValue()[0];
```

gets the current *x* position value from the Transform and stores it in the `worldPosX` variable. The println statement in the next line of code is designed to test whether this assignment works at runtime by checking in the Java Console. Note carefully how the *x* value is obtained from the Transform. The `translation` field of `boxTrans` contains its positional values in a FloatArrayField. The FloatArrayField class contains an accessor method named `getValue()`, which returns a reference to the actual array of (in this case) three `floats`. The statement `getValue()[0]` returns the first of these three `floats`—the one representing the *x* position value.

These syntactical rules take some getting used to for the beginner. Take the time to learn them, and they will quickly become second nature. Although they can seem forbidding at first, they directly reflect the principles of object-oriented programming.

At this point, the panel is properly initialized. The panel has the necessary reference to the Transform controlling the box in the scene and has stored its current *x* position in a separate variable. Now we need to consider interactivity. The panel is registered to handle mouse events, so look over the `onDeviceInput()` method. I'll assume you've reviewed the mouse-dragging code in the previous chapter, and therefore recognize the basics. Pressing the mouse button down stores the *x* location of the pixel over which the cursor is located in `pixelStartX`. This is the start point of the drag. With each dragging interval, the new *x* location of the cursor is stored in `pixelEndX`. A local variable named `dragDistance` stores the difference—the number of pixels dragged across in the horizontal direction.

This `dragDistance` of the cursor must now be converted into a distance to move the cube in world space. Translation distances in VRML, and therefore in Shout3D, are measured in meters. I decided, just as a guess, to move the cube one meter in world space for every 100 pixels dragged. Thus, the following line of code divides the `dragDistance` by 100 and assigned the result to a `float` variable.

```
float deltaX = dragDistance/100f;
```

Notice how the denominator of the fraction is explicitly cast as a `float`, using the `f`. This is a good example of the little things the new Java programmer must understand. `DragDistance` is an integer, representing a number of pixels, but we need to end up with a floating point result to represent a distance in 3D space. By explicitly dividing the `int` by a `float`, we can be sure to get a `float` result because Java will evaluate this expression to produce the result with the greatest precision. In any case, every 100 pixels of drag will produce one meter of `deltaX`. The term "delta," the Greek letter that corresponds to our English "D," is often used in mathematics and programming to mean *difference* or *change*. In this case, deltaX holds the change in the *x* position of the cube attributable to the current mouse drag. The next line of code therefore adds this delta to the current *x* position to get the new *x* position.

The variable worldPosX now contains the proper *x* position of the cube. But this is not enough; we now need to take this value and put in the Transform node. This is accomplished with the set1Value() method, which assigns the value in worldPosX to the first (the [0]) element in the translation array.

```
boxTrans.translation.set1Value(0, worldPosX);
```

 It's important to understand that the scene is not affected until a change is made to values within nodes. Often, as in this example, it makes sense to use variables as "work spaces" to figure out a result. Here, worldXPos is being used as a place to compute the current x position of the cube. But nothing will change within the scene until this result is reflected in the Transform node. We could have avoided using this "workspace" variable, but it makes the code easier to understand.

 Take the time to edit TemplatePanel.java to create TranslatePanel.java. The complete source code is available on the CD, but to practice typing in the code yourself will be invaluable. When you compile, there are sure to be error messages, and you will benefit from the opportunity to see what mistakes you've made. When you've successfully compiled the panel, and then the applet, edit Template.html to reference TranslateApplet.class and translate.wrl, and save the file as translate.html. Run this file in your Web browser and drag the cube across the screen. Pretty neat, huh? You've programmed your first piece of the 3D interactivity in Java. (If your scene isn't loading, check the Java Console for error messages.) All of the necessary files (listed below) are included on the CD for reference.

TranslatePanel.java

TranslatePanel.class

TranslateApplet.java

TranslateApplet.class

translate.wrl

translate.html

As you play with this demo, note how you can drag your cursor out of the applet window as long as you began within the window. This is because the mousedown event establishes the focus within the Shout3DPanel and therefore will continue to send drag messages to the TranslatePanel for as long as you continue to drag. On the other hand, if you begin outside the window and drag into it, nothing will happen because mouse events are not being channeled to the TranslatePanel. If the cube is moving too slowly for your taste, you can speed it up by changing the conversion ratio between pixels and meters in the TranslatePanel code. For example, the expression `dragDistance/50f` will move the box twice as fast—one meter in 3D space for every 50 pixels dragged. Try this (or any ratio you want) and recompile the panel class to see the result.

Adding the Second Dimension

Let's improve our project to add the vertical dimension. As the user drags vertically, the cube will translate in the *y* direction in 3D space. Open `TranslateApplet.java` and edit it to refer to TranslateXYApplet and TranslateXYPanel, as follows. Then save the file as `TranslateXYApplet.java`. Remember not to compile until after you've compiled the corresponding panel.

```
package applets;
import  shout3d.*;

public class TranslateXYApplet extends Shout3DApplet {


  public void initShout3DPanel(){
    panel = new TranslateXYPanel(this);
  }

}//end of class
```

Let's think through the panel class a bit before we look at the code. We now need to store cursor locations for both *x* and *y* screen dimensions. We also need to store the position of the object in at least two dimensions in 3D space. Rather than create separate *x* and *y* position variables for this second purpose, let's create an array of three `float`s to hold the entire 3D (*x*,*y*,*z*) position. This will make it easier to implement full 3D interactivity later on. The event handling method must track both horizontal and vertical drag distances and convert them into *x* and *y* position changes.

Consider the code in Listing 8.3. Changes or new elements are highlighted in boldface.

LISTING 8.3 TRANSLATEXYPANEL (*TRANSLATEXYPANEL.JAVA*)

```java
package applets;

import shout3d.*;
import shout3d.core.*;
import shout3d.math.*;

public class TranslateXYPanel extends Shout3DPanel implements
➥DeviceObserver{

  Transform boxTrans;
  float[] worldPos = new float[3];
  int pixelStartX;
  int pixelStartY;
  int pixelEndX;
  int pixelEndY;


  public TranslateXYPanel (Shout3DApplet applet){
     super(applet);
  }

  public void customInitialize() {
    addDeviceObserver(this,"MouseInput", null);

    boxTrans = (Transform) getNodeByName("mytrans");

    //get reference to position array
    //from the transform
    //and store in worldPos
    worldPos = boxTrans.translation.getValue();

    //print out values in worldPos
    //to Java Console
    System.out.println("Box's x position is " + worldPos[0]);
    System.out.println("Box's y position is " + worldPos[1]);
    System.out.println("Box's z position is " + worldPos[2]);    }
```

```
protected void finalize() {
  removeDeviceObserver(this,"MouseInput");

}


public boolean onDeviceInput(DeviceInput di, Object userData) {
  MouseInput mi = (MouseInput) di;

  switch (mi.which){
    case MouseInput.DOWN:
      pixelStartX = mi.x;
      pixelStartY = mi.y;
      return true;

    case MouseInput.DRAG:
      pixelEndX = mi.x;
      pixelEndY = mi.y;

      //get pixel distances dragged
      int dragDistanceX = pixelEndX - pixelStartX;
      int dragDistanceY = pixelEndY - pixelStartY;

      //convert pixel distance to meters
      // at 50 pixels/1 meter
      float deltaX = dragDistanceX/50f;
      float deltaY = -(dragDistanceY/50f);

      //add deltas to current X and Y
      //to get new position
      worldPos[0] = worldPos[0] + deltaX;
      worldPos[1] = worldPos[1] + deltaY;

      //put the updated position array
      //in the transform node.
      boxTrans.translation.setValue(worldPos);

      //reset the starting pixel for next drag
      pixelStartX = pixelEndX;
      pixelStartY = pixelEndY;
```

```
        return true;

    }//end of switch

    return false;
}


} //end of class
```

The fields declared at the top of the class now include pixelStartY and pixelEndY to track vertical cursor movement. And, in place of a single float variable to hold worldPosX, we use a float[], allocated to hold three elements, for worldPos. As a result, worldPos is initialized in the customInitialize() method with the entire translation array from the Transform, and the println statements will display all three initial values in the Java Console.

In the onDeviceInput() method, the cursor drag distances are measured in both *x* and *y*, and these are converted to the world space distances—deltaX and deltaY. For greater responsiveness, these conversions are at 50 pixels per meter. Note how deltaY is a negative ratio. In Java, the *y* pixel direction starts at the top of the window and increases as you move *down*. In VRML and Shout3D (and every 3D system I'm aware of), vertical values increase as you move *up*. Thus, dragging the mouse down produces positive drag distances, which must be converted to negative values to make sure the Transform moves in the same direction as the cursor.

The first two elements of the worldPos array are updated by the deltas, and the entire array is put to the Transform using the translation's setValue() method.

Edit your TranslatePanel.java to reflect all the changes and save it as TranslateXYPanel.java. Compile this file, correcting any errors until you get a successful result, then compile TranslateXYApplet.java. Update your translate.html file to reference TranslateXYApplet, and load it into your browser. You should now be able to drag the cube all over the screen. The finished files are also available on the CD.

Adding the Third Dimension

Adding the control over translation in *z* will be easy, but we need to think like interface designers. It's obvious that horizontal and vertical dragging should control horizontal and vertical movement. But moving the object in depth is more debatable. I felt that, given the default location of the Viewpoint, dragging down should pull the object closer to the viewer, and dragging up should push it away. Of course, vertical dragging is already being used for the *y* dimension, so we need to make use of the different mouse buttons.

In the panel class TranslateXYZPanel, the effect of dragging is made conditional on the choice of buttons. If the left button is used, the code is the same as it was in TranslateXYPanel. If the right button is used, only vertical drag distances are measured, and these are applied to the *z* value of the object's position.

Note a couple of things in the code in Listing 8.4. It's not necessary to create left and right conditional options for the mousedown event. This event will store both the *x* and *y* location of the current pixel, but if the right button is used, the `pixelStartX` value will never be used in dragging. Also, the positive delta values produced by dragging downward make sense here because the positive *z* direction is toward the default Viewpoint location. (This is a good example of something you just have to experiment with.)

LISTING 8.4 TRANSLATEXYZPANEL (*TRANSLATEXYZPANEL.JAVA*)

```java
package applets;
import shout3d.*;
import shout3d.core.*;
import shout3d.math.*;


public class TranslateXYZPanel extends Shout3DPanel implements
➡DeviceObserver{

  Transform boxTrans;
  float[] worldPos = new float[3];
  int pixelStartX;
  int pixelStartY;
  int pixelEndX;
  int pixelEndY;


  public TranslateXYZPanel (Shout3DApplet applet){
    super(applet);
  }

  public void customInitialize() {
    addDeviceObserver(this,"MouseInput", null);
```

```
        boxTrans = (Transform) getNodeByName("mytrans");

        worldPos = boxTrans.translation.getValue();

        System.out.println("Box's x position is " + worldPos[0]);
        System.out.println("Box's y position is " + worldPos[1]);
        System.out.println("Box's z position is " + worldPos[2]);
    }



    protected void finalize() {
        removeDeviceObserver(this,"MouseInput");

    }



    public boolean onDeviceInput(DeviceInput di, Object userData) {
        MouseInput mi = (MouseInput) di;

        switch (mi.which){

            case MouseInput.DOWN:
                pixelStartX = mi.x;
                pixelStartY = mi.y;
                return true;

            case MouseInput.DRAG:

                //if left button used
                if(mi.button == 0) {

                    pixelEndX = mi.x;
                    pixelEndY = mi.y;

                    int dragDistanceX = pixelEndX - pixelStartX;
                    int dragDistanceY = pixelEndY - pixelStartY;

                    float deltaX = dragDistanceX/50f;
                    float deltaY = -(dragDistanceY/50f);
```

```
            worldPos[0] = worldPos[0] + deltaX;
            worldPos[1] = worldPos[1] + deltaY;

            boxTrans.translation.setValue(worldPos);

            pixelStartX = pixelEndX;
            pixelStartY = pixelEndY;

            return true;
        }//end of 0 if

        //if right button used
        if (mi.button == 1) {

            pixelEndY = mi.y;

            //get y pixel distances only
            int dragDistanceY = pixelEndY - pixelStartY;

            //vertical drag converted
            //to 3D depth delta
            float deltaZ = dragDistanceY/50f;

            //add delta to current Z
            worldPos[2] = worldPos[2] + deltaZ;

            //put the updated position array
            //in the transform node.
            boxTrans.translation.setValue(worldPos);

            //reset the starting pixel for next drag
            pixelStartY = pixelEndY;

            return true;

        }//end of 1 if

    }//end of switch
```

```
        return false;
    }


    } //end of class
```

After you've figured this code out, you can edit, save, and compile a TranslateXYZPanel and TranslateXYZApplet. Try them out in an HTML file, or use the finished files from the CD:

`TranslateXYZPanel.java`

`TranslateXYZPanel.class`

`TranslateXYZApplet.java`

`TranslateXYZApplet.class`

`translateXYZ.html`

Interactive Rotation

Rotation in 3D graphics is a subtle and difficult subject, whether for the programmer or the animator working within a standard animation package. It's important to understand that these difficulties are not unique to Shout3D, and that Shout has gone to great lengths to provide practical rotation tools. Interactive rotations will always require careful planning and coding; even the simple example we will consider here raises plenty of issues.

Using Quaternions

There are two ways to describe rotations that are commonly used in 3D graphics. Anyone familiar with a 3D graphics package knows the standard approach in which rotations are made separately around the three separate axes—x, y, and z. This is called the *Euler* method of rotations, and it is so standard that it is the only method available in most 3D packages. The Euler method is the most useful for animators because its rotations can be graphed as function curves, and because the concept of turning around one axis and then another is conceptually workable. However, the very fact that complex rotations require rotations around two (or all three) of the axes is the source of much complication. This is because rotations around the different axes must be computed in a fixed order. We will see the consequences of this reality in the project we build here. Euler rotations are often described in navigation terms as *heading, pitch and roll*, or *heading, pitch and bank*, or even *yaw, pitch and roll*. In each of these

- the first rotation (heading or yaw) is around the vertical axis (y)
- the second (pitch) is around the horizontal axis (x)
- the third (bank or roll) is around the depth axis (z)

The first thing to note is that this order places y before x. Of course, the MAX user faces the additional confusion of working with a package that, contrary to standards, reverses the normal direction of y and z—with the z direction in MAX being the vertical in world space. If you're already getting confused, you're perfectly normal. Rotations can get your head spinning pretty quickly.

The second method of describing rotations is called the *axis-angle* method. It is commonly used in graphics programming, but 3D artists who use packages other than MAX probably never will have encountered it. MAX is unique in using the axis-angle method for storing rotational animation keys in its default rotation controller—TCB Rotation. This approach in MAX is very controversial because axis-angle numerical values (other than for the simplest rotations) are incomprehensible and because these values can't be graphed. Therefore, a great many animators make sure they are using MAX's Euler controllers when animating.

The axis-angle description of rotations is inherently superior to the Euler approach because any rotation can be described directly, rather than as the result of separate rotations around the x, y, and z axes. The axis-angle approach allows you to pick any direction as the axis of rotation, and not just the three standard perpendicular axes. Shout, like VRML, uses the axis-angle approach in the `rotation` field of Transform nodes. However, to make life easier for mere human beings, the Shout3D library provides a tool that translates between Euler and axis-angle values.

The Quaternion class is based on the quaternion, which is a way of storing rotations in an array of four `floats`. You can think of the quaternion as a middle ground from which to pass back and forth between Euler and axis-angle values. You can use either Euler or axis-angle values to set the quaternion, and then you can extract either Euler or axis-angle values from the quaternion.

Preparing the Model

Any object that will be interactively rotated requires proper consideration prior to export, whether in VRML or from MAX in .s3d format. Things will be easiest if an object's Transform is unrotated in the exported scene. If you have rotated an object in MAX, you should use the Reset Transform tool in the Hierarchy panel to "zero out" your rotations. This has the effect of moving the rotations into a subsidiary (nested) Transform, as you'll see when you export and look at the .s3d file. But at least the parent Transform that you'll actually control begins with zero values.

An even more important issue is the pivot point. Any animator knows the importance of the proper location of the point around which rotations will occur. MAX is a tricky program on the subject of pivot points because most objects are first created from a default local origin that is often not a good location for a rotational pivot point. For example, a MAX Box object is created from a local origin in the center of the bottom of the box. This is the center of local space—the point from which the positions of the vertices are measured when defining the geometry. When you move the pivot point from this location, typically to the center of the object, this center of local space does not change. Rather, a nested Transform is created, as though the object were parented to a null object. This means you have to know which Transform you want to control.

To get down to a practical instance, consider Listing 8.5. This .s3d file, rgb_cube.s3d on the CD, was exported from the MAX file rgb cube.max, also on the CD. Note the nested Transform structure. This is due to the fact that the pivot point was moved to the center of the box from its original location on the bottom of the box. The parent Transform represents the pivot point, with its location as the center of world space. The child Transform represents the local origin of the model (and the original pivot point), which remains at the bottom of the box. Thankfully, the Shout exporter applies the DEF name of the object (Box01) to the parent Transform which, being the one representing the pivot point, is the one we want to control.

LISTING 8.5 RED-GREEN-BLUE CUBE (*RGB_CUBE.S3D*)

```
DEF Box01 Transform {
translation 0 0 0
    children [
        Transform {
            translation 0 -1 0
            children [
                Shape {
                    appearance [
```

```
            MultiAppearance {
              material Material {
                diffuseColor 0 1 0
                  ...
              }
            }
            MultiAppearance {
              material Material {
                diffuseColor 0 0 1
                  ...
              }
            }
            MultiAppearance {
              material Material {
                diffuseColor 1 0 0
                  ...
              }
            }
          ]
          geometry MultiMesh {
            ...
          }
        }
      ]
    }
  ]
}
```

You may want to bring up the file in a text editor to see the whole thing, but this
abridgement is enough to show the nested Transform structure and the use of three
MultiAppearance nodes. The right and left faces of the cube, along the *x* axis, are colored red. The top and bottom faces along the *y* axis are green. And the front and back
faces along the *z* axis are blue. This color coding will help us understand the effect of
composite rotations.

The RotatePanel Class

Our first panel class to rotate the box interactively will use rotations only around two of
the three possible axes. In theory, this should be sufficient to rotate the object into any

possible orientation. I chose the heading (rotation around y) and pitch (rotation around x). There are many fundamental similarities between this rotation project and the translation panels we have already developed. In this case, a horizontal drag is converted into a heading rotation and the vertical drag will control pitch rotation.

The major new element here is the conversion of rotation values between Euler and axis-angle methods, using a Quaternion object. We create an array of three floats to hold the Euler rotation (heading, pitch, and roll), and an array of four values to hold the axis-angle value. Then we create a Quaternion object to serve as the translator being these two "languages." Take a look at the complete source code for RotatePanel.java in Listing 8.6.

LISTING 8.6 ROTATEPANEL (*ROTATEPANEL.JAVA*)

```
package applets;

import shout3d.*;
import shout3d.core.*;
import shout3d.math.*;


public class RotatePanel extends Shout3DPanel implements
➡DeviceObserver {


    //Node in scene to rotate
    Transform boxTrans;

    //pixels on screen
    int pixelStartX;
    int pixelStartY;
    int pixelEndX;
    int pixelEndY;

    //to store and compute angles
    float [] eulers = new float [3];
    float [] axisAngle = new float [4];
    Quaternion q = new Quaternion();


    public RotatePanel(Shout3DApplet applet){
```

```
        super(applet);
    }

    public void customInitialize() {

        addDeviceObserver(this,"MouseInput", null);
        boxTrans = (Transform) getNodeByName("Box01");

        //get starting rotation value from scene
        axisAngle = boxTrans.rotation.getValue();

        //put this rotation into the quaternion
        q.setAxisAngle(axisAngle);

        //get it back out as eulers
        q.getEulers(eulers);

    }


    protected void finalize() {

        removeDeviceObserver(this,"MouseInput");
    }


    public boolean onDeviceInput(DeviceInput di, Object userData) {
        MouseInput mi = (MouseInput) di;
        switch (mi.which){

            case MouseInput.DOWN:
                pixelStartX = mi.x;
                pixelStartY = mi.y;
                return true;

            case MouseInput.DRAG:

                pixelEndX = mi.x;
                pixelEndY = mi.y;
```

```
            int dragDistanceX = pixelEndX - pixelStartX;
            int dragDistanceY = pixelEndY - pixelStartY;

            //convert drag to rotation
            //at 50 pixels per radian (57.2 degrees)
            float headingDelta = dragDistanceX/50f;
            float pitchDelta = dragDistanceY/50f;

            //compute new heading and pitch
            eulers[0] = eulers[0] + headingDelta;
            eulers[1] = eulers[1] + pitchDelta;

            //Convert from Eulers to AxisAngle
            // using the Quaternion
            q.setEulers(eulers);
            q.getAxisAngle(axisAngle);

            //set the Transform to
            //updated axis angle values
            boxTrans.rotation.setValue(axisAngle);

            pixelStartX = pixelEndX;
            pixelStartY = pixelEndY;

            return true;

        }//end of switch

        return false;

    }


    }//end of class
```

The essence of this code is in the translation between the two rotation formats. In the `customInitialize()` method, after obtaining a reference to the Transform, we get the initial rotation value from the Transform in its axis-angle form and store it in the `axisAngle` array. Then we set the Quaternion object q to this rotation by calling

```
    q.setAxisAngle(axisAngle);
```

With the Quaternion properly set, we can extract the Euler equivalent of the rotation and put it in the `eulers` array.

```
q.getEulers(eulers);
```

At this point, the `eulers` array and the `axisAngle` array hold equivalent rotations. It's worthwhile to look over the Quaternion class in the Javadocs to get a sense of its range of methods.

Once the panel is initialized, we are ready to process drag events. The drags are converted into rotations in heading and pitch—Euler rotations. But the Transform can only be updated with axis-angle values. So we perform the same conversion in reverse. The updated Euler rotations, as stored in the `eulers` array, are used to set the Quaternion. Then the updated Quaternion is used to update the `axisAngle` array. Finally, the `axisAngle` array is used to set the Transform.

All angle values in Shout are in radians, rather than degrees. A radian is 57.3 degrees (180/3.1416). The drag conversion ratio used here is therefore 60 pixels per radian—about 1 degree for each pixel.

Create this RotatePanel file yourself, along with a corresponding RotateApplet. Compile them and create an HTML file to demo them using `rgb_cube.s3d` as the source. Copy `rgb_cube.s3d` from the CD into your `models` directory and give the demo a try. Or copy all these reference files from the CD to your Shout installation:

```
RotatePanel.java

RotatePanel.class

RotateApplet.java

RotateApplet.class

rgb_cube.s3d

rotate.html
```

Playing with the RotatePanel

Take some time to play with the RotatePanel demo. The scene appears with the box square to world space. Your first small rotations will make sense, but things will get screwy pretty fast. If you observe carefully, you'll note that the horizontal drag always works as expected, rotating in the world heading (around the world vertical axis). But a vertical drag *apparently* rotates around the local x axis—around the axis passing between the two red sides. Thus we'll never be able to get a red side on the top. This is a classic "order of rotations" problem. I stress the word "apparently" because the pitch and heading rotations are in fact applied cumulatively in world space. But every time you rotate, even in a single direction, all three rotations are reapplied in a specific order. Here, the roll rotation about the z axis is applied first but has no effect since the value is always 0. Then, the pitch rotation around the x axis is always applied before the heading. That means that the pitch rotation is always made when the object is square with world space—with the x axis pointing in the horizontal direction. Only then is the heading rotation applied, which rotates the already-rotated object again around world y.

This explanation, although correct, should have all but the most mathematical reader fairly confused. In practice, it's the effect of the order of rotations issues for Euler angles that matter more than the reasons. As you can see, we are unable to use just two rotations to freely orient the cube.

Adding the Third Axis

It's obvious we need a third rotational axis to be able to view the object in all possible orientations. This is a bit unfortunate because a user might not expect to need to use the right mouse button, or some alternative control like holding down the Control key while dragging. The interactivity would be less intuitive than we might like, but we can implement it in exactly the same way we implemented the z translation in the TranslateXYZPanel. Other than changing the name of the panel, RotateHPRPanel.java (as shown in Listing 8.7) differs from RotatePanel.java only in the addition of a right-button alternative to control the roll (rotation around the z axis).

LISTING 8.7 ROTATEHPRPANEL (*ROTATEHPRPANEL.JAVA*)

```
package applets;

import shout3d.*;
import shout3d.core.*;
import shout3d.math.*;


public class RotateHPRPanel extends Shout3DPanel implements
➥DeviceObserver {

    ...
```

```java
public RotateHPRPanel(Shout3DApplet applet){
   super(applet);
}

...

public boolean onDeviceInput(DeviceInput di, Object userData) {
   MouseInput mi = (MouseInput) di;
   switch (mi.which){

      case MouseInput.DOWN:
         pixelStartX = mi.x;
         pixelStartY = mi.y;
         return true;

      case MouseInput.DRAG:

         //if left button used
         if(mi.button == 0) {

            pixelEndX = mi.x;
            pixelEndY = mi.y;

            int dragDistanceX = pixelEndX - pixelStartX;
            int dragDistanceY = pixelEndY - pixelStartY;

            float headingDelta = dragDistanceX/50f;
            float pitchDelta = dragDistanceY/50f;

            eulers[0] = eulers[0] + headingDelta;
            eulers[1] = eulers[1] + pitchDelta;

            q.setEulers(eulers);
            q.getAxisAngle(axisAngle);

            boxTrans.rotation.setValue(axisAngle);

            pixelStartX = pixelEndX;
            pixelStartY = pixelEndY;
```

```
                            return true;
                        }//end of 0 if


                //if right button used
                if(mi.button == 1) {

                    pixelEndY = mi.y;
                    int dragDistanceY = pixelEndY - pixelStartY;

                    float rollDelta = dragDistanceY/50f;
                    eulers[2] = eulers[2] + rollDelta;

                    q.setEulers(eulers);
                    q.getAxisAngle(axisAngle);

                    boxTrans.rotation.setValue(axisAngle);

                    pixelStartY = pixelEndY;
                    return true;
                }//end of 1 if


            }//end of switch

            return false;

        }

    }//end of class
```

Build this project yourself (including the applet and HTML file) or copy these finished
RotateHPR files from the CD to your Shout installation:

RotateHPRPanel.java

RotateHPRPanel.class

RotateHPRApplet.java

RotateHPRApplet.class

rotateHPR.html

When you run `rotateHPR.html`, you'll see—using both the left and right mouse buttons—that you can orient the cube however you want. But order of rotations problems are still there and can make the interactivity highly unintuitive. In fact, if you rotate in the pitch such that the blue sides are on the top and bottom (the local *z* axis is aligned with the world *y* axis), the phenomenon known as *gimbal lock* sets in. Due to the order of rotations, roll rotation (vertical drag with the right button) produces the same result as heading rotation (horizontal drag with the left button).

This exploration of the problems of free interactive rotation leads to an important conclusion. Where you wish to give the user the power to view an object from all possible angles, a better approach may not be to rotate the object, but rather to swing the Viewpoint (camera) around the object. This is the approach taken in the Shout ExamineApplet, and it permits the user to view from any angle dragging only with the left mouse button.

Interactive Navigation

We can put rotational and translational control together to navigate an object around on a groundplane. We will create controls to rotate a pointed object in the heading and to move it in the direction that it's pointing.

You already know how to create both the positional and rotational controls with mouse dragging, and our code will be mostly a combination of the panel classes we've already written. However, there will be one new and very important element that may surprise you.

Rotating a Vector

When we drive a car or walk, we first rotate to point in the direction we wish to move, and then we move in that direction. As it turns out, this is not a good way of navigating in computer graphics. The following graphic illustrates the process we will use.

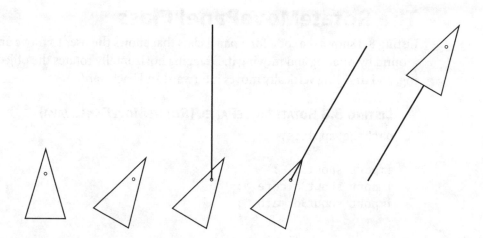

Say we want to rotate the triangular object 30 degrees in the clockwise direction and move it a certain distance in the direction it is pointing. First we rotate the object around its own axis. Then we create an *unrotated* vector, the length of the distance we want the object to move. We rotate this vector 30 degrees, the same amount that we rotated the object. Finally, we translate the object to the end of the rotated vector. The end result is the same as if the object had moved in the direction it was pointing.

The Quaternion object we are already using for rotations has a method named xform() that rotates a vector. You can think of this process as swinging a point in a circle around the center of world space. We measure the distance we want to move in the *z* direction. Thus, if we want to move the object 5 meters in the direction it's pointing, we first create the vector (0,0,5). Then we rotate this vector using the xform() method in the Quaternion. (Conveniently, the Quaternion will already be set to the rotation of the object.) After rotation, the new location of the vector will still be exactly 5 meters from the center. If we add the rotated vector value to the current location of the object, the object will be positioned in the proper location.

This idea confuses everyone at first. It's very logical, but can be hard to grasp because it runs directly counter to our intuition and experience. If you're having trouble with it, just accept it and use the code. I guarantee that it will sink it with a little practice.

The RotateMovePanel Class

Listing 8.8 shows the code for a panel class that allows the user to move an object around by rotating and moving it. Dragging horizontally rotates the object in its heading, and dragging vertically moves it forward and backward.

LISTING 8.8 ROTATEMOVEPANEL (*ROTATEMOVEPANEL.JAVA*)

```java
package applets;

import shout3d.*;
import shout3d.core.*;
import shout3d.math.*;


public class RotateMovePanel extends Shout3DPanel implements
➥DeviceObserver{

  Transform mover;

  int pixelStartX;
  int pixelStartY;
  int pixelEndX;
  int pixelEndY;

  float[] worldPos = new float[3];

  float [] eulers = new float [3];
  float [] axisAngle = new float [4];
  Quaternion q = new Quaternion();


  public RotateMovePanel (Shout3DApplet applet){
    super(applet);
  }

  public void customInitialize() {

    addDeviceObserver(this,"MouseInput", null);

    mover = (Transform) getNodeByName("vehicle");
```

```
    worldPos = mover.translation.getValue();

    axisAngle = mover.rotation.getValue();
    q.setAxisAngle(axisAngle);
    q.getEulers(eulers);

}


protected void finalize()  {

    removeDeviceObserver(this,"MouseInput");

}


public boolean onDeviceInput(DeviceInput di, Object userData) {

    MouseInput mi = (MouseInput) di;

    switch (mi.which){
      case MouseInput.DOWN:
        pixelStartX = mi.x;
        pixelStartY = mi.y;
        return true;


      case MouseInput.DRAG:

      //PIXEL OPERATIONS

        pixelEndX = mi.x;
        pixelEndY = mi.y;

        int dragDistanceX = pixelEndX - pixelStartX;
        int dragDistanceY = pixelEndY - pixelStartY;

        pixelStartX = pixelEndX;
```

```
pixelStartY = pixelEndY;


//ROTATING THE OBJECT

//convert x drag to rotation
// at 30 pixels/radian
float rotationDelta = -(dragDistanceX/30f);

//compute new heading
eulers[0] = eulers[0] + rotationDelta;

//Convert from Eulers to AxisAngle
// using the Quaternion
q.setEulers(eulers);
q.getAxisAngle(axisAngle);

//set the Transform to
//updated axis angle values
mover.rotation.setValue(axisAngle);



//TRANSLATING THE OBJECT

//covert y drag to distance
//at 2 meters per pixel
float translationDelta = dragDistanceY * 2.0f;

//make a distance vector
//in the z direction
float[] vector = {0,0, translationDelta};

//rotate the vector using
//value in quaternion
q.xform(vector);

//add rotated vector
//to current position
worldPos[0] = worldPos[0] + vector[0];
```

```
        worldPos[2] = worldPos[2] + vector[2];

        //set Transform to new position
        mover.translation.setValue(worldPos);

        return true;

    }//end of switch

    return false;
    }

} //end of class
```

This class was tailored to a specific scene that contains an object and flat groundplane. The DEF name of the object's Transform is `"vehicle"`, which is the name I gave the object when creating the scene in MAX. The groundplane is a 300×300 meter square, so I found, by experimenting, that a drag ratio of 2 meters per pixel felt responsive. I made a similar adjustment to the rotational drag. These are the kinds of settings that can only be determined when playing with an actual scene. The scene, in `rotatemove.s3d`, has a specifically positioned light and camera and doesn't rely on defaults. The original MAX file, `rotate_move.max` is included on the CD for reference.

Test this code out by copying the following files from the CD into your Shout installation:

`RotateMovePanel.java`

`RotateMovePanel.class`

`RotateMoveApplet.java`

`RotateMoveApplet.class`

`rotatemove.s3d`

`rotatemove.html`

Navigating the Viewpoint

We can use the methods we've developed thus far to navigate the Viewpoint (camera) through the scene, and thereby create the basis of an interactive "walkthrough."

Using Transforms

The easiest way to start is by repositioning the camera just behind the moving object and parenting the camera to that object. The object now serves as the traditional avatar and the Viewpoint follows the object through the scene, looking over its "shoulder." To make it a bit more interesting, I added some objects to the scene and made the ground-plane larger so there's more space to move around. No new coding is necessary. We'll just use the existing RotateMoveApplet and Panel with the modified scene file.

You can give this a try by copying the following files from the CD to your Shout installation:

```
rotatemoveavatar.s3d
```

```
rotatemoveavatar.html
```

The original MAX file is also available as `rotate_move_avatar.max`, so MAX users can play with variations.

You'll no doubt notice a jittery quality to navigation here. We've been taking a shortcut that reveals its weaknesses strikingly in this particular case. We'll see how to correct this problem at the very end of this chapter.

The approach we've taken thus far leads effortlessly into a more general idea that allows us to dispense with the avatar and navigate the Viewpoint directly. All the MoveRotatePanel needs is a Transform with the DEF name `"vehicle"` to navigate. Thus we can use a null object (a Dummy in MAX terms) as a parent to the camera. A null object is a pure Transform, a Transform that doesn't contain any geometry. (Don't confuse a null object in the language of 3D graphics with the keyword `null` in Java or other programming languages. The keyword `null` means the absence of an object.) By creating a Dummy, naming it "vehicle" and parenting the camera to that Dummy, we create a navigable camera. Try it yourself or use the `rotatemovenull.s3d` and `rotatemovenull.html` files from the CD. Once again, the MAX file is included for experimentation as `rotate_move_null.max`.

Working with the Viewpoint Node

You may be wondering why we haven't operated on the Viewpoint directly, rather than through an intermediary Transform. We can do so, but it requires a little additional knowledge. Unlike scene geometry, a Viewpoint in VRML (and therefore in Shout) doesn't need a Transform node. Rather, the position and rotation information is built directly into the Viewpoint. Take a look at the fields of the Viewpoint node in the Javadocs. The significant ones are fieldOfView, orientation, and position. fieldOfView is the angle of camera view, as would be determined for a physical camera by the focal length of the lens. The second two fields are precisely the same as the rotation and translation fields of a Transform node. I'm not sure why the VRML architects decided to use these different names, but it's a common source of confusion and error.

Thus, to apply the logic of the MoveRotatePanel to a Viewpoint, rather than a Transform, we must make a couple of changes to the panel class (see Listing 8.9). We must get a reference to the Viewpoint, rather than to a Transform, and we must use the correct field names for rotation and translation in the context of a Viewpoint node.

LISTING 8.9 ROTATEMOVEVIEWPOINTPANEL (*ROTATEMOVEVIEWPOINT.JAVA*)

```
package applets;

import shout3d.*;
import shout3d.core.*;
import shout3d.math.*;


public class RotateMoveViewpointPanel extends Shout3DPanel
➥implements DeviceObserver{

  Viewpoint camera;

  int pixelStartX;
  int pixelStartY;
  int pixelEndX;
  int pixelEndY;

  float[] worldPos = new float[3];

  float [] eulers = new float [3];
  float [] axisAngle = new float [4];
  Quaternion q = new Quaternion();


  public RotateMoveViewpointPanel (Shout3DApplet applet){
    super(applet);
  }
```

```
public void customInitialize() {

    addDeviceObserver(this,"MouseInput", null);

camera = (Viewpoint)
  getCurrentBindableNode("Viewpoint");

    worldPos = camera.position.getValue();

    axisAngle = camera.orientation.getValue();
    q.setAxisAngle(axisAngle);
    q.getEulers(eulers);

}


protected void finalize()  {

    removeDeviceObserver(this,"MouseInput");

}


public boolean onDeviceInput(DeviceInput di, Object userData) {

    MouseInput mi = (MouseInput) di;

    switch (mi.which){
      case MouseInput.DOWN:
        pixelStartX = mi.x;
        pixelStartY = mi.y;
        return true;

      case MouseInput.DRAG:

        //PIXEL OPERATIONS

        pixelEndX = mi.x;
        pixelEndY = mi.y;
```

```
        int dragDistanceX = pixelEndX - pixelStartX;
        int dragDistanceY = pixelEndY - pixelStartY;

        pixelStartX = pixelEndX;
        pixelStartY = pixelEndY;


        //ROTATING THE VIEWPOINT

        float rotationDelta = -(dragDistanceX/30f);
        eulers[0] = eulers[0] + rotationDelta;

        q.setEulers(eulers);
        q.getAxisAngle(axisAngle);

        camera.orientation.setValue(axisAngle);


        //TRANSLATING THE VIEWPOINT

        float translationDelta = dragDistanceY * 2.0f;

        float[] vector = {0,0, translationDelta};

        q.xform(vector);

        worldPos[0] = worldPos[0] + vector[0];
        worldPos[2] = worldPos[2] + vector[2];

        camera.position.setValue(worldPos);

        return true;

    }//end of switch

    return false;
    }

} //end of class
```

Notice the new way in which we are getting a reference to the Viewpoint node. We could have used the DEF name of the Viewpoint and obtained the reference with the getNodeByName() method, as we have been doing thus far. But the Viewpoint class is derived from the Bindable class. A scene can contain more than one Bindable node of a given type, but only one can be active at a given time. Thus you can put many Viewpoints in a scene, though only one will be operative at a given time. The active one is said to be "bound." Backgrounds and NavigationInfo nodes are also Bindable nodes that can be swapped during program execution.

Shout permits you to grab a reference to the currently bound node of each of the three types without using a DEF name. We use this technique here. The line

```
camera = (Viewpoint) getCurrentBindableNode("Viewpoint");
```

finds the currently bound Viewpoint node in the scene and returns a reference to this object, which is assigned to camera, a field declared at the top of the class.

Try creating this project yourself, or copy the following classes to your Shout installation:

```
RotateMoveViewpointPanel.java

RotateMoveViewpointPanel.class

RotateMoveViewpointApplet.java

RotateMoveViewpointApplet.class

rotatemoveviewpoint.s3d

rotatemoveviewpoint.html
```

The object that was formerly attached to the camera is has been eliminated, and now the scene file contains only a camera positioned in the same setting as before—between two rows of boxes on a groundplane.

Zooming the Camera

Since we have direct access to the Viewpoint, we might as well take advantage of it to provide for an interactive zoom. Unlike simply moving the Viewpoint, zooming changes the Viewpoint's field of view. This effect can be similar to moving the camera, but as any photographer knows, it changes the perspective.

We can cannibalize our earlier efforts to incorporate the same two-button mouse input. All the navigation will now be allocated to the left button, and a vertical drag of the right button will adjust the field of view. Like all angles, the field of view is expressed in radians rather than degrees. By now, the panel class in Listing 8.10 should be easy to understand.

LISTING 8.10 ROTATEMOVEVIEWPOINTPANEL (*ROTATEMOVEVIEWPOINT.S3D*)

```
package applets;

import shout3d.*;
import shout3d.core.*;
import shout3d.math.*;

public class RotateMoveZoomPanel extends Shout3DPanel implements
➥DeviceObserver{

  Viewpoint camera;
  float fov;

  int pixelStartX;
  int pixelStartY;
  int pixelEndX;
  int pixelEndY;

  float[] worldPos = new float[3];

  float [] eulers = new float [3];
  float [] axisAngle = new float [4];
  Quaternion q = new Quaternion();


  public RotateMoveZoomPanel (Shout3DApplet applet){
    super(applet);
  }

  public void customInitialize() {

    addDeviceObserver(this,"MouseInput", null);

    camera = (Viewpoint)
      getCurrentBindableNode("Viewpoint");
```

```java
    worldPos = camera.position.getValue();

    axisAngle = camera.orientation.getValue();
    q.setAxisAngle(axisAngle);
    q.getEulers(eulers);

    //get starting field of view
    fov = camera.fieldOfView.getValue();

}


protected void finalize()  {

    removeDeviceObserver(this,"MouseInput");

}


public boolean onDeviceInput(DeviceInput di, Object userData) {

    MouseInput mi = (MouseInput) di;

    switch (mi.which){
      case MouseInput.DOWN:
        pixelStartX = mi.x;
        pixelStartY = mi.y;
        return true;


      case MouseInput.DRAG:

        //if left button used
        if (mi.button == 0) {

          pixelEndX = mi.x;
          pixelEndY = mi.y;
          int dragDistanceX = pixelEndX - pixelStartX;
          int dragDistanceY = pixelEndY - pixelStartY;
          pixelStartX = pixelEndX;
```

```
pixelStartY = pixelEndY;

//ROTATION

float rotationDelta = -(dragDistanceX/30f);
eulers[0] = eulers[0] + rotationDelta;
q.setEulers(eulers);
q.getAxisAngle(axisAngle);
camera.orientation.setValue(axisAngle);

//TRANSLATION

float translationDelta = dragDistanceY * 2.0f;
float[] vector = {0,0, translationDelta};
q.xform(vector);
worldPos[0] = worldPos[0] + vector[0];
worldPos[2] = worldPos[2] + vector[2];
camera.position.setValue(worldPos);

return true;

}//end of 0 if


//if right button used
if (mi.button == 1)  {

  pixelEndY = mi.y;
  int dragDistanceY = pixelEndY - pixelStartY;

  //adjust field of view at
  //150 pixels dragged per
  //radian (57.2 degrees)
  float fovDelta = dragDistanceY/150.0f;
  fov = fov + fovDelta;

  camera.fieldOfView.setValue(fov);

  pixelStartY = pixelEndY;
  return true;
```

```
        }//end of 1 if

    }//end of switch

    return false;
  }

} //end of class
```

You can demo this project using the former scene, `rotatemoveviewpoint.s3d`. The other files to be copied from the CD are

`RotateMoveZoomPanel.java`

`RotateMoveZoomPanel.class`

`RotateMoveZoomApplet.java`

`RotateMoveZoomApplet.class`

`rotatemovezoom.html`

Customizing the Viewpoint

Our current panel class is pretty useful and could be used in a variety of scenes. But it would be even more useful if we could adjust certain parameters to better fit the requirements of the scene without having to recompile. We can do this by editing the panel to receive parameters from the <APPLET> tag in the HTML page.

To achieve this we need to do a couple of things. First, we must replace the hard number values in the drag conversion statements with variables that hold the conversion values. For example, the statement

```
float rotationDelta = -(dragDistanceX/30.f);
```

becomes

```
float rotatationDelta = - (dragDistanceX/rotationFactor);
```

The initial value of `rotationSpeed` is set to 30, and therefore nothing changes in the behavior of the panel class. However, now that we have a variable, we can set it using values gathered from the <APPLET> tag. If no parameter is included in the <APPLET>, the default value remains unchanged. Take a look at the improved panel class in Listing 8.11.

**LISTING 8.11 ROTATEMOVEZOOMPLUSPANEL
(*ROTATEMOVEZOOMPLUSPANEL.JAVA*)**

```java
package applets;

import shout3d.*;
import shout3d.core.*;
import shout3d.math.*;


public class RotateMoveZoomPlusPanel extends Shout3DPanel
➥implements DeviceObserver{

  Viewpoint camera;
  float fov;

  int pixelStartX;
  int pixelStartY;
  int pixelEndX;
  int pixelEndY;

  float[] worldPos = new float[3];

  float [] eulers = new float [3];
  float [] axisAngle = new float [4];
  Quaternion q = new Quaternion();

  float rotationFactor = 30.0f; //pixels per radian
  float translationFactor = .5f; //pixels per meter
  float rotationFactor = 150.0f; //pixels per meter

  public RotateMoveZoomPlusPanel (Shout3DApplet applet){
    super(applet);
  }

  public void customInitialize() {

    addDeviceObserver(this,"MouseInput", null);
```

```
    camera = (Viewpoint)
      getCurrentBindableNode("Viewpoint");

    worldPos = camera.position.getValue();

    axisAngle = camera.orientation.getValue();
    q.setAxisAngle(axisAngle);
    q.getEulers(eulers);

    fov = camera.fieldOfView.getValue();

    String rotationFactorString =
      applet.getParameter("rotationFactor");
    if (rotationFactorString != null){
      rotationFactor =
        Float.valueOf(rotationFactorString).floatValue();
    }

    String translationFactorString =
      applet.getParameter("translationFactor");
    if (translationFactorString != null){
      translationFactor =
        Float.valueOf(translationFactorString).floatValue();
    }

    String zoomFactorString =
      applet.getParameter("zoomFactor");
    if (zoomFactorString != null){
      zoomFactor =
        Float.valueOf(zoomFactorString).floatValue();
    }
  }


  protected void finalize() {

    removeDeviceObserver(this,"MouseInput");

  }
```

```java
public boolean onDeviceInput(DeviceInput di, Object userData) {

    MouseInput mi = (MouseInput) di;

    switch (mi.which){
      case MouseInput.DOWN:
        pixelStartX = mi.x;
        pixelStartY = mi.y;
        return true;

      case MouseInput.DRAG:

        //if left button used
        if (mi.button == 0) {

          pixelEndX = mi.x;
          pixelEndY = mi.y;
          int dragDistanceX = pixelEndX - pixelStartX;
          int dragDistanceY = pixelEndY - pixelStartY;
          pixelStartX = pixelEndX;
          pixelStartY = pixelEndY;


          //ROTATION

          float rotationDelta =
            -(dragDistanceX/Factor);
          eulers[0] = eulers[0] + rotationDelta;
          q.setEulers(eulers);
          q.getAxisAngle(axisAngle);
          camera.orientation.setValue(axisAngle);

          //TRANSLATION

          float translationDelta =
            dragDistanceY/translationFactor;
          float[] vector = {0,0, translationDelta};
          q.xform(vector);
          worldPos[0] = worldPos[0] + vector[0];
```

```
                    worldPos[2] = worldPos[2] + vector[2];
                    camera.position.setValue(worldPos);

                    return true;

                }//end of 0 if


                //if right button used
                if (mi.button == 1)  {

                    pixelEndY = mi.y;
                    int dragDistanceY = pixelEndY - pixelStartY;
                    float fovDelta = dragDistanceY/zoomFactor;
                    fov = fov + fovDelta;
                    camera.fieldOfView.setValue(fov);

                    pixelStartY = pixelEndY;
                    return true;

                }//end of 1 if

            }//end of switch

            return false;
        }

    } //end of class
```

The customInitialize() method looks for parameters entered in the <APPLET> tag. The parameters are entered as character strings and are therefore stored as String objects. If a string is actually found (i.e., the string is not equal to null), the value represented by the character string must be converted into a float. The following statement performs this conversion and places the value in the zoomFactor variable.

```
zoomFactor = Float.valueOf(zoomFactorString).floatValue();
```

This is the kind of valuable code that the beginner can just copy and accept at face value—much like the ubiquitous System.out.println()*. For those who are interested, this line uses a Float class object, not a mere* float *variable to achieve the conversion. This is a typical use of these kinds of "wrapper" objects, which exist for all the primitive data types—*int*,* boolean*, etc.*

To try out this parameterized version of the project, we need to add parameters to the <APPLET> tag. The following tag will result in much slower rotation and translation than the default values in the panel class.

```
<APPLET CODEBASE="../codebase"
➡CODE="applets/RotateMoveZoomPlusApplet.class"
➡ARCHIVE="shout3dClasses.zip" WIDTH=320 HEIGHT=240>
<param name="src" value="models/rotatemoveviewpoint.s3d">
<param name="headlightOn" value="true">

<param name="rotationFactor" value="240">
<param name="translationFactor" value="10">
```

These values will adjust the rotation to one radian (57.3 degrees) for each 240 pixels dragged, and the translation to one meter for every 10 pixels dragged. Install the following files from the CD and edit the HTML file to experiment with different parameter values to suit your tastes:

RotateMoveZoomPlusPanel.java

RotateMoveZoomPlusPanel.class

RotateMoveZoomPlusApplet.java

RotateMoveZoomPlusApplet.class

rotatemovezoom.html

Losing the Jitters

Earlier in this chapter, we noted a jittery quality to the navigation when the Viewpoint was parented to an avatar object. Now is a good time to clean up the problem.

For simplicity, we have been writing code that causes the mouse input to directly change values in the scene graph. This approach will not always be satisfactory. When user input affects more than a single scene value, it's possible that all of these values will not be changed within a single render cycle. For example, you may have input that causes many different objects to move together. It's likely that all the new translation values will not be set prior to the next render cycle. The movements will not be synchronized if they are spread out over successive render cycles.

In our particular case, the Viewpoint will often translate and rotate in a different frame than the avatar object, and the jittery effect is due to the fact that they are moving in and out of alignment with each other. To make sure that changes to both nodes are made prior to a given render cycle, we can move the code that sets the rotation and translation out of the onDeviceInput() method and into an onPreRender() method. The following listing improves the RotateMovePanel in just this way.

LISTING 8.12 IMPROVED ROTATEMOVE NAVIGATION (*BETTERROTATEMOVEPANEL.JAVA*)

```
package applets;

import shout3d.*;
import shout3d.core.*;
import shout3d.math.*;


public class BetterRotateMovePanel extends Shout3DPanel
➥implements DeviceObserver, RenderObserver {

    Transform mover;

    int pixelStartX;
    int pixelStartY;
    int pixelEndX;
    int pixelEndY;

    float[] worldPos = new float[3];

    float [] eulers = new float [3];
    float [] axisAngle = new float [4];
    Quaternion q = new Quaternion();
```

```
public BetterRotateMovePanel (Shout3DApplet applet){
    super(applet);
}

public void customInitialize() {

    addDeviceObserver(this,"MouseInput", null);
    getRenderer().addRenderObserver(this,null);

    mover = (Transform) getNodeByName("vehicle");

    worldPos = mover.translation.getValue();

    axisAngle = mover.rotation.getValue();
    q.setAxisAngle(axisAngle);
    q.getEulers(eulers);

}


protected void finalize()  {

    removeDeviceObserver(this,"MouseInput");
    getRenderer().removeRenderObserver(this);
}


public boolean onDeviceInput(DeviceInput di, Object userData)
{

    MouseInput mi = (MouseInput) di;

    switch (mi.which){
       case MouseInput.DOWN:
           pixelStartX = mi.x;
           pixelStartY = mi.y;
           return true;
```

```
case MouseInput.DRAG:

    //PIXEL OPERATIONS
    pixelEndX = mi.x;
    pixelEndY = mi.y;

    int dragDistanceX = pixelEndX - pixelStartX;
    int dragDistanceY = pixelEndY - pixelStartY;

    pixelStartX = pixelEndX;
    pixelStartY = pixelEndY;


    //ROTATING THE OBJECT

    //convert x drag to rotation
    // at 30 pixels/radian
    float rotationDelta = -(dragDistanceX/30f);

    //compute new heading
    eulers[0] = eulers[0] + rotationDelta;

    //Convert from Eulers to AxisAngle
    // using the Quaternion
    q.setEulers(eulers);
    q.getAxisAngle(axisAngle);


    //TRANSLATING THE OBJECT

    //covert y drag to distance
    //at 2 meters per pixel
    float translationDelta = dragDistanceY * 2.0f;

    //make a vector pointing
    //in z direction
    float[] vector = {0,0, translationDelta};

    //rotate the vector using
    //value in quaternion
```

```
            q.xform(vector);

            //add rotated vector
            //to current position
            worldPos[0] = worldPos[0] + vector[0];
            worldPos[2] = worldPos[2] + vector[2];


            return true;

        }//end of switch

        return false;
    }


    public void onPreRender(Renderer r, Object data){
        //set the Transform to
        //updated axis angle values
        mover.rotation.setValue(axisAngle);

        //set Transform to new position
        mover.translation.setValue(worldPos);
    }

    public void onPostRender(Renderer r, Object data){

    }

} //end of class
```

To check it out, install the following files from the CD and compare with rotatezoomavatar.html. The result will be much smoother.

BetterRotateMovePanel.java

BetterRotateMovePanel.class

BetterRotateMoveApplet.java

BetterRotateMoveZoomApplet.class

betterrotatemoveavatar.html

We've come a long way in this chapter, covering a great deal of ground. The most interesting aspect of the process is that it has been cumulative. The methods for interactive translation provide the basis for interactive rotation, and the two together provide a framework for interactive navigation. This is no lucky accident, but rather a reflection of the larger integrity of the Shout3D toolset for creating interactive 3D graphics. You'll find that seemingly unrelated concepts gel into a larger vision as you work with these exciting tools.

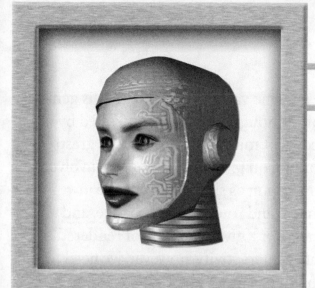

Animation Issues

SHOUT3D

Chapter 9

Animation is a variation in scene values over time that is generated independently of (although it may be controlled by) user interactivity. This concept may take a moment to grasp. The traditional 3D animator, working on projects that do not involve user interactivity, understands animation as simply the change in scene values over time. Objects move and rotate, colors change, and geometry morphs into new shapes over a given number of rendered frames. Once we add the element of interactivity, however, we need to refine our thinking. An animation might move an object across the screen. The user might also move an object interactively, using mouse drags as we did in the previous chapter. The lay person might consider the second alternative to be "animation," or at least "interactive animation," but the developer needs a clearer understanding.

Animation, in the sense that we will use the term, is changes in scene values that are driven by a clock rather than by the user. The user may control the animation but does not drive it directly. In the simplest example, a user might be given the power to start and stop an animation with mouse clicks, just as one starts and stops a video player. In this example, the distinction between the animation and user interactivity is easy to understand. A more complex example might allow the user to interactively control the speed of an animation or the direction of an animated object. In this example, the distinction between user interactivity and animation is less immediately evident, at least to the user. Yet the concept is directly analogous to driving a car or any other powered vehicle. The engine turns the crankshaft, and the rear wheels turn to move the car. The driver directs and modulates this energy for his or her purposes.

In this chapter, we will look at the interface between interactivity and animation. If all you wish to do is to display a single piece of animated content created in MAX or in any other 3D animation package with VRML export capabilities, no interactivity issues arise. The modswing demo in your Shout3D installation is a good example of a continuous looping keyframed animation created in MAX that involves no user interaction or control. The scene file is loaded into the basic Shout3DApplet. However, matters become much more interesting, and commercially useful, when you infuse an interactive element.

Understanding Realtime Animation

We have defined animation as clock-driven changes in scene values. To understand this concept, we must be clear about the distinction between realtime and pre-rendered animation. In pre-rendered animation, a sequence of images is created and displayed at a constant frame rate. We simply assume, as we must, that the video player or motion picture projector will maintain the correct speed. But this assumption can never be true of graphics rendered in realtime on a computer. Different systems will render at different speeds, and the frame rate may change from frame to frame depending on the complexity of the rendering task, among other things.

Thus realtime animation must be measured in time (seconds), not in frames. As each frame is to be rendered, a clock is consulted to determine how much time has passed since the previous frame. Based on this determination, the application must determine how animated values should be adjusted to properly correspond to the moment. A popular movie of the 1960s, "If It's Tuesday, This Must Be Belgium," mocked the rushed pace of a guided tour of Europe. But the idea is apt for our purposes. The application determines the current time, and then determines where everything should be at that moment before rendering the scene.

Take a simple example of an object moving at one meter per second. If the current frame rate is 10 frames per second, 0.1 seconds have elapsed since the previous frame was rendered. Therefore the object must be moved 0.1 meters before the current frame is rendered. As the frame rate increases, the object moves smaller distances between frames. As the rate decreases, the object advances in larger chunks. One way or another, the object is always where it should be at each rendered moment. The frame rate affects the smoothness of the animation, but it does not affect the timing.

Procedural Animation

Keyframed animation will almost always be produced in 3D animation packages and exported into the scene file, whether .wrl or .s3d. It's certainly possible to hand code Interpolators (and their TimeSensors) into the scene file, but this will make sense only for the simplest kinds of animation. By contrast, animation can be programmed directly in Java. This kind of *procedural animation* is extremely important, especially in the context of interactivity.

Keyframed animation will typically make more sense where the animation is complex and involves only limited interactive control. Procedural animation is more useful where the animation is simple and inter-activity plays a larger role.

Basic Translation

All realtime animation is clock-driven. For keyframed animation, the TimeSensor node monitors the clock. In procedural animation, the clock input is obtained by code we write in the onPreRender() or onPostRender() methods. You may remember that these methods of the RenderObserver interface are called immediately before and after a frame is rendered, giving you a chance to make adjustments to the scene graph before the next frame is rendered. If we wanted to make it hard on ourselves, we could compute the time elapsed since the last render and make the same kind of computations that the Interpolator nodes perform. But Shout makes things easier by providing a method that gets the current frame rate. This value (in frames per second) is necessarily computed by determining the time elapsed since the last render. For example, if the current frame rate is 10.0 fps, the previous frame was rendered 0.1 seconds ago.

Look over the panel class in Listing 9.1.

LISTING 9.1 SIMPLE PROCEDURAL ANIMATION (*PROCANIMPANEL.JAVA*)

```
package applets;

import shout3d.*;
import shout3d.core.*;
import shout3d.math.*;


public class ProcAnimPanel extends Shout3DPanel implements
➥RenderObserver{



    Transform t;
    float xPos;



    public ProcAnimPanel (Shout3DApplet applet){
```

```
        super(applet);
    }

    public void customInitialize() {
        getRenderer().addRenderObserver(this, null);

        t = (Transform) getNodeByName("trans");
        xPos = t.translation.getValue()[0];
    }

    protected void finalize()  {
        getRenderer().removeRenderObserver(this);
    }

    public void onPreRender (Renderer r, Object o) {

        //movement since previous frame
        //at .5 meter per second.
        float xDelta = .5f/getFramesPerSecond();

        //add to current x postion
        xPos = xPos + xDelta;

        //update Transform
        t.translation.set1Value(0, xPos);

    }


    public void onPostRender (Renderer r, Object o) {


    }

} //end of class
```

There isn't any user input in this panel, so we can dispense with the DeviceObserver interface. However, we need the RenderObserver interface. Note how the panel class is registered with the renderer in the `customInitialize()` method, and unregistered in the `finalize()` method. We include both the `onPreRender()` and `onPostRender()` methods. (All this code is in the standard `TemplatePanel.java` file included on the CD.) Thus, the two methods will be called before and after each render.

We won't need to use `onPostRender()`, and so we'll leave it empty. All of the action takes place in `onPreRender()`. First, we need to perform some setup in `customInitialize()`. We get a reference to the Transform from the scene, using its DEF name, and store it in a field named t. Then we get the current *x* position value from the Transform and store it in the `float` variable xPos.

Look at `onPreRender()`. To get our progress since the previous frame, we divide the desired speed by the current frame rate. This is so easy that it seems complicated. Frame rate is measured in "frames per second," so the inverse of this gives you "seconds per frame," which may be thought of as the number of seconds since the previous frame. Or think of it this way: Our desired speed is 0.5 meters per second. Assume that we are working on a very slow system and that our frame rate is a miserable 1 frame per second. This would produce an xDelta of 0.5/1, or 0.5 meters, which is exactly how far the object should move in one second. If our frame rate were 10 fps, the box would move .05 meters, which is exactly one-tenth of how far it should move in a second.

The next two steps are easy. The increment in xDelta is added to the current xPos to establish the new xPos, and the new xPos is supplied to the Transform to move the box on the screen.

Try coding this yourself to create a demo using the scene named `boxscene.wrl` from the CD. Or install all of the following files from the CD:

ProcAnimPanel.java

ProcAnimPanel.class

ProcAnimApplet.java

ProcAnimApplet.class

boxscene.wrl

procanim.html

When you run this demo, you'll certainly notice how the box seems to change speeds. There is a processing lag in which the box moves faster until it catches up with the position data that has already been computed, and then it begins moving at a steady speed until it passes right off the screen.

A Change of Direction

Let's add a bit more sophistication by making the object move back and forth. This is accomplished by adding a test that determines whether the current *x* position exceeds a chosen limit, and changing direction if it does. Things will be easier if we replace the literal speed value with a variable named speed. To change direction, we flip the sign of the speed value from positive to negative, or vice versa. A negative speed translates the object in the –*x* direction.

Take a look at the code in Listing 9.2.

LISTING 9.2 BACK-FORTH PROCEDURAL ANIMATION (*BACKFORTHPANEL.JAVA*)

```
package applets;

import shout3d.*;
import shout3d.core.*;
import shout3d.math.*;


public class BackForthPanel extends Shout3DPanel implements
➥RenderObserver{


    Transform t;
    float xPos;
    float speed = 1.0f; //in meters per second
    float limit = 3.0f;



    public BackForthPanel (Shout3DApplet applet){
        super(applet);
    }


    public void customInitialize() {
        getRenderer().addRenderObserver(this, null);

        t = (Transform) getNodeByName("trans");
        xPos = t.translation.getValue()[0];
    }
```

```
protected void finalize() {
   getRenderer().removeRenderObserver(this);
}


public void onPreRender (Renderer r, Object o) {

   float xDelta = speed/getFramesPerSecond();
   xPos = xPos + xDelta;

   if (xPos >= limit || xPos <= -limit) {

      speed = -speed;
   }

   t.translation.set1Value(0, xPos);

}


public void onPostRender (Renderer r, Object o) {


}


} //end of class
```

The if statement tests whether the new xPos value is equal to or greater than 3.0, or equal to or less than −3.0. (The || sign means "or.") If so, the current speed is flipped. The statement

```
speed = -speed;
```

is equivalent to

```
speed = -1 * speed;
```

Note that it would not be sufficient to test for xPos = limit or xPos = -limit. It's highly unlikely that the object would ever move to exactly these values. Thus, you must test whether these values are exceeded. Another way of writing this test would use the absolute value of xPos.

```
if (Math.abs(xPos) >= limit)
```

The absolute value of a number is simply its distance from zero, and therefore both –3 and +3 have the same absolute value.

This is a great example of the use of a static method, sometimes called a class method. A static method can be called without having to create any instances of the class. The Math class is composed solely of useful static methods that perform mathematical tasks, like computing trigonometric functions or raising a number to an exponential power. The methods can be called directly from the class name, Math, without creating a Math object. In fact, you can't instantiate a Math object. The Math class methods come up all the time. You'll find documentation in any decent Java reference book.

Try coding this example out yourself, or install the following CD files:

BackForthPanel.java

BackForthPanel.class

BackForthApplet.java

BackForthApplet.class

backforth.html

Swing It!

You probably noticed the rigid, linear feel to the last animation. The box moved at a constant speed throughout. We can use trigonometric functions to create natural-looking accelerations and decelerations.

Simple trigonometry plays a basic role throughout 3D computer graphics. Those who remember their high school trig will find our next experiment easy. Those who are rusty, or who have never been exposed to trigonometry, will want to think through the following introduction.

Imagine travelling around the circumference of a circle. You begin on the right side of the circle (3:00 o'clock), moving counterclockwise. You rise steeply, but level off as you reach the top of the circle. Then you descend back down on the left side, and the path becomes increasingly vertical. You pass the vertical midpoint on the way down (9:00 o'clock) and head for the bottom of the circle. Your descent levels out as you reach the bottom, but becomes increasingly vertical as you approach the point at which you began.

This journey corresponds roughly to the behavior of a swinging object. It slows down as it reaches its limits in both directions and accelerates into the midpoint of the swing.

The trigonometric functions named *sine* and *cosine* track the behavior of an object travelling around a circle. The sine function describes the vertical element of the motion. It starts at zero (the vertical midpoint), rises to the vertical maximum, falls back through zero to the vertical minimum (the bottom of the circle), and returns to zero again. If the circle has a radius of 1 unit, the sine goes from 0 to 1 to 0 to –1, and back to 0 to start another cycle. The cosine function tracks the horizontal movement. It starts at 1 (the rightmost point on the circle), goes to 0 (at 12:00 o'clock), continues to –1 (at the leftmost point on the circle), and passes through 0 on its way around the bottom of the circle. The sine and cosine functions follow the same paths, but their cycles begin at 0 or 1, respectively.

Take a look at the following illustration. Each cycle begins at the point at 0 degrees on the right side of the circle and travels counterclockwise. A complete cycle is 360 degrees and passes twice through all possible sine and cosine values between 1 and –1, just as a swinging object passes through all possible locations twice in a complete cycle back to where it began.

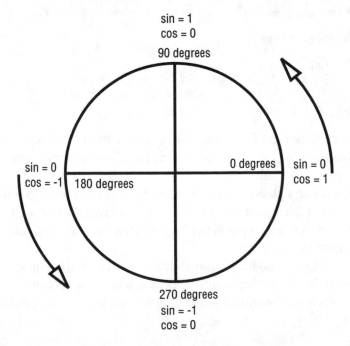

To make an object swing back and forth, we will apply sine values around the circle, and use these values to set the *x* position of the Transform. Since the sine values will vary between 1 and −1, we must multiply them by a number to produce a wider swing. We'll use the same limit value of 3 as in the previous project, and thus the multiplication will cause the box to swing between −3 and +3 in the *x* direction.

There is very little code here, but a great deal to learn. Take a careful look at Listing 9.3 to see if you can figure it out yourself before you go on.

LISTING 9.3 SWINGING PROCEDURAL ANIMATION (*SWINGPANEL.JAVA*)

```
package applets;

import shout3d.*;
import shout3d.core.*;
import shout3d.math.*;


public class SwingPanel extends Shout3DPanel implements
➥RenderObserver{


    Transform t;
    float cycleAngle = 0;
    float limit = 3.0f;
    float cycleTime = 4.0f; //seconds per cycle

    public SwingPanel (Shout3DApplet applet){
        super(applet);
    }


    public void customInitialize() {

        getRenderer().addRenderObserver(this, null);
        t = (Transform) getNodeByName("trans");

    }


    protected void finalize()  {
```

```
        getRenderer().removeRenderObserver(this);
    }


    public void onPreRender (Renderer r, Object o) {

        //change in angle around cycle

        float deltaAngle = (6.28f/cycleTime)/getFramesPerSecond();

        //update angle
      cycleAngle = cycleAngle + deltaAngle;

        //convert angle to x position
        float xPos   = (float) (Math.cos(cycleAngle) * limit);

        //update Transform
        t.translation.set1Value(0, xPos);
    }


    public void onPostRender (Renderer r, Object o) {


    }

  } //end of class
```

The main difficulty here for many readers will be the use of radian measures, rather than degrees. A radian is the angle of arc described by wrapping the radius of a circle around the circumference. The circumference of a circle is the length of the radius multiplied by 2 times pi. The value of pi is close to 3.14, and therefore, the circumference of a circle is 6.28 times the radius. A circle is 360 degrees, and therefore a radian is about 57.3 degrees (360/6.2832).

In effect, an animated rotation is being converted into back-and-forth translation. The most useful rotational unit is not the single radian, but rather the entire circle of 6.28 radians, because this produces a complete swing cycle. Thus the panel uses a cycle-Time variable, which represents the number of seconds in a complete cycle. Dividing this number by 6.28 produces the number of seconds to complete one radian. That result can be divided by the current frame rate, in the usual manner, to compute the amount of rotation since the previous render.

```
float deltaAngle = (6.28f/cycleTime)/getFramesPerSecond();
```

The current `cycleAngle` represents the distance traveled around the circle, in radians. This value is converted into distance along the *x* axis using a cosine function.

```
float xPos  = (float) (Math.cos(cycleAngle) * limit);
```

Look over the right side of this assignment statement carefully. The static `Math.cos()` method is used to compute the cosine of the current `cycleAngle`. The cosine will vary between 1 and –1, and thus this value must be multiplied by the `limit` to increase the range to 3 and –3. Cosine values begin at 1 (for `cycleAngle` = 0), and thus the box will begin the animation at the rightmost extreme of its range (at *x*=3). If we had used the sine instead of the cosine, the values would begin at 0, and the box would start in the middle (*x*=0). Note how the entire expression on the right side of the assignment statement must be cast to (`float`). This is because the Math.cos() method returns a `double` value (a double-precision floating point value). Multiplying this `double` by a `float`—the `limit` variable—produces a double because Java will preserve the highest possible precision. We cannot assign this double to the `float` variable `xPos` without first casting it to a `float`, because this assignment would involve a loss of precision that requires our explicit consent. If you failed to do this, the compiler would complain and point to the problem for easy correction.

Create this project yourself, or install the following files from the CD.

SwingPanel.java

SwingPanel.class

SwingApplet.java

SwingApplet.class

swing.html

When you run the demo, notice the pattern of acceleration and deceleration. The `cycleTime` is 4 seconds (2 seconds in each direction). Try a different `cycleTime` value and recompile the panel.

Bounce It!

For a more ambitious stab at procedural animation, we'll make the object bounce off the floor. This will involve a couple of new concepts. For one thing, we'll need to use absolute values to create the bounce. The sine or cosine values pass through both positive and negative values. We'll convert all the negative values into positive ones. Cosine values begin at 1, pass through 0 to –1, and then return through 0 to 1. But if all the negative values are converted to positive ones, the effect is as if the cosine passes from 1 to 0, back up to 1, down to 0 and back to 1. Note that this creates two bounce cycles (1 to 0 to 1) in a single cycle around the circle. The object bounces convincingly because it is not slowing down as it passes through 0. It just changes direction when it "hits the ground."

Another new concept involves decreasing the height of the bounce as the animation proceeds. The height is reduced by a decline factor, in this case, 8 percent per second. When the height is decreased past a certain minimum value, we'll stop the bouncing altogether. The cycle time of each bounce is decreased by the same factor as the height of the bounce for a more realistic effect.

Take some time to ponder the code in Listing 9.4, and see what you can figure out for yourself before continuing on with the explanation.

LISTING 9.4 BOUNCING PROCEDURAL ANIMATION (*BOUNCINGPANEL.JAVA*)

```java
package applets;

import shout3d.*;
import shout3d.core.*;
import shout3d.math.*;


public class BouncingPanel extends Shout3DPanel implements
➡RenderObserver{


    Transform t;
    float cycleAngle = 0.0f;
    float startHeight = 3.0f;
    float startCycleTime = 2.0f;
    // As time passes, the bounce height gets lower and
    // each bounce cycle takes less time.
    // This variable records how much of the original
```

```
// height or cycle time is left.
float declineFactor = 1.0f;
boolean bouncing = true;

public BouncingPanel (Shout3DApplet applet){
    super(applet);
}


  public void customInitialize() {

    getRenderer().addRenderObserver(this, null);
    t = (Transform) getNodeByName("trans");

  }


  protected void finalize()  {
    getRenderer().removeRenderObserver(this);
  }

  public void onPreRender (Renderer r, Object o) {

    if (bouncing) {

      //compute decline factor at 8 percent per second
      declineFactor = declineFactor -
➡(.08f/getFramesPerSecond());

      float cycleTime = startCycleTime * declineFactor;

      //use 3.14 because there are
      //two complete bouces in a cycle
      float deltaAngle = (3.14f/cycleTime)/getFramesPerSecond();
      cycleAngle = cycleAngle + deltaAngle;

      float height = startHeight * declineFactor;
      float yPos   = (float) (Math.cos(cycleAngle) * height);
```

```
        //no negative height
        yPos = Math.abs(yPos);

        t.translation.set1Value(1, yPos);

        //stop bouncing when height is low
        if (height < .1) {
            bouncing = false;
        }
    }


}


    public void onPostRender (Renderer r, Object o) {


    }

} //end of class
```

We store only the starting (maximum) bounce height and cycle times as fields, because these values will be reduced during the animation by the declineFactor. The declineFactor begins at 1.0 (100 percent). We also create a boolean flag to signal whether the object is bouncing.

The entire block of code within the onPreRender() method is made conditional upon whether the bouncing flag is true. The statement

```
    if (bouncing)
```

is equivalent to

```
    if (bouncing == true)
```

As bouncing is true when the animation begins, the code within the block will execute. However, when the height value decreases below 0.1 meters, the flag is flipped and the code within onPreRender() will no longer run.

The declineFactor begins at 1.0, but is reduced at a rate of 8 percent per second. The current declineFactor is applied to the startCycleTime to determine the length of the current cycleTime. This adjusted cycleTime is used to compute the current angle in the cycle around the circle. However, as we have two bounces per 360-degree cycle, we use a factor of 3.14, rather than 6.28. This allows the `startCycleTime` value to correspond to a single bounce. For example, the value of 2.0 means that the initial bounce will be 2 seconds long—1 second down and 1 second up.

The current `height` is computed using the `declineFactor`, and is used to arrive at the correct *y* position of the object. However, this `yPos` value is converted to its absolute value, so that any negative values become positive. This generates the bounce.

Try creating this yourself, or install the following files from the CD.

`BouncingPanel.java`

`BouncingPanel.class`

`BouncingApplet.java`

`BouncingApplet.class`

`bouncing.html`

Interactive Control

Procedural animation lends itself readily to user interactivity by allowing mouse or keyboard input to modify the values on which the animation depends. The most useful example is using mouse drags to control the speed and direction of translations or rotations.

In the panel class in Listing 9.5, dragging the mouse up or down in the window changes speed and direction of the translating box. The vertical length of the drag sets the speed at a rate of 1 meter/sec for every 70 pixels dragged. Dragging upwards generates a negative speed value, reversing the direction of translation. When the mouse button is released, the speed is set to 0.

As you look over the following code, notice how we have dispensed with explicitly implementing the RenderObserver interface. The Shout3DPanel class already implements it, and this implementation is inherited by all classes (like this one) that are extended from Shout3DPanel. Thus we never really had to write `implements RenderObserver` *in our code, or to bother to write empty* `onPreRender()` *or* `onPostRender()` *methods. Empty versions of these methods are inherited from the super class. We've been taking the long route thus far to make sure that the concepts involved are well understood by the Java newcomer. We won't need to do this anymore.*

LISTING 9.5 INTERACTIVE SPEED CONTROL (*CHANGESPEEDPANEL.JAVA*)

```java
package applets;

import shout3d.*;
import shout3d.core.*;
import shout3d.math.*;


public class ChangeSpeedPanel extends Shout3DPanel implements
➥DeviceObserver {


    Transform t;
    float xPos;
    float speed = 0.0f; //in meters per second
    float limit = 3.0f;

    //screen pixels
    int pixelStartY;
    int pixelEndY;

    public ChangeSpeedPanel (Shout3DApplet applet){
        super(applet);
    }

    public void customInitialize() {
        getRenderer().addRenderObserver(this, null);
        addDeviceObserver(this,"MouseInput", null);

        t = (Transform) getNodeByName("trans");
        xPos = t.translation.getValue()[0];
    }

    protected void finalize() {
        getRenderer().removeRenderObserver(this);
        removeDeviceObserver(this,"MouseInput");
    }
```

```
    public boolean onDeviceInput(DeviceInput di, Object userData)
→{
        MouseInput mi = (MouseInput) di;
        switch (mi.which){

            case MouseInput.DOWN:

                pixelStartY = mi.y;
                return true;

            case MouseInput.UP:
                speed = 0.0f;
                return true;

            case MouseInput.DRAG:

                int pixelEndY = mi.y;
                int dragDistanceY = pixelEndY - pixelStartY;

                //convert drag to speed
                //at 1 meter/second for each 70 pixels.
                speed = dragDistanceY/70f;
                return true;

        }//end of switch

        return false;
    }


    public void onPreRender (Renderer r, Object o) {

        float xDelta = speed/getFramesPerSecond();
        xPos = xPos + xDelta;

        t.translation.set1Value(0, xPos);

    }
```

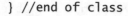

```
} //end of class
```

To test it out, install the following files from the CD. The scene file is the same boxscene.wrl that we've been using all along.

ChangeSpeedPanel.java

ChangeSpeedPanel.class

ChangeSpeedApplet.java

ChangeSpeedApplet.class

changespeed.html

This kind of interactive control makes great sense in Viewpoint navigation. Instead of translating or rotating a camera directly from a mouse drag, you can procedurally animate the camera and control its speed and direction with the mouse. This creates a smooth, "power-steering" feel for the user, and allows the Viewpoint to keep moving without continuous dragging. We'll start using this important technique in the next chapter.

Keyframed Animation

The traditional 3D animator is familiar with the concept of keyframes, and the vast majority of animated Shout3D content produced in MAX or other 3D packages will use keyframed animation. Keyframed animation involves assigning particular values to particular frames, and allowing the program to interpolate the values "in-between."

For example, assume that we want an object to move at 1 meter per second in the x direction for a total of 10 seconds. In our 3D package, we must first consult our frame rate. In MAX, the default is 30 fps , the standard video frame rate. Thus 10 seconds will consume 300 frames. We set a keyframe at frame 1 with a world x position value of 0. Then we go to frame 300, at set another keyframe for the object with a world x position value of 10. (For convenience, I'm equating MAX units with meters, which is what they will become upon conversion to VRML or Shout3D.) If the interpolation between these two values is linear—if the function curve between them is a straight line—we can be confident that the object will translate at a constant rate of 1 meter per second.

In VRML, a PositionInterpolator node would represent this same animation.

```
PositionInterpolator {
  Key  [ 0, 1 ]
  KeyValue  [ 0 0 0,
             10 0 0 ]
}
```

The two keys are set, respectively, at the start (0 percent) and the end (100 percent) of the time required for the animation. The first key has a position value of (0,0,0) and the second has a value of (10,0,0). Note how this information is independent of the total time of the animation. It could be 1 second long, or 100 hours long, but the keys and their values would apply to the start and end of the desired time period.

The time period, called the cycleInterval, is established by the TimeSensor node. The TimeSensor watches the clock. When it's time to render a frame, it determines how long it's been since the current cycleInterval began and converts it into a fraction. For example, assume that the cycleInterval is 10 seconds and that the current time is precisely 3 seconds after the cycleInterval began. The TimeSensor computes the current fraction to be 0.3 and sends this value to the PositionInterpolator. The PositionInterpolator computes the proper position value by interpolating between the key values. The value three-tenths of the way between the two key values would be (3,0,0), the proper location for the object at that moment. This value is sent to the Transform node to actually move the object in the scene. The entire VRML scene (using a Box primitive) would read like this:

```
DEF trans Transform {
  children  Shape {
    appearance  Appearance {
      material  Material {
      }

    }

    geometry  Box {
    }

  }

  translation  0 0 0
}
```

```
DEF timer TimeSensor {
   startTime  0
   cycleInterval  10
   loop  TRUE
}
DEF mover PositionInterpolator {
   key  [ 0, 1 ]
   keyValue  [ 0 0 0,
            10 0 0 ]
}
ROUTE timer.fraction TO mover.fraction
ROUTE mover.value TO trans.translation
```

Note the use of ROUTE statements to copy values from one node to another. ROUTE statements can only make sense if nodes are DEF named to uniquely identify them, so I named all the necessary nodes. If you are not already familiar with VRML animation, take the time to understand this simple example well. The TimeSensor, named `timer`, computes the current fraction of the `cycleInterval` and stores it in the field named `fraction`. This field is not indicated in the .wrl file because there would be no purpose in doing so, but it exists just as much as `startTime` or `loop`. The first ROUTE statement copies the `fraction` value in the TimeSensor to the `fraction` field of the Position-Interpolator (again, a field not listed in the scene file). The PositionInterpolator uses the current fraction to compute the current position, which it forwards to the Transform in the second ROUTE statement.

Note that the first field name in a ROUTE statement that comes from a file exporter will usually have the suffix `_changed` and that the second will usually have the prefix `set_`. This convention is a holdover from VRML that is not required in Shout3D, but Shout3D will read either style successfully. So the following two ROUTE statements would be equivalent:

```
ROUTE timer.fraction TO mover.fraction
ROUTE timer.fraction_changed TO mover.set_fraction
```

Take a closer look at the TimeSensor. The `startTime` field contains the time when the first `cycleInterval` should start. VRML computes time from an origin back in 1970, so a `startTime` of 0 occurred over 30 years ago. Since this `startTime` has already passed at any moment when one might load this VRML file, the TimeSensor will begin operation immediately. The `loop` field is set to a Boolean value, which, being `true` in this case, will cause the animation to repeat continuously.

We are exploiting a special VRML convention here. If the startTime *has already passed, and the loop flag is set to* true, *the animation will begin running immediately on load. However, if the loop flag is set to* false, *the animation will not run on load (even for a single cycle), regardless of the fact that the* startTime *has passed. An animation that is to run only once must be triggered by user input in VRML.*

As discussed in an earlier chapter, Shout3D has greatly improved upon VRML by offering Bezier and TCB interpolation in addition to the linear version. But aside from their greater subtlety in computing interpolated values between keyframes, these interpolators operate in the same manner as is described here.

Controlling the TimeSensor

To give users interactive control over keyframed animation, you must generally give them access to the TimeSensor. We'll experiment with a simple animation exported from 3D Studio MAX in which a cone travels across the screen. The file is named movingcone.s3d, and can be found on the CD.

Starting and Stopping a Keyframed Animation

Simple calls to start and stop the TimeSensor are easy to code. Listing 9.6 shows a panel class that starts the TimeSensor if it's stopped, and stops it if it's started.

LISTING 9.6 INTERACTIVE STARTING AND STOPPING A KEYFRAMED ANIMATION (*STARTSTOPPANEL.JAVA*)

```
package applets;

import shout3d.*;
import shout3d.core.*;
import shout3d.math.*;


public class StartStopPanel extends Shout3DPanel implements
➥DeviceObserver {


    TimeSensor timer;
    boolean started = false;

    public StartStopPanel (Shout3DApplet applet){
```

```
          super(applet);
      }


      public void customInitialize() {
          addDeviceObserver(this,"MouseInput", null);
          timer =(TimeSensor) getNodeByName("world-TIMER");



      }

      protected void finalize()  {
          removeDeviceObserver(this,"MouseInput");


      }


      public boolean onDeviceInput(DeviceInput di, Object userData)
  ➡{
          MouseInput mi = (MouseInput) di;

          switch (mi.which){

          case MouseInput.DOWN:

              //if animation is not started
              if (!started) {

                  timer.start();
                  started = true;
                  return true;
              }


              //if already started
              else   {
                  timer.stop();
                  started = false;
                  return true;
                }
```

```
    }//end of switch

    return false;

}
```

```
} //end of class
```

This class assumes that the animation does not run automatically on load, and therefore the initial value of the `started` flag is `false`. Animation exported from MAX into .s3d will loop automatically by default. To change this, you must edit the TimeSensor node in a text editor to change the `loop` field to `false`. It won't start automatically, and it also won't loop. If you want it to loop, but don't want the animation to start until you direct it to, you need to edit the `startTime` field. This field is not written out and contains the default value of 0. If you add the field name and set its value to −1, the animation will loop once started, but will not start until directed to. In `movingcone.s3d`, I edited the TimeSensor to read as follows:

```
DEF world-TIMER TimeSensor {
   loop TRUE
   startTime -1
   cycleInterval 3.333
}
```

Note the DEF name "world-Timer." This is a default name produced by the Shout MAX exporter, and so I kept it and referred to it in the panel class. If you want to change the default DEF name, make sure you change it everywhere it occurs in the .s3d file, including in the ROUTE statements at the bottom.

Install the following files from the CD and try out the demo.

`StartStopPanel.java`

`StartStopPanel.class`

`StartStopApplet.java`

`StartStopApplet.class`

`movingcone.s3d`

`startstop.html`

Pausing and Unpausing

You'll no doubt notice that when you restart the TimeSensor in the previous example, it jumps back to the beginning of the animation. In other words, it starts sending out time fractions from 0. By contrast, pausing and unpausing the TimeSensor allows picking up from where you left off. The panel class in Listing 9.7 will start the animation in the first place, and then pause and unpause it. Pausing and unpausing only have meaning once the animation is started.

LISTING 9.7 INTERACTIVE PAUSING AND UNPAUSING (*StartPausePanel.java*)

```
package applets;

import shout3d.*;
import shout3d.core.*;
import shout3d.math.*;

public class StartPausePanel extends Shout3DPanel implements
➥DeviceObserver {


    TimeSensor timer;
    boolean started = false;

    public StartPausePanel (Shout3DApplet applet){
        super(applet);
    }


    public void customInitialize() {
        addDeviceObserver(this,"MouseInput", null);
        timer =(TimeSensor) getNodeByName("world-TIMER");


    }

    protected void finalize()  {
        removeDeviceObserver(this,"MouseInput");

    }
```

```
    public boolean onDeviceInput(DeviceInput di, Object userData)
➡{
        MouseInput mi = (MouseInput) di;

        switch (mi.which){

            case MouseInput.DOWN:

                //if animation is not started
                if (!started) {

                    timer.start();
                    started = true;
                    return true;
                }


                //if already started
                else    {

                    //if it's paused, unpause it
                    //or vice versa
                    if (timer.isPaused())  {
                        timer.setPaused(false);
                        return true;
                    }
                    else {
                        timer.setPaused(true);
                        return true;
                    }
                }

        }//end of switch

        return false;

    }


} //end of class
```

The reference files on the CD are:

StartPausePanel.java

StartPausePanel.class

StartPauseApplet.java

StartPauseApplet.class

startpause.html

Swapping Animations

There are many possibilities for changing between different keyframed animations. If the different animations apply to a single scene, it makes sense to use an approach that changes the animation without requiring the user to reload a new scene file. If the animations represent different scenes, however, you'll have load a new scene into the Shout3D viewer.

Swapping Interpolators

The easiest way to organize alternative animations of the same scene elements is to create separate .s3d files of the same scene, with different animations. You then consolidate all of the TimeSensors, Interpolators, and their ROUTE statements into one of the .s3d files. Make sure that only one (or none) or the TimeSensors are set to run on load. Java methods can be used to switch between the TimeSensors.

Look over the scene file in Listing 9.8.

LISTING 9.8 SCENE WITH TWO ALTERNATIVE TIMESENSORS (TWOTIMESENSORS.S3D)

```
DEF Box01 Transform {
  children [
    Shape {
      appearance   Appearance {
      material   Material {
        diffuseColor   0.898 0.6039 0.8431
      }
       }

      geometry Box {
```

```
        }
      }
    ]
    translation    0 0 0
}


#Horizontal animation

DEF timer TimeSensor {
    startTime 0
    cycleInterval  2
    loop TRUE
}



DEF Box01-POS-INTERP PositionInterpolator {
    key    [ 0, 1 ]
    keyValue [
            #horizontal
            0 0 0,
            5 0 0 ]
}



#Vertical Animation

DEF timer2 TimeSensor {
    startTime -1
    cycleInterval    8
    loop TRUE
}


DEF Box01-POS-INTERP2 PositionInterpolator {
    key    [ 0, 1 ]
    keyValue [
         #vertical
```

```
        0 0 0,
        0 4 0 ]
   }
```

```
ROUTE timer.fraction_changed TO Box01-POS-INTERP.set_fraction
ROUTE Box01-POS-INTERP.value_changed TO Box01.set_translation

ROUTE timer2.fraction_changed TO Box01-POS-INTERP2.set_fraction
ROUTE Box01-POS-INTERP2.value_changed TO Box01.set_translation
```

In this scene, the two animations are in separate PositionInterpolators, each driven by its own TimeSensor with the correct cycleInterval. The first TimeSensor is set to run automatically upon loading (startTime 0). The second TimeSensor will not run until the user starts it.

The panel class in Listing 9.9 is easy to understand. With each click, the active TimeSensor stops and the inactive one starts.

LISTING 9.9 SWAPPING BETWEEN TIMESENSORS (CHANGETIMESENSORSPANEL.JAVA)

```java
package applets;

import shout3d.*;
import shout3d.core.*;
import shout3d.math.*;


public class ChangeTimeSensorsPanel extends Shout3DPanel
➥implements DeviceObserver {

   TimeSensor timer;
   TimeSensor timer2;

   boolean firstAnim = true;


   public ChangeTimeSensorsPanel (Shout3DApplet applet){
       super(applet);
   }

   public void customInitialize() {
```

```
        addDeviceObserver(this,"MouseInput", null);


        timer = (TimeSensor) getNodeByName("timer");
        timer2 = (TimeSensor) getNodeByName("timer2");


    }


    protected void finalize()  {
        removeDeviceObserver(this,"MouseInput");

    }



    public boolean onDeviceInput(DeviceInput di, Object userData)
    {
        MouseInput mi = (MouseInput) di;
        switch (mi.which){

        case MouseInput.DOWN:

            if(firstAnim) {

                timer.stop();
                timer2.start();

                firstAnim = false;
                return true;
            }
            else {

                timer2.stop();
                timer.start();

                firstAnim = true;
                return true;
            }
```

```
        }//end of switch

    return false;
    }



    }//end of class
```

To test all this out, copy the following files from the CD to your Shout3D installation.

```
ChangeTimeSensorsPanel.java

ChangeTimeSensorsPanel.class

ChangeTimeSensorsApplet.java

ChangeTimeSensorsApplet.class

twotimesensors.s3d

changetimesensors.html
```

Swapping Between Segments

Another approach to changing animations within the same scene is a bit more subtle. It involves lining the animations up back-to-back in a single Interpolator (or set of Inter-polators), all driven by a single TimeSensor. This would be the natural output of a MAX animated scene in which all of the alternative animations are arranged in order within a single MAX file—each one beginning the frame after the previous one ends. We then can use a ScalarInterpolator to isolate only an appropriate segment of the total length to run at any given time.

Compare the scene in Listing 9.10 with the one in Listing 9.8.

LISTING 9.10 SCENE WITH TWO ANIMATED SEGMENTS (*TWOSEGMENTS.S3D*)

```
DEF Box01 Transform {
  children [
    Shape {
      appearance   Appearance {
        material   Material {
          diffuseColor   0.898 0.6039 0.8431
        }
      }
```

```
      geometry Box {
      }
    }
  ]
  translation   0 0 0
}

DEF timer TimeSensor {
  startTime -1
  cycleInterval   10
  loop TRUE
}

DEF si ScalarInterpolator {
  key     [ 0, 1 ]
  keyValue  [ 0, 0.4 ]
}

DEF Box01-POS-INTERP PositionInterpolator {
  key   [ 0, .19, .20, 1 ]
  keyValue [
      #horizontal
      0 0 0,
      5 0 0,

      #vertical
      0 0 0,
      0 4 0 ]
}
```

```
ROUTE timer.fraction_changed TO si.set_fraction
ROUTE si.value_changed TO Box01-POS-INTERP.set_fraction
ROUTE Box01-POS-INTERP.value_changed TO Box01.set_translation
```

The single animation given by Box01-POS-INTERP is divided into two segments. The first section translates horizontally from (0,0,0) to (5,0,0) in only 20 percent of the time length of the total. The second section translates upward from (0,0,0) to (0,4,0) in the remaining 80 percent of the total time. In order to isolate one of the two segments, we must interpose a ScalarInterpolator between the TimeSensor and the PositionInterpolator. The TimeSensor, as you may remember, is generating time fractions between 0 and 1. The ScalarInterpolator will be used to change this range to either 0–0.19 or 0.2–1. That way, the TimeSensor will drive only one of the two segments. We must also change the cycleInterval of the TimeSensor to correspond to the proper length of the segment.

The ScalarInterpolator has keys at 0 and 1, and corresponding keyValues. The keyValues that I've provided here are entirely arbitrary because these values will ultimately be replaced when they are set by the panel class controlling the scene. Take a look at the TimeSensor. The cycleInterval of 10 seconds will also end up being overwritten by the panel class so as to provide the proper duration for each segment. The startTime is set to –1. This means that the animation will not run until the user triggers it by starting the TimeSensor. Finally, note that the loop field is set to true. Thus, each of the two segments will continuously loop.

The panel class in Listing 9.11 swaps animation segments each time the user clicks in the Shout3D panel. The first click will necessarily start the first segment running. Take some time to consider this code because there is a lot to learn.

LISTING 9.11 SWAPPING BETWEEN TWO SEGMENTS (CHANGESEGMENTSPANEL.JAVA)

```java
package applets;

import shout3d.*;
import shout3d.core.*;
import shout3d.math.*;


public class ChangeSegmentsPanel extends Shout3DPanel implements
➥DeviceObserver {


    TimeSensor timer;
    ScalarInterpolator si;
    float[] first = {0.0f, .19f};
    float[] second = {.2f, 1.0f};
    boolean firstseg = false;

    public ChangeSegmentsPanel (Shout3DApplet applet){
        super(applet);
```

```
      }

   public void customInitialize() {
      addDeviceObserver(this,"MouseInput", null);


      timer = (TimeSensor) getNodeByName("timer");
      si = (ScalarInterpolator) getNodeByName("si");

   }


   protected void finalize()  {
      removeDeviceObserver(this,"MouseInput");

   }


   public boolean onDeviceInput(DeviceInput di, Object userData)
   {
      MouseInput mi = (MouseInput) di;
      switch (mi.which){

         case MouseInput.DOWN:

            if(firstseg) {

               timer.loop.setValue(false);
               timer.stop();
               timer.cycleInterval.setValue(8.0);
               si.keyValue.setValue(second);
               timer.start();
               timer.loop.setValue(true);
               firstseg = false;
               return true;
            }
            else {
               timer.loop.setValue(false);
               timer.stop();
```

```
                    timer.cycleInterval.setValue(2.0);
                    si.keyValue.setValue(first);
                    timer.start();
                    timer.loop.setValue(true);

                    firstseg = true;
                    return true;
             }

       }//end of switch

       return false;
   }


   }//end of class
```

We can't reset (stop and start) a TimeSensor while it's looping, so we must turn the looping off first. With looping off, we stop the TimeSensor and set it to the proper `cycleInterval` for the segment we wish to run. (You cannot change the `cycleInterval` while the TimeSensor is running.) Then we set the `keyValue` array of the scalar interpolator to correspond to the appropriate segment. The TimeSensor is restarted and looping is turned back on.

If you prefer non-looping animation, you can eliminate the lines of code that turn the looping on and off. The scene file must also have the loop field of the TimeSensor set to false.

To test it out, copy the following files from the CD to your Shout3D installation.

ChangeSegmentsPanel.java

ChangeSegmentsPanel.class

ChangeSegmentsApplet.java

ChangeSegmentsApplet.class

twosegments.s3d

changesegments.html

Swapping Scenes

The concept of swapping scenes is a bit larger than swapping animations, as it applies to unanimated scenes as well. But this is a good place to consider it.

The simplest way to change scenes is to cause the user to load a new HTML page with a new <APPLET> tag. This, of course, means loading a new Shout3D viewer. It will often make more sense to load a new scene into the existing viewer on the current HTML page. There are a couple of possibilities. One is to use the loadSceneFromURL() method in the Shout3DApplet or Shout3DPanel classes to download new scenes from the server only when the user wishes to view them. Another possibility is to download all of the alternative scenes at the start and allow the user to switch between them. This second method obviously increases the initial download time in exchange for rapid swapping.

Whichever method is used, the parameters set in the <APPLET> tag in the HTML file will govern all of the alternative scenes. Thus you won't be able to change backgrounds if one is set as a parameter. Bring the background information into the scene files in the form of Background nodes, rather than providing it in <APPLET> parameters. For example, let's say we want to swap between the modswing and ratpack demos found in your Shout3D installation. If you open the HTML files for these demos, you'll see the background information provided as parameters. I edited the scene files to provide the same information as nodes.

I added the following Background node to the ratpack scene and saved it as ratpack2.s3d.

```
Background {
    color 1 1 1
}
```

I added a Background node to the modswing scene and saved it as modswing2.s3d.

```
Background {
    texture ImageTexture {
        url "images/shared/wooden_stage_bg.jpg"
    }
}
```

The appropriate HTML file loads modswing2.s3d without setting any background parameters.

```
<APPLET CODEBASE="../codebase"
➥CODE="applets/ChangeScenesApplet.class"
➥ARCHIVE="shout3dClasses.zip" WIDTH=320 HEIGHT=240>
<param name="src" value="models/modswing2.s3d">
</APPLET>
```

We'll try a panel class that loads both scenes at the start. The concept is straightforward, but there are few issues worth attention. Look over the code in Listing 9.12 first.

LISTING 9.12 SWAPPING BETWEEN TWO SCENES (*CHANGESCENESPANEL.JAVA*)

```
package applets;

import shout3d.*;
import shout3d.core.*;
import shout3d.math.*;

public class ChangeScenesPanel extends Shout3DPanel implements
➥DeviceObserver{

    //must create an array (list) of URLs,
    // even though there is only one URL in the array
    String[] URL = new String[1];

    Transform ratpack;
    Transform modswing;
    boolean mod = true;


    public ChangeScenesPanel(Shout3DApplet applet){
       super(applet);
    }



    public void customInitialize () {

       addDeviceObserver(this,"MouseInput", null);
```

```
        URL[0] = "models/ratpack2.s3d";
        ratpack = new Transform();
        loadURL(URL, ratpack);

        modswing = (Transform) getScene();

    }

    protected void finalize()  {
        removeDeviceObserver(this,"MouseInput");

    }

    public boolean onDeviceInput(DeviceInput di, Object userData)
    {
        MouseInput mi = (MouseInput) di;
        switch (mi.which){

            case MouseInput.DOWN:

                if(mod) {

                    setScene(ratpack);
                    mod = false;
                    return true;
                }

                else {
                    setScene(modswing);
                    mod = true;
                    return true;
                }

        }//end of switch

        return false;
    }


}
```

To set a scene in the viewer, we call the setScene() method inherited from the Shout3DPanel class. This method takes the root node of the scene we wish to display. Thus, we need to obtain references to the root nodes (root Transforms) of the two scenes to store in the fields named modswing and ratpack. The modswing2.s3d scene is automatically loaded as the current scene because it's the scene file indicated in the <APPLET> tag. Thus, we can get a reference to its root node using the getScene() method inherited from the Shout3DPanel class.

By contrast, the ratpack2.s3d scene will not be loaded unless we cause it to load. We do this during initialization, using the loadURL() method. To load a scene in this way, we need a character string specifying the path to the desired file from the current codebase directory, and a Transform node to reference the root of the scene after loading it. As is common in Shout3D, the loadURL() method requires an array of Strings, even if there is only one String in the array. Thus, we create a String[] with only a single element and initialize it with the path to the ratpack2.s3d scene file. The loadURL () method loads the scene and places a reference to its root Transform in the ratpack field.

Try it out yourself. Copy the following files from the CD to your Shout3D installation.

ChangeScenesPanel.java

ChangeScenesPanel.class

ChangeScenesApplet.java

ChangeScenesApplet.class

ratpack2.s3d

modswing2.s3d

changescenes.html

The projects in this chapter have barely scratched the surface of what is possible at the nexus of interactivity and animation. The game project later in this book will integrate a number of the techniques introduced here. Yet there is much farther to go because, at this point in time, creative ideas for merging interactivity and animation are only beginning to develop. I encourage you to exercise your imagination in this area.

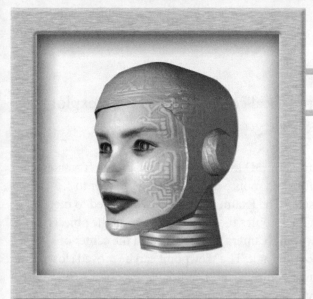

A Project with Custom Nodes

SHOUT3D

Chapter 10

I n this chapter we'll build a practical commercial project, exploring a number of new topics as we go along.

The ExamineApplet provided in your Shout3D installation is very useful. It rotates the camera around the scene using an animated mouse drag, enabling the user to see an object (or group of objects) from all sides. The ExamineApplet was designed to meet a very general need in a transparent way. It computes the total volume of all the objects in the scene as a bounding box. The Viewpoint (camera) rotates around the center of this bounding box and always remains pointing at it. The Viewpoint can be moved closer and farther from this center point, creating a zooming effect, although it is not the true photographic zoom that would result from changing the Viewpoint's `fieldOfView` angle. The ExamineApplet computes an initial Viewpoint distance from the center of the scene volume in a way that insures that the entire scene will be viewable when it first displays.

It would be nice to have a targeted Viewpoint that can be added to any scene without having to use the ExamineApplet. All 3D artists are familiar with the concept of a targeted camera, which is effectively tethered to an object. Translating the camera causes it to rotate so as to remain pointed toward the target object. Neither VRML nor Shout3D have a TargetViewpoint node. If you export a MAX scene with a TargetCamera, all you'll get is a regular VRML Viewpoint object. But we can create our own TargetViewpoint node and add it to the Shout3D class library. In this way we create a custom node that we can use again and again, simply by adding it to the scene file.

Building the Custom Node

Just as we build custom panel and applet classes by extension from Shout's base panel and applet classes, so will we build custom node classes by extending existing node classes in the Shout library. At a minimum, any class must be extended from the base node class, but more often we will extend a class that is already derived from node. In this case, we'll extend the Viewpoint class to add the features of our new TargetViewpoint class.

The Concept of a TargetViewpoint

Before we can do any coding, we need to understand how a targeted camera operates. In a standard 3D animation package like MAX, you can move (translate) the targeted camera wherever you want, and it will remain pointing toward the target object. But you are not free to rotate the camera in a way that will keep it from pointing at its target. This approach makes sense because it allows a camera to remain pointing toward the target, regardless of where either the camera or the target object move.

Our needs here are a little different. We are less concerned with the cinematic problem of holding on to a camera's "interest," but rather we wish to use a targeted camera as a way of examining an object from all sides (without the problems of trying to rotate the object itself). We want to be able to move the Viewpoint in a circle around a point of our choosing and always remain directed toward that point. We also want to be able to adjust our distance from that point. Thus it makes more sense to rotate the Viewpoint in the heading and pitch rather than translate it. Imagine a globe marked by lines of longitude and latitude. Heading rotation corresponds to setting our longitude in the East or West direction. Pitch rotation corresponds to setting our latitude in North and South. Whatever position on the globe we place our Viewpoint, it should remain pointed toward the center of the globe.

This problem turns out to be fairly easy to solve by building from ideas that we have already considered. We'll start by using the world origin as the center point and address the problem only in two dimensions. In the following illustration, we are looking down at the groundplane from above. In its default state, the Viewpoint is positioned along the positive z axis, pointing toward the world origin. Both the Viewpoint and the vector connecting it to the origin are unrotated.

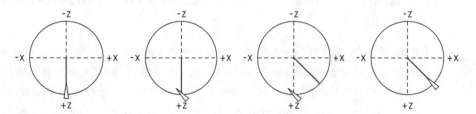

Next, the Viewpoint is rotated in the heading by 45 degrees. Then the vector is also rotated the same amount. By moving the rotated Viewpoint to the end of the rotated vector, the Viewpoint remains pointed at the center.

Thus we see that as long as the same rotation is applied to both the camera and the vector, the camera will remain properly targeted. The length of the vector (the radius of the circle) is the distance from the Viewpoint to the center. This distance can be changed without affecting the targeting operation. These concepts are equally applicable when the Viewpoint is rotated in both pitch and heading, rather than only in heading.

Coding the Custom Node

Now that we have a concept, we can start to implement it in a custom node. We start with a Viewpoint node. This node has `position` and `orientation` fields. We need to add `heading`, `pitch`, and `distance` fields. These new fields will be used to compute the proper `position` and `orientation` values. For the time being, we'll stick to using the world origin as the target point. This is no great inconvenience for most purposes because the object to be examined can be placed at the world origin.

The FieldObserver Interface

The key to the operation of this node is the FieldObserver interface. The FieldObserver interface provides the vehicle for communication within and between nodes. In this case, we want to set things up so that anytime a `heading`, `pitch`, or `distance` value is changed, a method is called within the TargetViewpoint node that recomputes the `position` and `orientation`. To achieve this, we must cause the TargetViewpoint node to implement the FieldObserver interface. This interface (like the DeviceObserver interface) contains only a single method. The `onFieldChange()` method is called whenever a value changes in a field with which the DeviceObserver has registered. Here, for example, the TargetViewpoint node (as a DeviceObserver) will register with the `heading`, `pitch`, and `distance` fields. Once registered, these fields will call the `onFieldChanged()` method of the TargetViewpoint node whenever they change values. The `onFieldChanged()` method will use the new values to recompute the new `position` and `orientation` of the Viewpoint.

 The fact that changes in field values can trigger actions in nodes, and therefore changes in other fields, explains the importance of using the `setValue()` methods. Often, the value in a field is determined by reference to another object, and therefore it changes automatically along with that object. But only if the `setValue()` method has explicitly called for a changed value will the interested FieldObservers be notified of the new value.

As it turns out, the Viewpoint node, like many of the Shout nodes, already implements the FieldObserver interface. (Look up the Viewpoint node in the API documentation to confirm this for yourself.) This has a couple of important consequences. One is that it's not strictly necessary to declare that our TargetViewpoint class implements FieldObserver. Since the superclass, Viewpoint, already implements this interface, any class extended from Viewpoint also implements it automatically. This is the same situation we've already encountered with respect to the Shout3DPanel class implementing the RenderObserver interface. There's no harm in adding the words `implements` `FieldObserver` to the class declaration, so we'll do it to begin with to highlight the fact that we are making explicit use of this interface by overriding the `onFieldChange()` method.

The second consequence of the fact that the Viewpoint class already implements the FieldObserver interface is much more important. The Viewpoint class needs to hear from certain fields and respond to changes in those fields. We don't know what Viewpoint's `onFieldChange()` method is doing, because this information is hidden from us in the API. But we do know that we can't interfere with it. Remember that our TargetViewpoint won't work if the underlying Viewpoint doesn't work, so we need to code our `onFieldChange()` method to make sure that messages intended for Viewpoint get through.

A First Pass at the Code

There's a lot to learn in this first version of the TargetViewpoint class. Take some time to feel your way around Listing 10.1 before continuing with the discussion.

LISTING 10.1 DEVELOPING A TARGETED CAMERA (*TARGETVIEWPOINT1.JAVA*)

```
package custom_nodes;

import   shout3d.core.*;
import   shout3d.math.*;


public class TargetViewpoint1 extends Viewpoint implements
➥FieldObserver {


    final public FloatField heading = new FloatField(this,
➥"heading",  Field.ANY, 0);

    final public FloatField pitch = new FloatField(this, "pitch",
➥Field.ANY, 0);

    final public FloatField distance = new FloatField(this,
➥"distance", Field.NON_NEGATIVE_FLOAT, 10);

    Quaternion q = new Quaternion();
```

```java
        float[] eulers = {0.0f, 0.0f, 0.0f};

        //default constructor
        public TargetViewpoint1(){
            this(null);
        }

        //constructor that takes
        //a viewer argument
        public TargetViewpoint1(Shout3DViewer viewer){

            //call Viewpoint's constructor
            super(viewer);

            //register node as FieldObserver
            heading.addFieldObserver(this, null);
            pitch.addFieldObserver(this, null);
            distance.addFieldObserver(this, null);

            //compute position and orientation
            setViewpoint();
        }


        protected void finalize() throws Throwable {

            heading.removeFieldObserver(this);
            pitch.removeFieldObserver(this);
            distance.removeFieldObserver(this);

            super.finalize();
        }


        public void onFieldChange(Field theField, Object userData) {

            //if TargetViewpoint fields have changed
            if ( theField == heading || theField == pitch || theField
    ➡== distance) {
                setViewpoint();
```

```
        }

        //if something else has changed
        else {

            // call Viewpoint's onFieldChange()
            super.onFieldChange(theField, userData);
        }
    }


    public void setViewpoint() {

        //set quaternion to current heading and pitch
        eulers[0] = heading.getValue();
        eulers[1] = pitch.getValue();
        q.setEulers(eulers);

        //set distance vector
        //and rotate it
        if ( distance.getValue() < 0.0f) {
            distance.setValue(0.0f);
        }
        float[] vector = {0.0f, 0.0f, distance.getValue()};
        q.xform(vector);

        //set Viewpoint rotation and
        //translate to end of vector
        float[] axisAngle = new float[4];
        q.getAxisAngle(axisAngle);
        orientation.setValue(axisAngle);
        position.setValue(vector);


    }
}
```

After you've had a good long look, you'll surely have lots of questions. Let's get rid of some preliminaries first. Note at the top of the listing how this class is packaged in custom_nodes, and thus its full moniker is java.custom_nodes.TargetViewpoint1. We'll be storing it the custom_nodes directory of your Shout installation. Note also the two class packages that are imported. The `core` package is always essential, but we need the `math` package as well to use the Quaternion class.

Let's jump out of order for a moment and go directly to the last method in the class, `setViewpoint()`. This is the method that will use the current `heading`, `pitch`, and `distance` values to compute the `position` and `orientation` of the Viewpoint. The `heading` and `pitch` values are used to set a Quaternion, and this Quaternion is used to rotate the vector. The same rotation is extracted from the Quaternion in axis-angle format to rotate the Viewpoint, which is translated to the end of the rotated vector. These are all the elements of the process illustrated a few pages back. Note how the vector is set to the length of the current `distance`, which may not be less than zero.

Creating Field Objects

The `heading`, `pitch`, and `distance` values are all taken from Field objects declared and created at the top of the class. Instead of storing the `heading`, for example, as a simple `float` variable, we create a FloatField class object. This is something new, and it is very important. We are already familiar with the fact that the Shout nodes contain fields that are class objects rather than simple data types. To get and set the values in these objects, we need to use `getValue()` and `setValue()` methods. But there are other fields in our TargetViewpoint1 class. How about the Quaternion named `q` and the `float []` named `eulers`? Why aren't these placed inside field objects, too?

These latter two fields are not intended to be public. They are used only within the TargetViewpoint1 class for its own internal computational purposes. By contrast, the `heading`, `pitch`, and `distance` fields must be available to other classes. We must, for example, be able to change these values from a panel class if we want to make them interactive. Just as important, we want the Shout viewer to be able to set these fields when it loads a scene file that contains a TargetViewpoint1 node. The `heading`, `pitch`, and `distance` fields are precisely the kinds of public fields that must be documented in the API, just as `position` and `orientation` are for the Viewpoint class. These are the fields we want the users of our class to know about and have access to.

Let's look at the first Field object declaration to understand it:

```
final public FloatField heading = new FloatField(this, "heading",
➥Field.ANY, 0);
```

The object is an instance of the FloatField class and is named `heading`. It is declared to be `public` and `final`. The `public` designation allows us to call the methods of the object in the `heading` field from objects of any Java class (such as Shout3DPanel class objects). Like all class references, `heading` contains a reference to an object, rather than the object itself. The object is created (instantiated) by the `new` statement. The `final` designation means that once a FloatField object is so instantiated, the reference in `heading` can never be changed. Look up the FloatField class in your online Javadocs and find its constructor detail information. The constructor takes four arguments. The first is the node that the FloatField belongs to. Passing the keyword `this` makes the current class, TargetViewpoint, the owner of the FloatField object. The second argument is a string representing the name of the object. Look up the Field class in your online Javadocs to see the methods common to all of the various field types. You'll find methods to get the name and owner node that are set in the constructor.

The third argument is the usage. Look up the UsageTypes interface in your online Javadocs and check out the long list of constants associated with integer values. These constants indicate limitations on data values appropriate for a specific purpose. For example, position values could only be represented by an array of three `floats`. In this case, however, the heading could be a float of any possible value, positive or negative. Thus the argument is `Field.ANY`.

The final argument is the default or starting value. If the heading is not set otherwise, its value will be 0. Actually, when the node is read from a scene file, it is first constructed using the default value. If a different value is provided in the scene file, this value is immediately set using the `setValue()` method. This bit of internal mechanics will become significant to you later on, so keep it in the back of your mind.

Two Different Constructors

The TargetViewpoint1 class has two constructors—a default version that takes no arguments and another version that accepts a Shout3DViewer object as an argument. Look up the Viewpoint class in your online Javadocs and you'll see that Viewpoint has two constructors, with the same argument signatures. Whenever you instantiate a class in Java, a constructor of each of its ancestor classes must be called. For example, when a Viewpoint object is created, its superclass Bindable is constructed, which in turn must construct its superclass node, which in turn must construct Object (the base class in the entire Java hierarchy). This is an important insight into object-oriented programming that has many practical implications.

All Bindable nodes need two constructors. A default constructor without arguments simply creates the node. But to work properly, a Bindable node must have a reference to a Shout3DViewer object (either a Shout3DPanel or a Shout3DApplet) with which it is associated. The purpose is to assure that only one Bindable of a given type is bound at a given moment. Assume you have a scene with multiple Viewpoints. When you bind a Viewpoint, you want to be sure that all other Viewpoints are unbound. This can happen automatically if the panel class is aware of all the Viewpoints in the scene and can communicate with them. Thus a truly complete Bindable node must be constructed with a reference to the panel.

But you don't need to know the precise reason Bindable nodes (such as the Viewpoint node) have two constructors. All you need to know is that they do. Therefore, when coding the TargetViewpoint1 class, we must provide both constructors. If a TargetViewpoint1 object is constructed using the default constructor, the default constructors of Viewpoint and Bindable will be used as well. If, as is the general case, TargetViewpoint1 is constructed with an argument to its Shout3DViewer object (the Shout3DPanel in which the Viewpoint is operating), this argument will be passed along to the Viewpoint and Bindable constructors so they can set things up properly. When a Bindable node is read from a scene file, it is constructed with a Shout3DViewer argument.

We could create two complete parallel constructors, but our node uses an interesting technique. The complete construction code is in the second constructor, the one that takes the argument. The first thing this constructor does is to explicitly call the Viewpoint constructor, passing along the Shout3DViewer object. This ensures that the ancestor classes will be properly constructed. Then the constructor goes about the special business of its own class, which we'll consider in a moment.

The default constructor, on the other hand, simply calls the second constructor, passing it a null argument. The statement

```
this(null);
```

is effectively the same as

```
TargetViewpoint1(null);
```

and therefore calls the only constructor that takes a single argument. (Note that a `null` argument is not the same as no argument at all, as represented by empty parentheses.) Thus, if the default constructor is used, it immediately hands off to the second constructor. But due to the absence of a Shout3DViewer object in the argument, the call to the super constructor (the construction of the super or parent class) will also pass a `null` up the chain, and the ancestor classes will be constructed without a reference to the Shout3DViewer.

Registering the FieldObserver

The TargetViewpoint1 class implements the FieldObserver interface. It contains an `onFieldChange()` method that will be called whenever values in certain specified fields change. These fields may be fields of the class itself, providing intraclass communication, or fields of other classes, to provide interclass communication. We want any changes in the value of our `heading`, `pitch`, and `distance` fields to trigger a recomputation of the `position` and `orientation` fields. Thus we must register the TargetViewpoint1 node as a FieldObserver of its own fields.

Look up the Field class in your online Javadocs and note that all Fields have an `addFieldObserver()` method. When a TargetViewpoint1 object is constructed, this method is called for each of the three fields. The first argument, `this`, indicates that the current class, TargetViewpoint1, is the object registering as a FieldObserver.

As we have seen with the DeviceObserver and RenderObserver interfaces, we must remember to unregister when the class object is destroyed. The `finalize()` method of any Java object is called for such cleanup purposes, and (in this case) contains the calls that remove the DeviceObserver from the three Field objects. This code necessarily overrides the `finalize()` method in the Viewpoint class. Remember that the Viewpoint class is already a DeviceObserver and therefore needs to unregister with its own fields. Thus, after cleaning up TargetViewpoint, we call `super.finalize()` to make sure that Viewpoint's cleanup work is accomplished.

Note that the `finalize()` *method contains the statement* `throws Throwable`. *The subject of exception handling in Java (how Java responds to problems during program execution) is beyond the scope of this book and is covered in any basic text on Java. The* `super.finalize()` *method requires such a* `throws` *statement, and if you omit it, the compiler will complain.*

Setting the Position and Orientation

We've already noted how the `position` and `orientation` values are computed in the `setViewpoint()` method. This method is first called at the end of the constructor so that the Viewpoint is properly set based on the default `heading`, `pitch`, and `distance` values. But these values can change. They will be changed immediately if values were specified in the scene file. For example, we might add a TargetViewpoint1 object to an .s3d file by typing in the node and specifying a distance of 5, instead of the default of 10.

```
TargetViewpoint1 {
   distance 5
}
```

In this case, a TargetViewpoint1 object will be created with the distance of 10, and then the new value from scene file will be used in a `setValue()` call to the `distance` FloatField object. This change in value will trigger a call to onFieldChange(), which will in turn call setViewpoint() to recompute the position and orientation.

The heading, pitch, and distance values can also change at any subsequent time in response to user interaction programmed in the panel or applet classes. (We will soon be using mouse drags to change these values.) Once again, the onField-Change() method will call the setViewpoint() method to recompute the Viewpoint.

Let's take a close look at onFieldChange() to understand its structure.

```
public void onFieldChange(Field theField, Object userData) {

    //if TargetViewpoint fields have changed
    if ( theField == heading || theField == pitch || theField
➡== distance) {
        setViewpoint();
    }

    //if something else has changed
    else {

        // call Viewpoint's onFieldChange()
        super.onFieldChange(theField, userData);
    }
}
```

The method receives a Field argument, which is a reference to the Field object that triggered the call (the Field that changed). Remember that the Viewpoint class is already a FieldObserver with its own onFieldChange() method set up to handle inputs. Just as with the constructor and the finalize() methods, we need to make sure that this superclass method is preserved. Thus we test for the Field object triggering the call. If that Field is heading or pitch or distance, we call set Viewpoint(). If it is not, it should be handled by the superclass' onFieldChange() method.

Testing the Node

Let's give this code a test drive to see how it handles. The source code and compiled files can be found on the CD. Copy TargetViewpoint1.java and Target Viewpoint1.class to the custom_nodes directory of your Shout installation.

To test out the new Viewpoint, I've created a scene with a box centered on the world origin. Its faces are color-coded to help you understand the operation of the rotating Viewpoint.

Right (+x)   light red

Left (+x)   dark red

Top (+y)   light green

Bottom (−y)   dark green

Front (+z)   light blue

Bottom (−z)   dark blue

The scene contains nothing but this box (an IndexedFaceSet), a Background node set to white, and a default TargetViewpoint1 object, added by hand to the top of the scene file as follows:

```
TargetViewpoint1 {}
```

The scene is named `targetviewpoint1.s3d`. Copy it from the CD to the `models` folder of your Shout installation.

Static Testing

We'll start without any interactivity at all and see how the new Viewpoint responds to different values in the scene file. Create an HTML file that loads the scene into the basic Shout3DApplet, as in Listing 10.2. Or just copy `targetviewpoint1static.html` from the CD into your `demos` directory.

LISTING 10.2 STATIC TESTING OF THE TARGETVIEWPOINT
(*TARGETVIEWPOINT1STATIC.HTML*)

```
<HTML>
<HEAD>
<TITLE>targetviewpoint1static</TITLE>
</HEAD>
<BODY>
<APPLET CODEBASE="../codebase" CODE="shout3d/Shout3DApplet.class"
➥ARCHIVE="shout3dClasses.zip" WIDTH=320 HEIGHT=240>
<param name="src" value="models/targetviewpoint1.s3d">
<param name="headlightOn" value="true">
</APPLET>
</BODY>
</HTML>
```

Run this demo, and you will be viewing the box with the default values, with the Viewpoint looking down the *z* axis from the front at a distance of 10 meters from the world origin. The front (light blue) face of the box will be the only one visible.

So far, so good. Edit the scene file to rotate the heading one radian. (Remember that the angle values are in radians, not degrees.)

```
TargetViewpoint1 {
    heading 1
}
```

Save the file and refresh your browser. The box will appear to rotate one radian (57.3 degrees) in the clockwise direction (as judged from above), so the right (light red) face is now visible. But notice that the Viewpoint is swinging around the object in the counter-clockwise direction. This is an important point. The viewer will instinctively perceive the Viewpoint rotations as the (opposite) rotations of the object being viewed.

Now let's try the pitch rotation. Delete the heading rotation and set the pitch rotation to .5 radians, as follows.

```
TargetViewpoint1 {
    pitch .5
}
```

Save the file and refresh your browser again. The front (light blue) face of the box will appear to be rotating backwards. This may seem the opposite of what you expected. A positive pitch value tilts the Viewpoint upward. To remain pointing at the center of the box (the center of world space), the camera must swing down into the "Southern Hemisphere."

Let's get closer to the object by reducing the distance to 5 meters. Add some heading rotation and reverse the pitch direction to make it more interesting.

```
TargetViewpoint1 {
    heading .7
    pitch -.5
    distance 5
}
```

No confusion here. It works just as expected.

The only issue might be the perspective. The default fieldOfView angle may produce too much perspective distortion when we get this close to the object. The default fieldOfView angle of a VRML Viewpoint is about 45 degrees (.785 radians). Since our TargetViewpoint1 is still a Viewpoint, we can set its fieldOfView field in the scene file. Try .5 radians (28.65 degrees) for a telephoto lens feel with flattened perspective. Then move the Viewpoint back to about 7 meters to make up for the decreased viewing angle.

```
TargetViewpoint1 {
   heading .5
   pitch -.5
   distance 7
   fieldOfView .5
}
```

The result is much more effective.

Consider how valuable this new Viewpoint node is, even without user interactivity. You can add a camera by hand to a file and position (and reposition) it freely to get the angle you want—all without going back to MAX or any other 3D application to set up a camera.

Dynamic Testing

The real test of our new node is user interactivity. It's a simple procedure to write a panel class to do the job. The panel class in Listing 10.3 sets the current heading and pitch by dragging the left mouse button and adjusts the distance by dragging the right mouse button.

> **LISTING 10.3 INTERACTIVE TESTING OF THE TARGETVIEWPOINT (*TARGETVIEWPOINT1TESTPANEL.JAVA*)**

```
package applets;

import shout3d.*;
import shout3d.core.*;
import custom_nodes.*;


public class TargetViewpoint1TestPanel extends Shout3DPanel
➥implements DeviceObserver {


    int pixelStartX;
    int pixelStartY;
    int pixelEndX;
    int pixelEndY;

    TargetViewpoint1 cam;


    public TargetViewpoint1TestPanel(Shout3DApplet applet){
        super(applet);
    }

        public void customInitialize() {

        addDeviceObserver(this,"MouseInput", null);
```

```
            cam = (TargetViewpoint1)
      getCurrentBindableNode("Viewpoint");

        }


        protected void finalize()  {
            removeDeviceObserver(this,"MouseInput");
        }



        public boolean onDeviceInput(DeviceInput di,
    ➥Object userData) {
            MouseInput mi = (MouseInput) di;
            switch (mi.which){

                case MouseInput.DOWN:
                    pixelStartX = mi.x;
                    pixelStartY = mi.y;
                    return true;

                case MouseInput.DRAG:

                    //if left button used
                    if(mi.button == 0) {

                    pixelEndX = mi.x;
                    pixelEndY = mi.y;

                    int dragDistanceX = pixelEndX - pixelStartX;
                    int dragDistanceY = pixelEndY - pixelStartY;

                    //convert drag to rotation
                    //at 70 pixels per radian (57.3 degrees)
                    float headingDelta = dragDistanceX/70f;
                    float pitchDelta = dragDistanceY/70f;

                    //compute new heading and pitch
                    float temp = cam.heading.getValue() - headingDelta;
```

```
                        cam.heading.setValue(temp);
                        temp = cam.pitch.getValue() - pitchDelta;
                        cam.pitch.setValue(temp);

                        pixelStartY = pixelEndY;
                        pixelStartX = pixelEndX;

                        return true;

                    }//end of 0 if

                    //if right button used
                    if(mi.button == 1) {

                        pixelEndY = mi.y;
                        int dragDistanceY = pixelEndY - pixelStartY;

                        float distanceDelta = dragDistanceY/150f;
                        float temp = cam.distance.getValue() + distanceDelta;
                        cam.distance.setValue(temp);

                        pixelStartY = pixelEndY;
                        return true;

                    }//end of 1 if

                }//end of switch

                return false;

            }


    }//end of class
```

Create a matching applet and an HTML demo file, or copy the following files from
the CD:

```
TargetViewpoint1TestPanel.java
```

```
TargetViewpoint1TestPanel.class
```

```
TargetViewpoint1TestApplet.java

TargetViewpoint1TestApplet.class

targetviewpoint1interactive.html
```

Give it a spin! The interactivity is easy and intuitive, and there are no rotational problems that prevent the user from examining the object from any orientation.

Improving the TargetViewpoint

The TargetViewpoint1 class works well, and it might provide all the functionality we need; however, a truly complete TargetViewpoint would have an adjustable center. It could be made to point at, and revolve around, any specified point in the scene rather than just the world origin. This is surprisingly easy to do. We store the desired center location in a field, but we perform all the computations just as we have been doing using (0,0,0) as the center. Then we take the computed location of the Viewpoint and translate it by the same distance that the desired center is from (0,0,0).

Take a look at the following illustration, which demonstrates the process in two dimensions. We want to rotate the Viewpoint around the point (x,z), which is away from the origin (0,0), as seen at left. In the next two steps, the rotation is computed around (0,0). Finally, at right, the rotated camera is translated back. By adding the x and z values of the desired center to the x and z values computed for the Viewpoint after rotation around (0,0), we get the Viewpoint in the proper location.

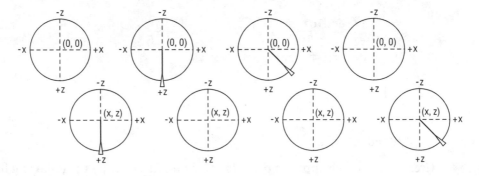

Adding a Center Field

Listing 10.4 shows the completed version of the TargetViewpoint custom node, with the additions shown in bold.

LISTING 10.4 THE FINISHED TARGET VIEWPOINT CUSTOM NODE (*TARGETVIEWPOINT.JAVA*)

```java
package custom_nodes;

import  shout3d.core.*;
import  shout3d.math.*;


public class TargetViewpoint extends Viewpoint  {

    float[] origin = {0.0f, 0.0f, 0.0f};

    final public FloatField heading = new FloatField(this,
➥"heading",  Field.ANY, 0);

    final public FloatField pitch = new FloatField(this, "pitch",
➥Field.ANY, 0);

    final public FloatField distance = new FloatField(this,
➥"distance", Field.NON_NEGATIVE_FLOAT, 10);

    final public FloatArrayField center = new
➥FloatArrayField(this, "center", Field.COORD3, origin);

    Quaternion q = new Quaternion();
    float[] eulers = {0.0f, 0.0f, 0.0f};


    public TargetViewpoint(){
        this(null);
    }

    public TargetViewpoint(Shout3DViewer viewer){

        super(viewer);
```

```
    heading.addFieldObserver(this, null);
    pitch.addFieldObserver(this, null);
    distance.addFieldObserver(this, null);
    center.addFieldObserver(this,null);

    setViewpoint();
}


protected void finalize() throws Throwable {

    heading.removeFieldObserver(this);
    pitch.removeFieldObserver(this);
    distance.removeFieldObserver(this);
    center.removeFieldObserver(this);

    super.finalize();
}


public void onFieldChange(Field theField, Object userData) {

    if ( theField == heading || theField == pitch || theField
➡== distance || theField == center) {
        setViewpoint();
    }
    else {
        // call super class--Viewpoint
        super.onFieldChange(theField, userData);
    }
}


public void setViewpoint() {

    //set quaternion to current heading and pitch
    eulers[0] = heading.getValue();
    eulers[1] = pitch.getValue();
    q.setEulers(eulers);
```

```
//set distance vector
//and rotate it
if ( distance.getValue() < 0.0f) {
   distance.setValue(0.0f);
}
float[] vector = {0.0f, 0.0f, distance.getValue()};
q.xform(vector);


//translate vector relative
//to target center
vector[0] = vector[0] + center.getValue()[0];
vector[1] = vector[1] + center.getValue()[1];
vector[2] = vector[2] + center.getValue()[2];


//set Viewpoint rotation and
//translate to end of vector
float[] axisAngle = new float[4];
q.getAxisAngle(axisAngle);
orientation.setValue(axisAngle);
position.setValue(vector);


   }
}
```

A center field is added as a FloatArrayField object because three floating point values are required to specify position in (x,y,z). The constructor for the FloatArrayField object requires a reference to such an array, holding the default values. Unless other values are provided in the scene file, the TargetViewpoint will function as it did before—rotating around (0,0,0).

The computation in setViewpoint() is the same as before except that we now add the center values to translate the Viewpoint to its proper position around that point. If the default center of (0,0,0) is used, this step has no effect.

The node registers as a FieldObserver of the center field. This allows us to interactively change (or to procedurally animate) the center, perhaps to track a moving object. But even if we do not intend to change the center value, we must still register the node as a FieldObserver with that field. This is because of the way in which field values are initially set, as mentioned before. When the TargetViewpoint node is constructed, it is initialized with its default values. Only then are these values changed by values read in from the scene file. If a nondefault `center` value is set in this way, we must be sure that `setViewpoint()` is called to compute the proper Viewpoint position. In short, even setting the initial values from the scene file is a "change" from the default initialization that requires recomputation.

TargetViewpoint no longer explicitly `implements` `FieldObserver` *in the class declaration. As previously noted, the Viewpoint class from which TargetViewpoint is extended is already a FieldObserver, and this interface is therefore necessarily inherited.*

Testing It Out

Copy the following files from the CD into your Shout installation to test out the final version of the TargetViewpoint custom node. (Remember to place the custom node files in the `custom_nodes` directory.)

```
TargetViewpoint.java

TargetViewpoint.class

targetviewpoint.s3d
```

The .s3d file is the same as before, except that the box has been translated to (3,4,5) in world space. The TargetViewpoint is therefore assigned a `center` at the same location, and some nondefault `heading`, `pitch`, and `distance` values. I also dropped in a Still-CameraProgressiveAntialiase custom node, to get rid of the jaggedness that renders along the edges of the box.

```
StillCameraProgressiveAntialiase {}

TargetViewpoint {
    center 3 4 5
    heading -.5
    pitch -.8
    distance 7
}

...
```

```
DEF Box01 Transform {
     translation 3 4 5
     ...
}
```

If everything works out, the box (however rotated) should be right in the middle of the viewing window.

Static Test

Try a static test using the basic Shout3DApplet as in Listing 10.5.

LISTING 10.5 STATIC TESTING THE FINISHED TARGETVIEWPOINT NODE.
(*TARGETVIEWPOINTSTATIC.HTML*)

```
<HTML>
<HEAD>
<TITLE>targetviewpointstatic</TITLE>
</HEAD>
<BODY>
<APPLET CODEBASE="../codebase" CODE="shout3d/Shout3DApplet.class"
➥ARCHIVE="shout3dClasses.zip" WIDTH=320 HEIGHT=240>
<param name="src" value="models/targetviewpoint.s3d">
<param name="headlightOn" value="true">
</APPLET>
</BODY>
</HTML>
```

Create this file yourself, or copy targetviewpointstatic.html from the CD to your demos folder. Give it a try.

Animated Drag

Our improved TargetViewpoint deserves an improved interactivity test. The panel class in Listing 10.6 animates the Viewpoint using drag controls for the kind of "power steering" we considered in the previous chapter. The drag distance sets the speed of the rotation or zooming.

LISTING 10.6 INTERACTIVE TESTING OF THE FINISHED TARGETVIEWPOINT NODE (*TARGETVIEWPOINTTESTPANEL.JAVA*)

```java
package applets;

import shout3d.*;
import shout3d.core.*;
import custom_nodes.*;


public class TargetViewpointTestPanel extends Shout3DPanel
➡implements DeviceObserver {


    int pixelStartX;
    int pixelStartY;

    float headingSpeed = 0.0f;
    float pitchSpeed = 0.0f;
    float distanceSpeed = 0.0f;

    TargetViewpoint cam;


    public TargetViewpointTestPanel(Shout3DApplet applet){
        super(applet);
    }

     public void customInitialize() {

    addDeviceObserver(this,"MouseInput", null);
    getRenderer().addRenderObserver(this, null);
    cam = (TargetViewpoint)
➡getCurrentBindableNode("Viewpoint");
```

```
        }


    protected void finalize() {
        removeDeviceObserver(this,"MouseInput");
        getRenderer().removeRenderObserver(this);
    }



    public boolean onDeviceInput(DeviceInput di,
➥Object userData) {
        MouseInput mi = (MouseInput) di;
        switch (mi.which){

            case MouseInput.DOWN:
                pixelStartX = mi.x;
                pixelStartY = mi.y;
                return true;

            case MouseInput.UP:
                headingSpeed = 0.0f;
                pitchSpeed = 0.0f;
                distanceSpeed = 0.0f;
                return true;

            case MouseInput.DRAG:

              //if left button used
              if(mi.button == 0) {

                int pixelEndX = mi.x;
                int pixelEndY = mi.y;

                int dragDistanceX = pixelEndX - pixelStartX;
                int dragDistanceY = pixelEndY - pixelStartY;

                //convert drag to rotation speeds
```

```
            //at 1/70 radians/sec for each pixel dragged
➥//i.e., dragging 70 pixels creates
            //speed of 1 radian per second
            headingSpeed = dragDistanceX/70f;
            pitchSpeed = dragDistanceY/70f;


            return true;

        }//end of 0 if

        //if right button used
        if(mi.button == 1) {

            int pixelEndY = mi.y;
            int dragDistanceY = pixelEndY - pixelStartY;

            //convert drag to zoom speed
            //at 1/150 meters/sec for each pixel draggedpixels
➥per meters/second
            //i.e., dragging 150 pixels creates
            //speed of 1 meter per second

            distanceSpeed = dragDistanceY/150f;

            return true;

        }//end of 1 if

    }//end of switch

    return false;

}

public void onPreRender (Renderer r, Object o) {

    float headingDelta = headingSpeed/getFramesPerSecond();
    float temp = cam.heading.getValue() - headingDelta;
    cam.heading.setValue(temp);
```

```
        float pitchDelta = pitchSpeed/getFramesPerSecond();
        temp = cam.pitch.getValue() - pitchDelta;
        cam.pitch.setValue(temp);

        float distanceDelta = distanceSpeed/getFramesPerSecond();
        temp = cam.distance.getValue() + distanceDelta;
        cam.distance.setValue(temp);

    }

}//end of class
```

 Copy the following classes from the CD to your Shout installation and check out this panel using the `targetviewpoint.s3d` scene from the previous example.

TargetViewpointTestPanel.java

TargetViewpointTestPanel.class

TargetViewpointTestApplet.java

TargetViewpointTestApplet.class

targetviewpointinteractive.html

A Multiple Viewpoint Application

Let's show off our new Viewpoint node with a useful application. We'll build a project that allows the user to add new cameras on the fly and toggle between them. Then we'll add improved interface features that will introduce us to a new range of possibilities.

Adding Viewpoints on the Fly

There are many ways of designing our project. We'll limit ourselves to a maximum of three Viewpoints. We'll start with one and allow the user to add two more. These will be stored in an array of three TargetViewpoints.

Using Keyboard Input

Since we'll need both mouse buttons to control the TargetViewpoints, we'll use the keyboard to create new ones and switch between them. Up until now, we've only been using mouse input in our projects. We needed only to register our panel classes to receive MouseInput objects, and our `onDeviceInput()` methods have been structured with the assurance that only MouseInput arguments were being received. Now, we need to receive both MouseInput and KeyboardInput objects, and thus we register the panel class in the `customInitialize()` method as follows:

```
addDeviceObserver(this,"DeviceInput", null);
```

Since any kind of DeviceInput object can now be received, the `onDeviceInput()` method must first determine whether it is getting a MouseInput object or a KeyboardInput object. This is achieved by testing the class type of the DeviceInput object, as follows:

```
//if mouse input
if (di instanceof MouseInput) {
    ...
}

//if keyboard input
if (di instanceof KeyboardInput) {
    ...
}
```

If the object is KeyboardInput, we need to sort out details. Take a look at the Keyboard-Input class in your online Javadocs to get the idea. For our purposes, we need concern ourselves only with key presses, as opposed to key releases. And we wish to respond only to the 'c' key (to create a new camera) and to the '1,' '2,' and '3' keys at the top of keyboard to switch between Viewpoints. Thus the structure is

```
KeyboardInput ki = (KeyboardInput) di;
    if (ki.which == KeyboardInput.PRESS) {

        if (ki.key == 'c' || ki.key == 'C') {
            //create new camera
            return true;
        }


        if (ki.key == '1') {
```

```
        //bind camera 1
          return true;
      }


      if (ki.key == '2') {
        //bind camera 2
        return true;
      }


      if (ki.key == '3') {
        //bind camera 3
        return true;
      }

      return false;  //not one of the desired keys
    }


        return false; //a key release, not a key press
```

Although it's not the most elegant approach, I've created a pattern of return statements in a way that is easy to understand. If any of the desired keys is pressed, onDeviceInput() returns a true value. If either the wrong key is pressed, or any key is released, it returns false to indicate that no action has been taken.

The Basic Panel

Our basic panel class stores TargetViewpoints in an array named cameras. The currentCam field holds the number of the currently bound Viewpoint. This raises a rather typical programming issue: The Viewpoints in the array must be indexed starting at zero, as cameras[0], cameras[1], and cameras[2]. It might make sense to set the currentCam variable in the same way. However, we can already anticipate a user interface of some kind in which the user will expect the alternatives to be numbered 1, 2, and 3. Thus, currentCam will use the values 1, 2, and 3, and currentCam *n* will correspond to cameras[*n*-1]. The totalCams field will hold the total number of cameras in the scene. Both currentCam and totalCams are initialized to 1.

Look over the panel class in Listing 10.7. To keep it simple, I've used only the basic (nonanimated) dragging methods.

**LISTING 10.7 DEVELOPING A MULTIPLE VIEWPOINT APPLICATION
(*MULTIVIEWPOINTS1PANEL.JAVA*)**

```
package applets;

import shout3d.*;
import shout3d.core.*;
import custom_nodes.*;


public class MultiViewpoints1Panel extends Shout3DPanel
➥implements DeviceObserver {


    int pixelStartX;
    int pixelStartY;
    int pixelEndX;
    int pixelEndY;

    TargetViewpoint[] cameras = new TargetViewpoint [3];
    int currentCam = 1;
    int totalCams = 1;


    public MultiViewpoints1Panel(Shout3DApplet applet){
        super(applet);
    }

    public void customInitialize() {

        addDeviceObserver(this,"DeviceInput", null);
        cameras[currentCam-1] = (TargetViewpoint)
➥getCurrentBindableNode("Viewpoint");


    }


    protected void finalize()  {
        removeDeviceObserver(this,"DeviceInput");
    }
```

```
public boolean onDeviceInput(DeviceInput di,
➥Object userData) {

    //if mouse input
    if (di instanceof MouseInput) {
     MouseInput mi = (MouseInput) di;
     switch (mi.which){

        case MouseInput.DOWN:
            pixelStartX = mi.x;
            pixelStartY = mi.y;
            return true;

        case MouseInput.DRAG:

            //if left button used
            if(mi.button == 0) {

            pixelEndX = mi.x;
            pixelEndY = mi.y;

            int dragDistanceX = pixelEndX - pixelStartX;
            int dragDistanceY = pixelEndY - pixelStartY;

            float headingDelta = dragDistanceX/70f;
            float pitchDelta = dragDistanceY/70f;

            float temp = cameras[currentCam-1].heading.getValue()
➥- headingDelta;
            cameras[currentCam-1].heading.setValue(temp);

            temp = cameras[currentCam-1].pitch.getValue()
➥- pitchDelta;
            cameras[currentCam-1].pitch.setValue(temp);

            pixelStartY = pixelEndY;
            pixelStartX = pixelEndX;
```

```
            return true;

        }//end of 0 if


        //if right button used
        if(mi.button == 1) {

            pixelEndY = mi.y;
            int dragDistanceY = pixelEndY - pixelStartY;

            float distanceDelta = dragDistanceY/150f;
            float temp =
➤cameras[currentCam-1].distance.getValue() + distanceDelta;
            cameras[currentCam-1].distance.setValue(temp);

            pixelStartY = pixelEndY;
            return true;
        }//end of 1 if


    }//end of switch

    return false;
    }//end of mouse input

    if (di instanceof KeyboardInput) {

    KeyboardInput ki = (KeyboardInput) di;
    if (ki.which == KeyboardInput.PRESS) {
        if (ki.key == 'c' || ki.key == 'C') {

            //create new camera and
            //add it to the array
                if (totalCams < 3) {
                totalCams++;
                currentCam = totalCams;
                cameras[currentCam-1] = new TargetViewpoint(this);

                    //add to scene and bind
                    Node [] kids = {cameras[currentCam-1]};
```

```
                getScene().addChildren(kids);
                cameras[currentCam-1].isBound.setValue(true);
                cameras[currentCam-1].center.setValue(cameras[0]
➥.center.getValue());


            }
        return true;
        }//end of 'c'


        if (ki.key == '1') {
            if (totalCams >=  1) {
                //bind camera 1
                currentCam  = 1;
                cameras[currentCam- 1].isBound.setValue(true);
            }
         return true;
        }//end of '1'


        if (ki.key == '2') {
            if (totalCams >=  2) {
                currentCam  = 2;
                cameras[currentCam- 1].isBound.setValue(true);
            }
         return true;
        }//end of '2'


        if (ki.key == '3') {
            if (totalCams >=  3) {
                currentCam  = 3;
                cameras[currentCam- 1].isBound.setValue(true);
            }
         return true;
        }//end of '3'

        return false;
    }
```

```
        return false;

    }//end of keyboard input

    return false;

}//end of onDeviceInput()


}//end of class
```

The drag operates on the currently bound camera in the TargetViewpoint array. When the panel is initialized, there is only a single TargetViewpoint—the one loaded from the scene file. We get a reference to this TargetViewpoint and store it in `cameras[0]`.

When the 'c' key is pressed—and there are less than three cameras in the scene—a new TargetViewpoint is created. Its reference is stored in the next available element in the array. We increment the `totalCams` variable, and set `currentCam` to correspond to the new Viewpoint. But just creating the Viewpoint doesn't add it to the scene. Thus we create an array of nodes and put the new TargetViewpoint in it as the only element. This array is added to the scene by making it a child of the root Transform, which is returned by the `getScene()` method.

```
    getScene().addChildren(kids);
```

Finally, we bind the new Target Viewpoint, making it the currently active camera, and set its `center` to match that of the TargetViewpoint from the scene file.

You'll often run across circumstances in which you want to pass a single value to a method that only accepts an array. The `addChildren()` method of the Group (and therefore the Transform) class is a good example. We want to add only a single TagetViewpoint to the root Transform, so we must create a node array to hold only this single object, and then pass this array to `addChildren()`.

When the user presses the number keys, the appropriate section of code determines whether that camera exists. If it does, it is made the current camera and is bound to make it active.

Check this project out by copying the following files from the CD to your Shout installation:

```
MultiViewpoints1Panel.java
```

```
MultiViewpoints1Panel.class
```

```
MultiViewpoints1Applet.java

MultiViewpoints1Applet.class

multiviewpoints1.html
```

This demo uses the `targetviewpoint.s3d` file that we've been using already. Rotate the camera and then create another using the 'c' key. Rotate the new camera and toggle between them using the '1' and '2' keys.

Improving the Zoom

The current zoom implementation is not really adequate for general purposes because the zoom speed is fixed in the panel. It's set to change the speed by 1 meter/second for every 150 pixels of vertical drag. That makes sense for our present test scene because the camera begins at a distance of 10 meters from the center. But what about a scene in which the initial camera distance was 200 meters from the center? Our fixed zoom speed would be far too slow. We need a more general approach that sets the zoom speed based on the initial camera distance.

The current speed we have is comfortable in its context, so we can generalize it. If the user drags 150 pixels, it will take 10 seconds to move the camera from its initial distance to zero distance. The `distanceSpeed` variable is currently computed as

```
distanceSpeed = dragDistanceY/150f;
```

Note that dividing by 150 is the same as multiplying by $\frac{1}{150}$. Let's replace the $\frac{1}{150}$ pixel value with a variable called `zoomPixelFactor`, so that

```
distanceSpeed = dragDistanceY*zoomPixelFactor;
```

To compute the zoomPixelFactor, we can work from the assumption that its value should be $\frac{1}{150}$ if the initial camera distance is 10 meters. Thus we get

```
zoomPixelFactor = (initialDistance/10)/150;
```

Think this through. If the `initialDistance` value is 10, the `zoomPixelFactor` is $\frac{1}{150}$, giving us the same zoom speed that we currently have in our scene. If the `initialDistance` is 100 meters, the `zoomPixelFactor` is $\frac{1}{15}$. This will increase the `distanceSpeed` (the zooming rate) by 10 times. Now, the camera will move at a rate of 10 meters/second for every 150 pixels that the user drags.

Adding a Counter Label

Everything is working just fine, but it's a little tough for the user because there's no indication of which camera is currently active. We need a text label in the upper-left corner of the screen to provide this information. This is a great opportunity to try out the PostRenderEffect class. The PostRenderEffect class allows us to edit the pixels produced by each render cycle or to draw on top of them.

Creating a PostRenderEffect

PostRenderEffect is a node class, and thus PostRenderEffect objects can be added directly to the scene file. We create our own PostRenderEffect classes by extending PostRenderEffect. The PostRenderEffect class provides an empty framework. Look this class up in the online Javadocs and note that it is an abstract class—a class that cannot be instantiated and serves only as a base from which to build extended classes. It contains an abstract method named `filter()`, which must be overridden in extended classes in order to provide functionality. The `filter()` method is called after each render and is passed a number of important arguments. These include the complete array of rendered pixels (the frame buffer), the 3D depth values associated with each pixel (the *z* buffer) and the height and width of the panel window. The `filter()` method is also passed the Graphics object for the panel, often called the *graphics context*.

The graphics context is a central concept in Java graphics, and anyone with the slightest experience writing Java applets is familiar with it. This book is not the right place to discuss general Java graphics programming or the Abstract Windowing Toolkit (AWT), but the subject is simple enough to get started with even the most limited background. Essentially, the graphics context holds information about color, fonts, and line weights for drawing. You set these values, and then call the various methods of the Graphicsclass to perform the drawing actions. Any general Java reference book will provide you with all you need to know on this subject.

Listing 10.8 shows a class that draws a text string in the upper-left corner of the panel.

LISTING 10.8 A 2D TEXT DISPLAY INDICATING THE CURRENT CAMERA (*CAMERACOUNTER.JAVA*)

```
package custom_nodes;

import shout3d.core.*;
import shout3d.*;
```

```
import java.awt.*;


public class CameraCounter extends PostRenderEffect{

    final public IntField  number = new IntField(this, "number",
➥Field.NON_NEGATIVE_INT, 1);

    //the constructor
    public CameraCounter(){

    }


    public void filter(Graphics g, int surface_pixel_bits[],
➥float z_buffer[], int deviceWidth, int deviceHeight){

        String message = "Camera "+ number.getValue();
        g.setFont( new Font("SansSerif", Font.BOLD, 16));
        g.setColor(java.awt.Color.gray);
        g.drawString(message, 20, 20);

    }
}
```

Look first at the filter() method. We create a string composed of the word "Camera" followed by the current value in the number field. We then set the font and the color in the graphics context, and finally draw the string, beginning at the screen coordinates (20,20) in the upper-left corner. The Graphics object is in the java.awt package, which accounts for the new import statement at the top of the class.

As with every class, we need a constructor. An empty one will do here, as there are no special actions to perform. There is a single field, composed of a public IntField object, initialized to a value of 1. This field must be public so that its value can be changed by the panel class to reflect the current camera number.

That's all there is to it. This is an example of a custom node built for a one-shot function. It only makes sense coupled with an appropriate panel class designed to use it. By contrast, the TargetViewpoint is general purpose, and can be used wherever a Viewpoint node might be used.

Copy the CameraCounter.java and CameraCounter.class files from the CD to your custom_nodes directory.

The Full Panel Class

Let's put everything together into an improved panel class. The finished MultiViewpointsPanel in Listing 10.9 creates a CameraCounter object and updates the number value whenever the current camera changes. The drag is once again animated for a smoother interactive feel. And for an additional refinement, the panel stores all the initial TargetViewpoint values so they can be applied to each new camera as it is created. Thus, each new camera starts with precisely the same view as the first one.

LISTING 10.9 THE COMPLETE MULTIPLE CAMERA APPLICATION
(*MULTIVIEWPOINTSPANEL.JAVA*)

```java
package applets;

import shout3d.*;
import shout3d.core.*;
import custom_nodes.*;


public class MultiViewpointsPanel extends Shout3DPanel implements
➥DeviceObserver {


    int pixelStartX;
    int pixelStartY;

    float headingSpeed = 0.0f;
    float pitchSpeed = 0.0f;
    float distanceSpeed = 0.0f;
    float zoomPixelFactor = 0.0f;

    TargetViewpoint[] cameras = new TargetViewpoint [3];
    int currentCam = 1;
    int totalCams = 1;


    float initialHeading;
    float initialPitch;
```

```
float initialDistance;
float[] initialCenter;
float initialFieldOfView;

CameraCounter counter;

public MultiViewpointsPanel(Shout3DApplet applet){
  super(applet);
}

public void customInitialize() {

  addDeviceObserver(this,"DeviceInput", null);
  getRenderer().addRenderObserver(this, null);
  cameras[0] = (TargetViewpoint)
    getCurrentBindableNode("Viewpoint");

  //store initial values
  initialHeading = cameras[0].heading.getValue();
  initialPitch = cameras[0].pitch.getValue();
  initialDistance = cameras[0].distance.getValue();
  initialCenter = cameras[0].center.getValue();
  initialFieldOfView = cameras[0].fieldOfView.getValue();

  //set zoom factor
  //based on initial distance
  zoomPixelFactor = (initialDistance/10)/150;

  //create CameraCounter
  //and add to scene
  counter = new CameraCounter();
  Node[]tempArray = {counter};
  getScene().addChildren(tempArray);
  counter.number.setValue(currentCam);

}


protected void finalize() {
```

```java
        removeDeviceObserver(this,"DeviceInput");
        getRenderer().removeRenderObserver(this);
    }



    public boolean onDeviceInput(DeviceInput di, Object
➥userData) {

        //if mouse input
        if (di instanceof MouseInput) {
          MouseInput mi = (MouseInput) di;
          switch (mi.which){

            case MouseInput.DOWN:
                pixelStartX = mi.x;
                pixelStartY = mi.y;
                return true;

            case MouseInput.UP:
              headingSpeed = 0.0f;
              pitchSpeed = 0.0f;
              distanceSpeed = 0.0f;
              return true;

            case MouseInput.DRAG:

                //if left button used
                if(mi.button == 0) {

                    int pixelEndX = mi.x;
                    int pixelEndY = mi.y;

                    int dragDistanceX = pixelEndX - pixelStartX;
                    int dragDistanceY = pixelEndY - pixelStartY;

                    headingSpeed = dragDistanceX/70f;
                    pitchSpeed = dragDistanceY/70f;

                    return true;
```

```
        }

    //if right button used
    if(mi.button == 1) {

        int pixelEndY = mi.y;
        int dragDistanceY = pixelEndY - pixelStartY;
        distanceSpeed = dragDistanceY*zoomPixelFactor;
        return true;
    }

  }//end of switch

  return false;

}//end of mouse input



//if keyboard input
if (di instanceof KeyboardInput) {

  KeyboardInput ki = (KeyboardInput) di;

  if (ki.which == KeyboardInput.PRESS) {

    if (ki.key == 'c' || ki.key == 'C') {

      //create new camera and
      //add it to the array
      if (totalCams < 3) {

        totalCams++;
        currentCam = totalCams;
        cameras[currentCam-1] = new
          TargetViewpoint(this);

        //add to scene and bind
        Node [] kids = {cameras[currentCam-1]};
        getScene().addChildren(kids);
```

```
            //set to initial values
            cameras[currentCam-1].isBound.setValue(true);
            cameras[currentCam-1]
              .heading.setValue(initialHeading);
            cameras[currentCam-1]
              .pitch.setValue(initialPitch);
            cameras[currentCam-1]
              .distance.setValue(initialDistance);
            cameras[currentCam-1]
              .center.setValue(initialCenter);
            cameras[currentCam-1]
              .fieldOfView.setValue(initialFieldOfView);

            //update CameraCounter display
            counter.number.setValue(currentCam);


        }
        return true;
    }


    if (ki.key == '1') {
      if (totalCams >=  1) {

        currentCam  =  1;
        cameras[currentCam- 1].isBound.setValue(true);
        counter.number.setValue(currentCam);
      }
      return true;
    }


    if (ki.key == '2') {
      if (totalCams >=  2) {

        currentCam  =  2;
        cameras[currentCam- 1].isBound.setValue(true);
        counter.number.setValue(currentCam);
      }
      return true;
    }
```

```
        if (ki.key == '3') {
          if (totalCams >=  3) {

            currentCam  =  3;
            cameras[currentCam- 1].isBound.setValue(true);
            counter.number.setValue(currentCam);
          }
          return true;
        }

      return false;
    }//end of key PRESS

    return false;

  }//end of keyboard input

  return false;

}//end of onDeviceInput()



public void onPreRender (Renderer r, Object o) {

  float headingDelta = headingSpeed/getFramesPerSecond();
  float temp = cameras[currentCam-1].heading
➡.getValue() - headingDelta;
  cameras[currentCam-1].heading.setValue(temp);

  float pitchDelta = pitchSpeed/getFramesPerSecond();
  temp = cameras[currentCam-1].pitch.getValue() - pitchDelta;
  cameras[currentCam-1].pitch.setValue(temp);

  float distanceDelta =  distanceSpeed/getFramesPerSecond();
  temp = cameras[currentCam-1].distance
➡.getValue() + distanceDelta;
  cameras[currentCam-1].distance.setValue(temp);
```

```
    }//end of onPreRender()


    }//end of class
```

Once you've got a handle on this, copy the following classes from the CD to your Shout installation and give it a test drive. Your panel will display the name of the current camera. Pretty cool!

```
MultiViewpointsPanel.java

MultiViewpointsPanel.class

MultiViewpointsApplet.java

MultiViewpointsApplet.class

multiviewpoints.html
```

Camera 2

SHOUT 3d

Creating a Graphical User Interface

Our MultiViewpointsPanel is easy to use and works well, but the user must learn the keyboard commands in order to operate it. Let's try a different approach using a button and a list box, which will appear directly beneath the 3D viewing area.

To do this, we will use standard Java GUI (graphical user interface) components. This requires a word of explanation. Java provides rather complete tools for creating graphical user interfaces through the classes in the AWT (Abstract Windowing Toolkit) package. These tools are very simple in Java 1.02, the earliest version of Java. They were much improved in Java 1.1, and many Java developers work entirely with the 1.1 version tools. However, to keep things simple, the GUI we'll develop here will use only the older, 1.02 version of AWT.

As I previously stressed, we cannot cover the AWT here. Any introductory book on Java applets will provide you with more than you need to know. Rather, we will only see the AWT in action.

A Panel Within an Applet

Thus far, we have created Shout3DPanel objects that completely fill the applet space. In order to use GUI components like buttons and list boxes, we must create a panel that is smaller than the applet so there is surrounding space within the applet to hold the components.

Look up the Shout3DPanel class in your online Javadocs and note that there are three versions of the constructor. This is what is called an *overloaded* constructor. Each of the different versions has a different *signature*, in that each accepts different arguments. When you create a Shout3DPanel, the arguments you use in the new statement will determine which of the three constructors is called.

The basic constructor takes only the applet that is creating the panel as an argument. It creates a panel that fills the entire applet space. The two other constructors allow you more flexibility. The second constructor allows you to specify the width and height of the panel, which is positioned in the top-left corner of the applet.

```
public Shout3DPanel(Shout3DApplet applet, int width, int height)
```

The third constructor allows you to position the top-left corner of the panel at a specified (x,y) pixel location in the applet.

```
public Shout3DPanel(Shout3DApplet applet, int x, int y, int
➥width, int height)
```

We'll need only an empty strip at the bottom of the applet to hold our components, so the second constructor will do. The dimensions of entire applet will be 320×240. Thus we'll construct a panel with a width of 320 pixels and a height of 210 pixels, leaving 30 pixels of exposed applet at the bottom.

Since the panel is created by the applet in its initShout3DPanel() method, we'll need to call the correct constructor there.

```
public void initShout3DPanel(){
        panel = new MultiViewpointsGUIPanel(this, 320, 210);
```

The constructor in the panel class must be prepared to receive the three arguments, and to pass them on to the corresponding superclass constructor (for Shout3DPanel). This will do the trick.

```
public MultiViewpointsGUIPanel(Shout3DApplet applet, int width,
➥int height){
    super(applet, width, height);
}
```

Adding the Components

Java AWT components are objects. In our applet, we'll instantiate them and store their references in fields. A Button object is a simple labeled button. A Choice object is a basic drop-down list. A Panel is a general Container class object that can be used for organizing Components within its space. We will create a Button and a Choice object, add them to a Panel, and then put the Panel at the bottom of the applet.

Take a look at the following code, which is relevant portion of the complete Multi-ViewpointsGUIApplet in Listing 10.11 a little further on.

```
import  shout3d.*;
import java.awt.*;


public class MultiViewpointsGUIApplet extends Shout3DApplet {

    int Total = 1;
    Button newcam;
    Choice list;
    Panel bottomPanel;



    public void initShout3DPanel(){
        panel = new MultiViewpointsGUIPanel(this, 320, 210);
    }

    setLayout(new BorderLayout());
    newcam = new Button("NEW CAMERA");
    list = new Choice();
    list.addItem("Camera "+ total);
```

```
        bottomPanel = new Panel();
        bottomPanel.add(newcam);
        bottomPanel.add(list);
        add(bottomPanel, "South");
    }

    ...

}//end of class
```

The code to create the new GUI objects has all been added to the initShout3DPanel() method. Programmers familiar with programming applets would initially be inclined to put this code in an init() method. However, in Shout3D, the elements must be added after the creation of the panel in order for the layout to work properly.

Applets have a setLayout() method that allows you to choose between certain layout options. We'll use the BorderLayout, which permits you to place components around the perimeter of the applet. We create a button labeled "NEW CAMERA" and assign its reference to the newcam field. Then we create a Choice and assign its reference to the list variable. The default Choice object is empty, so we add an item labeled Camera 1 (using the total variable).

With the components ready, we create a Panel and add the components to it. Finally we add the Panel to the bottom of the applet (using the "South" argument). This is all so straightforward that you should be able to follow it even if you lack any exposure to the Java AWT. At this point, our interface is all set up.

Hooking it Up

Right now, the button and drop-down list are mere decorations. To put them to work, we must connect them up to methods to perform actions. We'll do this using a standard Java 1.0 approach. The `action()` method of the applet Applet class is called an time a GUI component is used. We'll override the `action()` method to identify which of the two components was used, and respond accordingly. This is especially easy in our case because there is only one possible meaning to clicking on a button or selecting an item from a list box.

The basic idea is as follows:

```
public boolean action(Event e, Object o) {

    //user pressed button;
    if (e.target = newcam) {

        //(create a new camera)
        return true;
    }

    //user selects from list
    if (e.target == list) {

        //(bind the selected camera)
        return true;
    }

    return false;

}//end of action method
```

The action method receives an Event object as an argument. It contains information about the event that triggered the method call, just as the MouseInput or Keyboard-Input objects do in the Shout class library. In particular, the Event object has a `target` field that contains a reference to the GUI component that generated the method call. This makes it easy to determine which component was used.

When you compile an applet using the old Java 1.0 event model, you'll receive a warning from the compiler that you are using methods that have been deprecated. This means that they have been replaced by newer methods in more recent versions of Java, but they are still supported. You can ignore this warning and use the applet as compiled.

The next step is to implement the desired functionality. We can do this in two basic ways. On the one hand, we can just write the desired code right here in the applet. On the other, we can write a method in the panel class and call that method from the applet. We'll try both techniques.

The Revised Panel Class

We'll return to our MultiViewpointsPanel class and modify it to eliminate all of the code that responds to KeyboardInputs. And since the drop-down list will tell the user which camera is active, we won't need the CameraCounter object either. The code we previously used to create a new Viewpoint in response to the 'c' key is isolated in a method named `createCamera()` that can be called by the applet. Since this method will not create a new camera if there are already three of them, we write this method to return true or false, depending on whether a camera in created. We won't actually use this return value for any purpose, but it's good planning for the future. Listing 10.10 shows the complete MultiViewpointsGUIPanel.

LISTING 10.10 MULTIPLE CAMERAS CONTROLLED BY A BUTTON AND A DROP-DOWN LIST IN A SURROUNDING APPLET (*MULTIVIEWPOINTSGUIPANEL.JAVA*)

```
package applets;

import shout3d.*;
import shout3d.core.*;
import custom_nodes.*;


public class MultiViewpointsGUIPanel extends Shout3DPanel
➥implements DeviceObserver {


    int pixelStartX;
    int pixelStartY;

    float headingSpeed = 0.0f;
```

```
float pitchSpeed = 0.0f;
float distanceSpeed = 0.0f;
float zoomPixelFactor = 0.0f;

TargetViewpoint[] cameras = new TargetViewpoint [3];
int currentCam = 1;
int totalCams = 1;


float initialHeading;
float initialPitch;
float initialDistance;
float[] initialCenter;
float initialFieldOfView;


public MultiViewpointsGUIPanel(Shout3DApplet applet, int width,
➥int height){
  super(applet, width, height);
}


public void customInitialize() {

  addDeviceObserver(this,"MouseInput", null);
  getRenderer().addRenderObserver(this, null);
  cameras[0] = (TargetViewpoint)
    getCurrentBindableNode("Viewpoint");

  //store initial values
  initialHeading = cameras[0].heading.getValue();
  initialPitch = cameras[0].pitch.getValue();
  initialDistance = cameras[0].distance.getValue();
  initialCenter = cameras[0].center.getValue();
  initialFieldOfView = cameras[0].fieldOfView.getValue();

  zoomPixelFactor = (initialDistance/10)/150;

}
```

```java
protected void finalize() {
  removeDeviceObserver(this,"MouseInput");
  getRenderer().removeRenderObserver(this);
}


public boolean onDeviceInput(DeviceInput di, Object userData) {

  MouseInput mi = (MouseInput) di;
  switch (mi.which){

    case MouseInput.DOWN:
        pixelStartX = mi.x;
        pixelStartY = mi.y;
        return true;

    case MouseInput.UP:
      headingSpeed = 0.0f;
      pitchSpeed = 0.0f;
      distanceSpeed = 0.0f;
      return true;

    case MouseInput.DRAG:

      //if left button used
      if(mi.button == 0) {

        int pixelEndX = mi.x;
        int pixelEndY = mi.y;

        int dragDistanceX = pixelEndX - pixelStartX;
        int dragDistanceY = pixelEndY - pixelStartY;

        headingSpeed = dragDistanceX/70f;
        pitchSpeed = dragDistanceY/70f;

        return true;
```

```
        }

        //if right button used
        if(mi.button == 1) {

            int pixelEndY = mi.y;
            int dragDistanceY = pixelEndY - pixelStartY;
            distanceSpeed = dragDistanceY*zoomPixelFactor;
            return true;
        }

    }//end of switch

    return false;

}//end of onDeviceInput()



public boolean createCamera() {

    if (totalCams < 3) {

        totalCams++;
        currentCam = totalCams;
        cameras[currentCam-1] = new TargetViewpoint(this);

        //add to scene and bind
        Node [] kids = {cameras[currentCam-1]};
        getScene().addChildren(kids);

        //set to initial values
        cameras[currentCam-1].isBound.setValue(true);
        cameras[currentCam-1]
            .heading.setValue(initialHeading);
        cameras[currentCam-1].pitch.setValue(initialPitch);
        cameras[currentCam-1]
            .distance.setValue(initialDistance);
        cameras[currentCam-1].center.setValue(initialCenter);
        cameras[currentCam-1]
```

```
         .fieldOfView.setValue(initialFieldOfView);

       return true;
     }
     return false;
   }//end of createCamera()



   public void onPreRender (Renderer r, Object o) {

     float headingDelta = headingSpeed/getFramesPerSecond();
     float temp = cameras[currentCam-1].heading
➥.getValue() - headingDelta;
     cameras[currentCam-1].heading.setValue(temp);

     float pitchDelta = pitchSpeed/getFramesPerSecond();
     temp = cameras[currentCam-1].pitch.getValue() - pitchDelta;
     cameras[currentCam-1].pitch.setValue(temp);

     float distanceDelta = distanceSpeed/getFramesPerSecond();
     temp = cameras[currentCam-1].distance
➥.getValue() + distanceDelta;
     cameras[currentCam-1].distance.setValue(temp);

   }//end of onPreRender()


}//end of class
```

The Complete Applet Class

Now on to the complete applet. The applet has a panel field that contains reference to its panel object. This allows us to call any of the methods of the panel or access any of the panel's fields. But there is a slight complication. The panel field is a Shout3DPanel reference. Even though it actually contains a reference to a MultiViewpointsGUIPanel, the panel field does not know this and therefore does not recognize the fields and methods we have added in the extended class. For example, the applet could not make sense of a call to

```
panel.createCamera();
```

and the compiler will tell us so if we include it. So we have to create a variable that is explicitly a MultiViewpointsGUIPanel reference and use it to make calls to the panel class.

```
MultiViewpointsGUIPanel pnl = (MultiViewpointsGUIPanel) panel;
pnl.createCamera();
```

We take the existing `panel` reference, cast it to a MultiViewpointsGUIPanel object, and assign it to the new `pnl` variable for further use.

This is just the kind of problem that tends to baffle the new object-oriented programmer, so don't be troubled if you're confused. It will sink in with time, and the issue will certainly come up again.

Take some time to consider the complete applet in Listing 10.11.

LISTING 10.11 THE APPLET WITH BUTTON AND DROP-DOWN LIST (*MULTIVIEWPOINTSGUIAPPLET.JAVA*)

```
package applets;

import  shout3d.*;
import java.awt.*;


public class MultiViewpointsGUIApplet extends Shout3DApplet {

    int total = 1;
    Button newcam;
    Choice list;
    Panel bottomPanel;



    public void initShout3DPanel(){
        panel = new MultiViewpointsGUIPanel(this, 320, 210);

        setLayout(new BorderLayout());
        newcam = new Button("NEW CAMERA");
        list = new Choice();
        list.addItem("Camera "+ total);
        bottomPanel = new Panel();
```

```
        bottomPanel.add(newcam);
        bottomPanel.add(list);
        add(bottomPanel, "South");
    }


    public boolean action(Event e, Object o) {

        //user pressed button;
        //calls createCamera() in panel class
        if (e.target == newcam) {

            MultiViewpointsGUIPanel pnl = (MultiViewpointsGUIPanel)
➡panel;
            pnl.createCamera();
            total = pnl.totalCams;
            list.addItem("Camera "+ total);

            //call select to update list
            list.select(total - 1);

            //disable button, if necessary
            if(total == 3) {newcam.enable(false);}
            return true;
        }

        //user selects from list
        if (e.target == list) {

            int i = list.getSelectedIndex();
            MultiViewpointsGUIPanel pnl = (MultiViewpointsGUIPanel)
➡panel;
            pnl.currentCam  =  i + 1;
            pnl.cameras[i].isBound.setValue(true);
            return true;
        }

        return false;

    }//end of action method
```

```
}//end of class
```

If the user presses the button, the `createCamera()` method of the panel class is called. After the new Viewpoint is created, its name is added as new item in the list box. The item is then selected so that the drop-down list displays the name of the active camera. If there are three cameras in the scene, the button is disabled and is grayed-out in the applet.

If the user selects an existing camera from the list, the index of the selected item (0, 1, or 2) is used to update the `currentCam` field in the panel class and to bind the selected Viewpoint.

You can test out the applet by copying the following files from the CD to your Shout installation:

`MultiViewpointsGUIPanel.java`

`MultiViewpointsGUIPanel.class`

`MultiViewpointsGUIApplet.java`

`MultiViewpointsGUIApplet.class`

`multiviewpointsGUI.html`

Take the project for a drive and see how it performs. What ideas would you have for improving it, and how would you implement them? The projects in this chapter have covered a great deal of ground and tied many themes together to produce practical applications. Use them as a base camp for further exploration.

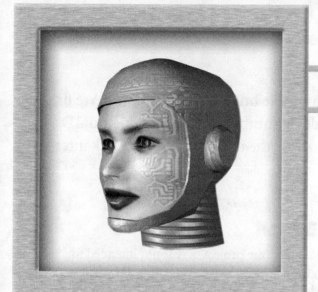

A Simple Game

SHOUT3D

Chapter 11

In this chapter we'll examine a simple but effective 3D game. We'll use the opportunity to consider a number of important Shout3D topics of wide applicability, such as the use of JavaScript, pick intersection, and resizable applets.

Designing the Game

I'm not a professional game designer, and our game project here is not intended to teach the methods and practices used in the games industry. This project has been fashioned primarily to explore the possibilities of Shout3D. But we still want to create a game that's challenging and fun to play.

Games on the Java Virtual Machine

Games that are created for play on standard consoles or as installed computer applications are carefully programmed to squeeze the maximum performance out of the user's hardware. Games played on computer platforms generally require 3D hardware acceleration (such as Direct3D or OpenGL) as supported in today's powerful video cards. A standard Java applet cannot make use of such acceleration, and the whole process of runtime interpretation in the Java Virtual Machine means that Java games cannot approach the speed of fully compiled programs. For the past few years, Java was not a reasonable way to produce action games of any kind—2D or 3D.

But things are changing rapidly. Massive increases in processor speeds are making Java action games possible right now, and further advances will undoubtedly make a dramatic difference. In this chapter, we will create an action game that is very responsive on late-model computers, even at large screen sizes. To do so, we will design graphics that, although relatively primitive, are nonetheless effective. The playing experience should never be compromised to graphics, and the designer can often rely heavily on the player's imagination if the action is fun and fast-moving.

Shout3D 2 offers optional OpenGL hardware acceleration. If a content author chooses to use it, the client receiving the content will be given the choice of whether or not to install a small plug-in application. If the client refuses to install the plugin—or if the client lacks an OpenGL accelerated graphics card—the content will be displayed in OpenGL software mode. Read the online documentation in your Shout3D installation for details.

Scan the Skies Overview

Our game is called *Scan the Skies*. The player is located on a space station and is being attacked from all directions. At any given moment, a missile is heading directly for the player. The goal is to find the attacker and shoot it down before it kills the player.

The game is a fully 3D experience. Attacking objects appear from random directions in space. The player begins with 40 seconds to find the attacker. If the player fails to find it and shoot it down, he or she is killed by the impact. If the player shoots it down, a new missile is launched and the player has 39 seconds to find and kill it. This process continues until—if the player succeeds in knocking down 20 missiles—he or she is allowed 20 seconds to find and kill all further attackers.

The player looks directly through the sights of a gun, rotating the gun by dragging the mouse until it is centered on the attacker. The player fires by releasing the mouse button. If the object is hit, it explodes (with accompanying sound). The score is incremented on the display and a "shot clock" is reset to begin ticking down the seconds in the next attack. If the player fails to kill the attacker before time runs out, the display resets and the player can click to begin another game.

This game is simple enough to be implemented in a remarkably small amount of code, yet interesting enough to be fun. It can also serve as the basis for experimentation and variation.

Basic Mechanics

The player is looking through a Viewpoint located at the center of world space. By rotating the Viewpoint in heading and pitch, the player can freely "scan the skies" using the kinds of rotational drag controls we have explored many times thus far. However, due to the inherent interaction of heading and pitch rotation, the player will have to learn some skills to manipulate the gun effectively. Since this interaction of heading and pitch corresponds to the way a true artillery piece is aimed (by setting its bearing around 360 degrees, and then adjusting the vertical angle), these skills are realistic ones.

The situation is complicated by the fact that there is no "up" or "down" in outer space. The gun can rotate past 90 degrees in the pitch, which turns the viewer upside down. The heading direction is therefore reversed. This, once again, is a wholly realistic experience as well as a challenge. To keep the player from getting lost, we'll need to provide a visual framework—a matter we'll consider shortly.

The missiles must originate at a distance from the Viewpoint and follow a path directly toward the world origin. This goal is easily achieved by parenting the missile to a Transform located at the center of world space. The missile's own Transform will have a translation (position) value set to (0,0,distance). As the distance value approaches zero, the missile draws closer toward its parent Transform, which is located at the world origin. By rotating the parent Transform, the missile can be made to approach from any direction because the Missile will be rotated around the parent Transform.

The following illustration conveys the idea in 2D. The square is the parent Transform and the circle is the missile. The distance is measured in the *z* direction. If the parent Transform is rotated, the circle is rotated as well, but maintains its distance. As the distance decreases, the circle approaches the parent along the parent's (rotated) *z* axis.

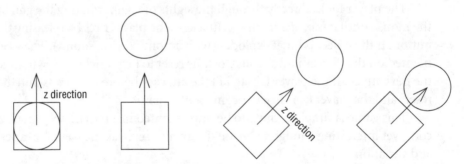

To launch a new missile, we need to generate random heading and pitch values. These values are used to rotate the parent Transform, and the child (the missile) is translated to its maximum distance. With each subsequent frame, the distance value is decreased and the missile approaches the Parent at an assigned speed, using the most basic kind of procedural animation we have already considered.

Firing the Gun

We will use a Picker object to fire at the approaching missile. We'll consider this important tool in more detail a bit later. For now, it's enough to understand that Shout provides for ray intersection. A ray is caused to pass through the space of the scene. If the ray intersects any geometry on its way, the Picker returns and stores data. This ray intersection tool is called a Picker because one of its most important functions is to provide a means by which a user can interactively "pick" objects in a scene. It is the vehicle behind all interactive object selection methods found in the standard 3D modeling and animation programs.

We need a ray that originates at the Viewpoint and moves in the direction the Viewpoint is pointing. This is easily achieved by causing the ray to move toward the pixel in the very center of the viewing panel. When the user releases the mouse button, the Picker object sends out a ray. We then can test to see if it intersects anything on its path. Since the missile will be the only piece of geometry in the scene, we don't need to determine exactly what was hit. If anything was hit, it must be the approaching missile.

Triggering the Explosion

If we have a successful hit, we need an explosion. The explosion will be a short animation of a PointSet object. A PointSet is simply a collection of points in the space of the scene. They do not respond to scene lighting and must therefore be assigned an emissive color or specific vertex colors. It's easy to make a simple explosion of this type animate a sphere that scales from 0 to some maximum size. A little careful work with Bezier interpolation in MAX makes for a more realistic feel, with very rapid expansion that suddenly tails off.

The animated sphere can be exported from MAX to an .s3d file. It's a simple matter to hand edit this scene file to convert the MultiMesh object (the sphere) to a PointSet object by changing the name and eliminating the irrelevant fields that pertain to edges and faces. This produces a PointSet explosion file, complete with Transform, Interpolator, and TimeSensor.

The explosion object must be translated to the correct spot before we set it off. Here's where the Picker comes in handy. We can store the precise point at which the ray intersected the missile and move the explosion object (the PointSet) there just before we start the animation. A pretty simple idea, but very powerful.

The Heads-Up Display

A heads-up display (HUD) is a 2D display that stays in front of the viewer at all times, as the dashboard of the car does while driving. We need a HUD that provides a sight for the gun and displays both the current score and the "shot clock" that counts down the elapsing seconds. The display must also be capable of providing text instructions—at a minimum, the instruction to click to start a new round.

The heads-up display will be implemented as a PostRenderEffect node. This node must be able to receive input from the panel class in order to update the display of the time and the score.

Building the Scene File

Building the scene elements of a game is not the kind of integrated experience typical of creating an animation for passive viewing. You must think in terms of individual scene assets and their relationships, and it often makes sense to build assets in separate stages, export them to .s3d (or VRML) format, and then assemble these elements in a single file by hand editing in a text editor.

The Primary Elements

I built the primary scene elements in a single MAX file. I created a Dummy object (a null object) precisely at the center of world space. I then created a simple sphere (collapsed to an EditableMesh) and also positioned it at the world origin. I parented (linked) the sphere to the Dummy, and named the objects CHILD and PARENT, respectively, so that they would be easily identified when working with the text file.

It's extremely important to make sure that objects are exported from MAX unrotated. MAX has the most remarkable way of sticking rotations to objects, and of hiding these rotations from you. Don't rely on dialog boxes to determine the state of rotations. Open up TrackView and find the rotation track of your object. By default, rotations are stated in axis-angle form. Make sure that the angle value is set to zero. If it is not, use the Reset Transform tool in the Hierarchy panel to "zero out" your rotations.

To create the Viewpoint, I positioned a Free Camera in the same MAX scene precisely at the world origin, and pointing in the −z direction. I was, once again, very careful to be sure that the camera was unrotated before export from MAX. I then performed a quick export to .s3d format. I opened the file and examined it carefully. To create games and other highly interactive projects, you must be able to read and edit a scene file with complete confidence. At this point, there were so few objects that the process was easy. If anything showed up rotated, I hand edited the rotation field to contain only zeros.

I then performed an important test: I edited the file to translate the CHILD (the sphere) some distance in the −z direction, from its original position at (0,0,0). I loaded this scene into the basic Shout3DApplet to check it out. With the camera pointing in the −z direction, I should expect to see the object as I pull it away from its parent null. The test was successful, and so I tested various −z distances. This kind of careful, incremental testing, directly with the scene file, is essential to building an interactive scene.

I moved on to another critical test. I rotated the PARENT Transform and rotated the Viewpoint by the same amount. For example, I rotated both of these exactly one radian around the y (vertical) axis using the values (0 1 0 1). (The first three values indicate the positive *y* axis, and the fourth value specifies a rotation of 1 radian around that axis.) I tested these rotations by typing them directly into the proper fields in the s3d file, like so:

```
DEF GUN Viewpoint{
    position 0 0 0
    orientation 0 1 0 1
    . . .
}

. . .

DEF PARENT Transform {
    translation 0 0 0
    rotation 0 1 0 1
    . . .
}
```

If the overall concept is sound, the sphere should still be in front of the camera, having rotated the same amount as the viewpoint. My test worked, and I was therefore confident in the underlying mechanism on which the entire game rests.

The Animated Explosion

As already mentioned, I created the explosion in a separate MAX file and exported it to .s3d format. I tested it extensively as an animated loop, and I experimented with different scaling values by changing them in the interpolator node in the text file. When I was satisfied, I copied this collection of nodes into the main .s3d file containing the other objects. I set the position of the explosion some distance in front of the camera, and loaded the combined file into a Shout3DApplet. The explosion looped properly within the camera's view.

This explosion must be triggered and should not loop, so I set its TimeSensor (named DETONATOR) as follows:

```
DEF DETONATOR TimeSensor {
    startTime -1
    loop FALSE
    cycleInterval 2.5
}
```

With a −1 `startTime`, the TimeSensor will never start on its own, and must be triggered. I played with different animation lengths before settling on 2.5 seconds.

I wanted the points to change color during the explosion. At a minimum, they had to turn black at the end of the animation so as to disappear into the black background. But I also wanted some color variations that would remind the viewer of fireworks. I decided to try a step approach in which the colors change suddenly at specific times, rather than smoothly interpolating into each other. I typed a FloatArrayStepInterpolator node directly into the file. Color values consist of three floating-point values (for red, green, and blue), and therefore are stored in `float` arrays. The StepInterpolator node is very simple. You associate colors with percentages of the `cycleInterval`.

```
DEF COLORSTEP FloatArrayStepInterpolator{
key [0, .25, .50, .95]
keyValue [ 1 0 0, 1 1 0, 0 1 0, 0 0 0 ]
}
```

In this case, the color is red until 25 percent of the way through the animation, whereupon it changes suddenly to yellow. Halfway through the `cycleInterval` it changes to green. The final five percent of the animation is black. To make these values operate on the PointSet, we need to route things up. The TimeSensor must feed the Interpolator, and the Interpolator must, in turn, route to the `emissiveColor` field of the material of the PointSet. I had to DEF name the appropriate Material node in the scene file so as to be able to route to it.

```
ROUTE DETONATOR.fraction_changed TO COLORSTEP.set_fraction
ROUTE COLORSTEP.value TO MAT1.emissiveColor
```

I tested this file in a Shout3DApplet and played with the color values until I was happy. Then I moved this object (a Transform named EXPLOSION) to (0,100,0) so it would be out of the view of the camera when the game begins.

Structural Elements

The game needs some graphical context or environment. The most attractive graphical approach would have been to create a suitable Panorama node. But after experimenting with Panoramas in other contexts, I felt that they would slow down the frame rate too much on older machines and when using larger windows. This is a classic trade-off typical of games. For example, you must always balance the appeal of high-quality, detailed geometry against its effect on frame rate. I wanted the game to run fast, and I was willing to try alternative graphical ideas to get there.

I decided to create a wireframe globe to surround the Viewpoint to create a strong sense of direction and spatial structure. Shout has a wireframe option for mesh objects, but I decided to create a classic VRML IndexedLineSet. Here I ran across an interesting problem: I wanted to make sure that there would be no diagonal edges triangulating the quadrangles of the sphere. The following image will illustrate.

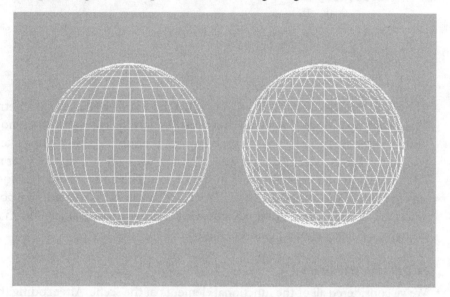

MAX geometry is always composed of triangles, although it permits the organization of triangles in ways that functionally allow a modeler to work with quads and n-gons. Shout3D exports MAX geometry only as triangles, but the MAX VRML97 exporter allows you to preserve quad geometry, so I used it to export a sphere to .wrl format. A few obvious hand edits were all that was needed to convert the IndexedFaceSet to an IndexedLineSet. Simply change the name of the node and eliminate any fields other than `coord` and `coordIndex` (the vertices and their connecting edges). Look up the IndexedLineSet in the Javadocs online documentation and you'll see a field named `lineWidth`, which is measured in pixels. I added this field by hand, and I also edited the Material node to create an `emissiveColor` of my choice.

It doesn't matter how big this globe is, as long as it is centered on (0,0,0). However you scale the globe, the camera's field of view always intersects the same fraction of the sphere.

The final structural element was a PointSet composed of a single point positioned right in the center of the camera's field of view.

```
geometry PointSet {
  coord Coordinate {
    point [
      0 0 -10
    ]
  }
  pointSize 5
}
```

The Shout renderer behaves unreliably when there is absolutely no geometry in the Viewpoint. Specifically, it will not draw PostRenderEffects reliably when no geometry is visible. Often this is not a serious problem, but it's important in a game like this one, which uses PostRenderEffects (as we'll see). I created a new Transform for the gun, and I parented both the Viewpoint and the point to it. The point would therefore always stay in front of the camera when the PARENT Transform is rotated. The point is used as a sight, in lieu of the traditional crosshairs. With the wire frame globe in the scene, there were already enough criss-crossing lines.

More Fireworks

We've considered all of the functional elements of the scene. After coding the game itself, I decided to add some more graphical excitement. Since I already knew how to make an explosion, I wondered whether adding some purely decorative fireworks would adversely affect frame rate. I was pleased to discover that I could add a number of them looping around the scene without slowing down the action at all.

Adding more explosions was easy, and it didn't clutter up the scene file because I could make use of VRML-style instancing. I edited the file to give a DEF name to the PointSet node in the first explosion. I was then able to create new explosions by copying, pasting, and replacing the entire long list of points with a simple USE statement. The USE statement refers to the node with the same DEF name.

```
DEF EXPLOSION2 Transform {
  translation 0 0 -50
  children [
    Shape {
      appearance [
```

```
            Appearance {
                material DEF MAT2 Material {
                    emissiveColor 0 1 0
                }
            }
        ]
        geometry  USE PS PointSet {
        }
    }
]
}
```

That gave me another idea. Instead of using the Step Interpolator, I added a standard ColorInterpolator to the scene file. This allows the colors to change fluidly, using linear interpolation. And since these explosions would loop continuously, they didn't need to fade into black. Here is the ColorInterpolation and its TimeSensor:

```
DEF COLORINTER ColorInterpolator {
key [0, .25, .50, 1.0]
keyValue [ 1 0 0, 1 1 0, 0 1 0, 1 0 0 ]
}
DEF FIREWORKS TimeSensor {
    startTime 0
    loop TRUE
    cycleInterval 2.5
}
```

I added the necessary routing statements, and the entire scene file was finished.

The Finished Scene File

Here is the completed scene file. The only element we haven't discussed is the ScanThe-SkiesDisplay custom node, which provides the heads-up display. We'll get to that in the next section, but now's a good time to look over the entire .s3d scene. Take some time to make sure you understand how the whole thing hangs together, and pay particular attention to the ROUTE statements that connect TimeSensors, Interpolators, and the fields being animated. You can find this file on the CD as scantheskies.s3d and as Listing 11.1 here.

LISTING 11.1 SCANTHESKIES (*SCANTHESKIES.S3D*)

```
DEF DISPLAY ScanTheSkiesDisplay {}

DEF GLOBE Transform {
  translation 0 0 0
  children [
    Shape {
      appearance Appearance {
        material Material {
          emissiveColor 0 .5 .3
        }
      }
      geometry IndexedLineSet {
    lineWidth 1
        coord Coordinate
      { point [
          0 50 0, 0 46.19 -19.13,
          -7.322 46.19 -17.68, -13.53 46.19 -13.53,
          -17.68 46.19 -7.322, -19.13 46.19 0,
          -17.68 46.19 7.322, -13.53 46.19 13.53,
          -7.322 46.19 17.68, 0 46.19 19.13,
          7.322 46.19 17.68, 13.53 46.19 13.53,
          17.68 46.19 7.322, 9.13 46.19 0,
          17.68 46.19 -7.322, 13.53 46.19 -13.53,
          7.322 46.19 -17.68, 0 35.36 -35.36,
          -13.53 35.36 -32.66, -25 35.36 -25,
          -32.66 35.36 -13.53, -35.36 35.36 0,
          -32.66 35.36 13.53, -25 35.36 25,
          -13.53 35.36 32.66, 0 35.36 35.36,
          13.53 35.36 32.66, 25 35.36 25,
          32.66 35.36 13.53, 35.36 35.36 0,
          32.66 35.36 -13.53, 25 35.36 -25,
          13.53 35.36 -32.66, 0 19.13 -46.19,
          -17.68 19.13 -42.68, -32.66 19.13 -32.66,
          -42.68 19.13 -17.68, -46.19 19.13 0,
          -42.68 19.13 17.68, -32.66 19.13 32.66,
          -17.68 19.13 42.68, 0 19.13 46.19,
          17.68 19.13 42.68, 32.66 19.13 32.66,
          42.68 19.13 17.68, 46.19 19.13 0,
          42.68 19.13 -17.68, 32.66 19.13 -32.66,
```

```
    17.68 19.13 -42.68, 0 0 -50, -19.13 0 -46.19,
   -35.36 0 -35.36, -46.19 0 -19.13, -50 0 0,
   -46.19 0 19.13, -35.36 0 35.36,
   -19.13 0 46.19, 0 0 50, 19.13 0 46.19,
    35.36 0 35.36, 46.19 0 19.13, 50 0 0,
    46.19 0 -19.13, 35.36 0 -35.36,
    19.13 0 -46.19, 0 -19.13 -46.19,
   -17.68 -19.13 -42.68, -32.66 -19.13 -32.66,
   -42.68 -19.13 -17.68, -46.19 -19.13 0,
   -42.68 -19.13 17.68, -32.66 -19.13 32.66,
   -17.68 -19.13 42.68, 0 -19.13 46.19,
    17.68 -19.13 42.68, 32.66 -19.13 32.66,
    42.68 -19.13 17.68, 46.19 -19.13 0,
    42.68 -19.13 -17.68, 32.66 -19.13 -32.66,
    17.68 -19.13 -42.68, 0 -35.36 -35.36,
   -13.53 -35.36 -32.66, -25 -35.36 -25,
   -32.66 -35.36 -13.53, -35.36 -35.36 0,
   -32.66 -35.36 13.53, -25 -35.36 25,
   -13.53 -35.36 32.66, 0 -35.36 35.36,
    13.53 -35.36 32.66, 25 -35.36 25,
    32.66 -35.36 13.53, 35.36 -35.36 0,
    32.66 -35.36 -13.53, 25 -35.36 -25,
    13.53 -35.36 -32.66, 0 -46.19 -19.13,
   -7.322 -46.19 -17.68, -13.53 -46.19 -13.53,
   -17.68 -46.19 -7.322, -19.13 -46.19 0,
   -17.68 -46.19 7.322, -13.53 -46.19 13.53,
   -7.322 -46.19 17.68, 0 -46.19 19.13,
    7.322 -46.19 17.68, 13.53 -46.19 13.53,
    17.68 -46.19 7.322, 19.13 -46.19 0,
    17.68 -46.19 -7.322, 13.53 -46.19 -13.53,
    7.322 -46.19 -17.68, 0 -50 0]
}
coordIndex [
   0, 1, 2, -1, 0, 2, 3, -1, 0, 3, 4, -1,
   0,4, 5, -1, 0, 5, 6, -1, 0, 6, 7, -1,
   0, 7, 8, -1, 0, 8, 9, -1, 0, 9, 10, -1,
   0, 10, 11, -1, 0, 11, 12, -1, 0, 12, 13, -1,
   0, 13, 14, -1, 0, 14, 15, -1, 0, 15, 16, -1,
   0, 16, 1, -1, 1, 17, 18, 2, -1,
   2, 18, 19, 3, -1, 3, 19, 20, 4, -1,
```

```
4, 20, 21, 5, -1, 5, 21, 22, 6, -1,
6, 22, 23, 7, -1, 7, 23, 24, 8, -1,
8, 24, 25, 9, -1, 9, 25, 26, 10,-1,
10, 26, 27, 11, -1, 11, 27, 28, 12, -1,
12, 28, 29, 13, -1, 13, 29, 30, 14, -1,
14, 30, 31, 15, -1, 15, 31, 32, 16, -1,
16, 32, 17, 1, -1, 17, 33, 34, 18, -1,
18, 34, 35, 19, -1, 19, 35, 36, 20, -1,
20, 36, 37, 21, -1, 21, 37, 38, 22, -1,
22, 38, 39, 23, -1, 23, 39, 40, 24, -1,
24, 40, 41, 25, -1, 25, 41, 42, 26, -1,
26, 42, 43, 27, -1, 27, 43, 44, 28, -1,
28, 44, 45, 29, -1, 29, 45, 46, 30, -1,
30, 46, 47, 31, -1, 31, 47, 48, 32, -1,
32, 48, 33, 17, -1, 33, 49, 50, 34, -1,
34, 50, 51, 35, -1, 35, 51, 52, 36, -1,
36, 52, 53, 37, -1, 37, 53, 54, 38, -1,
38, 54, 55, 39, -1, 39, 55, 56, 40, -1,
40, 56, 57, 41, -1, 41, 57, 58, 42, -1,
42, 58, 59, 43, -1, 43, 59, 60, 44, -1,
44, 60, 61, 45, -1, 45, 61, 62, 46, -1,
46, 62, 63, 47, -1, 47, 63, 64, 48, -1,
48, 64, 49, 33, -1, 49, 65, 66, 50, -1,
50, 66, 67, 51, -1, 51, 67, 68, 52, -1,
52, 68, 69, 53, -1, 53, 69, 70, 54, -1,
54, 70, 71, 55, -1, 55, 71, 72, 56, -1,
56, 72, 73, 57, -1, 57, 73, 74, 58, -1,
58, 74, 75, 59, -1, 59, 75, 76, 60, -1,
60, 76, 77, 61, -1, 61, 77, 78, 62, -1,
62, 78, 79, 63, -1, 63, 79, 80, 64, -1,
64, 80, 65, 49, -1, 65, 81, 82, 66, -1,
66, 82, 83, 67, -1, 67, 83, 84, 68, -1,
68, 84, 85, 69, -1, 69, 85, 86, 70, -1,
70, 86, 87, 71, -1, 71, 87, 88, 72, -1,
72, 88, 89, 73, -1, 73, 89, 90, 74, -1,
74, 90, 91, 75, -1, 75, 91, 92, 76, -1,
76, 92, 93, 77, -1, 77, 93, 94, 78, -1,
78, 94, 95, 79, -1, 79, 95, 96, 80, -1,
80, 96, 81, 65, -1, 81, 97, 98, 82, -1,
82, 98, 99, 83, -1, 83, 99, 100, 84, -1,
84, 100, 101, 85, -1, 85, 101, 102, 86, -1,
```

```
                        86, 102, 103, 87, -1, 87, 103, 104, 88, -1,
                        88, 104, 105, 89, -1, 89, 105, 106, 90, -1,
                        90, 106, 107, 91, -1, 91, 107, 108, 92, -1,
                        92, 108, 109, 93, -1, 93, 109, 110, 94, -1,
                        94, 110, 111, 95, -1, 95, 111, 112, 96, -1,
                        96, 112, 97, 81, -1, 113, 98, 97, -1,
                        113, 99, 98, -1, 113, 100, 99, -1,
                        113, 101, 100, -1, 113, 102, 101, -1,
                        113, 103, 102, -1, 113, 104, 103, -1,
                        113, 105, 104, -1, 113, 106, 105, -1,
                        113, 107, 106, -1, 113, 108, 107, -1,
                        113, 109, 108, -1, 113, 110, 109, -1,
                        113, 111, 110, -1, 113, 112, 111, -1,
                        113, 97, 112, -1]
                    }
                }
            ]
        }


DEF GUN Transform {
    translation 0 0 0
    children [
        DEF Camera01 Viewpoint{
            position 0 0 0
            orientation 0 0 0 0
            fieldOfView .8
            description "Camera01"
        }

        DEF POINT Transform {
            translation 0 0 0
            children [
                Shape {
                    appearance [
                        Appearance {
                            material Material {
                                emissiveColor 0 0 1
                            }
                        }
                    ]
```

```
                        geometry PointSet {
                            coord Coordinate {
                                point [
                                    0 0 -10
                                ]
                            }
                            pointSize 5
                        }
                    }

                ]

            }

        ]
    }


    DEF PARENT Transform {
        translation 0 0 0
        children [
            DEF CHILD Transform {
                translation 0 0 0
                children [
                    Transform {
                        children [
                            Shape {
                                appearance [
                                    MultiAppearance {
                                        material Material {
                                            diffuseColor 1 0 0.02353
                                        }
                                    }
                                ]
                                geometry MultiMesh {
                                    defaultFlatShaded FALSE
                                    coord DEF CHILD-COORD Coordinate {
                                        point [
                                            0 5 0 0 3.536 -3.536 -2.5
                                            3.536 -2.5 -3.536 3.536 0
                                            -2.5 3.536 2.5 0 3.536
```

```
                           3.536 2.5 3.536 2.5 3.536
                            3.536 0 2.5 3.536 -2.5 0 0
                          -5 -3.536 0 -3.536 -5 0 0
                          -3.536 0 3.536 0 0 5 3.536
                            0 3.536 5 0 0 3.536 0
                          -3.536 0 -3.536 -3.536
                          -2.5 -3.536 -2.5 -3.536
                          -3.536 0 -2.5 -3.536 2.5 0
                          -3.536 3.536 2.5 -3.536
                            2.5 3.536 -3.536 0 2.5
                          -3.536 -2.5 0 -5 0
                        ]
                    }
                coordIndex [
                    0 1 2 -1 0 2 3 -1 0 3 4 -1
                    0 4 5-1 0 5 6 -1 0 6 7 -1
                    0 7 8 -1 0 8 1 -1
                    1 9 10 -1 1 10 2 -1
                    2 10 11 -1 2 11 3 -1
                    3 11 12 -1 3 12 4 -1
                    4 12 13 -1 4 13 5 -1
                    5 13 14 -1 5 14 6 -1
                    6 14 15 -1 6 15 7 -1
                    7 15 16 -1 7 16 8 -1
                    8 16 9 -1 8 9 1 -1
                    9 17 18 -1 9 18 10 -1
                    10 18 19 -1 10 19 11 -1
                    11 19 20 -1 11 20 12 -
                    12 20 21 -1 12 21 13 -1
                    13 21 22 -1 13 22 14 -1
                    14 22 23 -1 14 23 15 -1
                    15 23 24 -1 15 24 16 -1
                    16 24 17 -1 16 17 9 -1
                    25 18 17 -1 25 19 18 -1
                    25 20 19 -1 25 21 20 -1
                    25 22 21 -1 25 23 22 -1
                    25 24 23 -1 25 17 24 -1
                ]
                appearanceIndex [
                    1 1 1 1 1 1 1
                    1 1 1 1 1 1 1
```

```
                              1 1 1 1 1 1
                              1 1 1 1 1 1
                              1 1 1 1 1 1
                              1 1 1 1 1
                              1 1 1 1 1 1
                      ]
                      textureMappings [
                      ]
                  }
                }
              ]
            }
          ]
        }
      ]
    }


DEF DETONATOR TimeSensor {
    startTime -1
    loop FALSE
    cycleInterval 2.5
}


DEF EXPLOSION-BEZSCALE-INTERP BezierVecInterpolator {
  key [
     0 1
  ]
  keyValue [
     0 0 0 0.9258 0.9169 -0.9199 1.048
     1.051 -1.045 .25 .25 -.25
  ]
}


DEF COLORSTEP FloatArrayStepInterpolator{
key [0, .25, .50, .95]
keyValue [ 1 0 0, 1 1 0, 0 1 0, 0 0 0 ]
}
```

```
DEF EXPLOSION Transform {
    translation 0 100 0
    scale .01 .01 .01
    children [
      Shape {
        appearance [
          Appearance {
            material DEF MAT1 Material {
              emissiveColor 0 1 0
            }
          }
        ]
        geometry  DEF PS PointSet {
          coord DEF GeoSphere01-COORD Coordinate {
            point [
                 0 10 0 8.944 4.472 0 2.764 4.472
                 -8.507 -7.236 4.472 -5.257 -7.236
                 4.472 5.257 2.764 4.472 8.507
                 7.236 -4.472 -5.257 -2.764 -4.472
                 -8.507 -8.944 -4.472 0 -2.764 -4.472
                 8.507 7.236 -4.472 5.257 0 -10 0 2.733
                 9.619 0 5.257 8.507 0 7.382 6.746 0
                 0.8444 9.619 -2.599 1.625 8.507 -5
                 2.281 6.746 -7.02 -2.211 9.619 -1.606
                 -4.253 8.507 -3.09 -5.972 6.746 -4.339
                 -2.211 9.619 1.606 -4.253 8.507 3.09
                 -5.972 6.746 4.339 0.8444 9.619 2.599
                 1.625 8.507 5 2.281 6.746 7.02 8.226
                 5.057 -2.599 6.882 5.257 -5 5.014 5.057
                 -7.02 0.07031 5.057 -8.627 -2.629 5.257
                 -8.09 -5.128 5.057 -6.938 -8.183 5.057
                 -2.733 -8.507 5.257 0 -8.183 5.057 2.733
                 -5.128 5.057 6.938 -2.629 5.257 8.09
                 0.07032 5.057 8.627 5.014 5.057 7.02
                 6.882 5.257 5 8.226 5.057 2.599 9.593
                 2.325 -1.606 9.511 0 -3.09 8.705 -2.325
                 -4.339 1.437 2.325 -9.619 0 0 -10 -1.437
                 -2.325 -9.619 -8.705 2.325 -4.339 -9.511
                 0 -3.09 -9.593 -2.325 -1.606 -6.816
                 2.325 6.938 -5.878 0 8.09 -4.492 -2.325
```

```
 8.627 4.492 2.325 8.627 5.878 0 8.09
 6.816 -2.325 6.938 9.593 2.325 1.606
 9.511 0 3.09 8.705 -2.325 4.339 4.492
 2.325 -8.627 5.878 0 -8.09 6.816 -2.325
-6.938 -6.816 2.325 -6.938 -5.878 0 -8.09
-4.492 -2.325 -8.627 -8.705 2.325 4.339
-9.511 0 3.09 -9.593 -2.325 1.606 1.437
 2.325 9.619 0 0 10 -1.437 -2.325 9.619
 5.128 -5.057 -6.938 2.629 -5.257 -8.09
-0.0703 -5.057 -8.627 -5.014 -5.057 -7.02
-6.882 -5.257 -5 -8.226 -5.057 -2.599
-8.226 -5.057 2.599 -6.882 -5.257 5
-5.014 -5.057 7.02 -0.07031 -5.057
 8.627 2.629 -5.257 8.09 5.128 -5.057
 6.938 8.183 -5.057 2.733 8.507 -5.257
 0 8.183 -5.057 -2.733 2.211 -9.619
-1.606 4.253 -8.507 -3.09 5.972 -6.746
-4.339 -0.8444 -9.619 -2.599 -1.625
-8.507 -5 -2.281 -6.746 -7.02 -2.733
-9.619 0 -5.257 -8.507 0 -7.382 -6.746
 0 -0.8444 -9.619 2.599 -1.625 -8.507
 5 -2.281 -6.746 7.02 2.211 -9.619 1.606
 4.253 -8.507 3.09 5.972 -6.746 4.339
 3.618 8.944 -2.629 6.179 7.404
-2.647 4.427 7.404 -5.058 -1.382 8.944
-4.253 -0.6079 7.404 -6.694 -3.443
 7.404 -5.773 -4.472 8.944 0 -6.554 7.404
-1.49 -6.554 7.404 1.49 -1.382 8.944
 4.253 -3.443 7.404 5.773-0.6079 7.404
 6.694 3.618 8.944 2.629 4.427 7.404
 5.058 6.179 7.404 2.647 10 0 0 9.554
-2.551 1.49 9.554 -2.551 -1.49 3.09 0
-9.511 4.37 -2.551 -8.625 1.535 -2.551
-9.547 -8.09 0 -5.878 -6.853 -2.551
-6.821 -8.605 -2.551 -4.41 -8.09 0
 5.878 -8.605 -2.551 4.41 -6.853 -2.551
 6.821 3.09 0 9.511 1.535 -2.551 9.547
 4.37 -2.551 8.625 8.09 0 -5.878 6.853
 2.551 -6.821 8.605 2.551 -4.41 -3.09
 0 -9.511 -4.37 2.551 -8.625 -1.535
 2.551 -9.547 -10 0 0 -9.554 2.551 1.49
```

```
                            -9.554 2.551 -1.49 -3.09 0 9.511 -1.535
                             2.551 9.547 -4.37 2.551 8.625 8.09 0
                             5.878 8.605 2.551 4.41 6.853 2.551
                             6.821 1.382 -8.944 -4.253 0.6079
                            -7.404 -6.694 3.443 -7.404 -5.773
                            -3.618 -8.944 -2.629 -6.179 -7.404
                            -2.647 -4.427 -7.404 -5.058 -3.618
                            -8.944 2.629 -4.427 -7.404 5.058
                            -6.179 -7.404 2.647 1.382 -8.944
                             4.253 3.443 -7.404 5.773 0.6079
                            -7.404 6.694 4.472 -8.944 0 6.554
                            -7.404 -1.49 6.554 -7.404 1.49
                    ]
                }
            pointSize 2
            }
        }
    ]
}


DEF FIREWORKS TimeSensor {
    startTime 0
    loop TRUE
    cycleInterval 2.5
}


DEF COLORINTER ColorInterpolator {
key [0, .25, .50, 1.0]
keyValue [ 1 0 0, 1 1 0, 0 1 0, 1 0 0 ]
}


DEF EXPLOSION2 Transform {
    translation 0 0 -50
    children [
        Shape {
            appearance [
                Appearance {
                    material DEF MAT2 Material {
```

```
                        emissiveColor 0 1 0
                     }
                  }
               ]
           geometry  USE PS PointSet {
           }
         }
      ]
   }

   DEF EXPLOSION3 Transform {
      translation 0 50 0
      children [
         Shape {
            appearance [
               Appearance {
                  material USE MAT2 Material {
                     emissiveColor 0 1 0
                  }
               }
            ]
            geometry  USE PS PointSet {
            }
         }
      ]
   }


   DEF EXPLOSION4 Transform {
      translation 0 -50 0
      children [
         Shape {
            appearance [
               Appearance {
                  material USE MAT2 Material {
                     emissiveColor 0 1 0
                  }
               }
            ]
            geometry  USE PS PointSet {
            }
```

```
            }
        ]
    }

    DEF EXPLOSION5 Transform {
        translation -10 0 0
        children [
            Shape {
                appearance [
                    Appearance {
                        material USE MAT2 Material {
                            emissiveColor 0 1 0
                        }
                    }
                ]
                geometry   USE PS PointSet {
        }
            }
        ]
    }


    ROUTE DETONATOR.fraction_changed TO
    ➥EXPLOSION-BEZSCALE-INTERP.set_fraction
    ROUTE EXPLOSION-BEZSCALE-INTERP.value_changed TO
    ➥EXPLOSION.set_scale
    ROUTE DETONATOR.fraction_changed TO COLORSTEP.set_fraction
    ROUTE COLORSTEP.value TO MAT1.emissiveColor

    ROUTE FIREWORKS.fraction_changed TO
    ➥EXPLOSION-BEZSCALE-INTERP.set_fraction
    ROUTE EXPLOSION-BEZSCALE-INTERP.value_changed TO
    ➥EXPLOSION2.set_scale
    ROUTE EXPLOSION-BEZSCALE-INTERP.value_changed TO
    ➥EXPLOSION3.set_scale
    ROUTE EXPLOSION-BEZSCALE-INTERP.value_changed TO
    ➥EXPLOSION4.set_scale
    ROUTE EXPLOSION-BEZSCALE-INTERP.value_changed TO
    ➥EXPLOSION5.set_scale
```

```
ROUTE FIREWORKS.fraction_changed TO COLORINTER.set_fraction
ROUTE COLORINTER.value TO MAT2.emissiveColor
```

Coding the Java

With the scene assets all assembled, it's time to code the game.

The game will not require any GUI components, and the panel will completely fill the applet. Thus we do not need to worry about coding an applet and can rely on the simple applet template. All the action will be in the panel class. However, you will also need to code a PostRenderEffect node for the heads-up display. Let's get that out of the way first.

The ScanTheSkiesDisplay Node

You can go a lot further with the heads-up display than I did. I kept it simple to better serve as a learning tool.

The display requires four elements:

1. A message to start or restart the game by clicking the mouse

2. The score of successful hits in the current game

3. The "shot clock" counting down the remaining seconds before impact

4. A sighting box in the center of the screen to aim the gun

The score and the remaining time are values that must be computed by the game itself in the panel class. Thus, these must be public fields in the display node so the panel can change them as the game proceeds.

The ScanTheSkiesDisplay node is extended from PostRenderEffect. It displays the shot clock in the upper-left corner of the panel window, the current score in the upper right, and the message "CLICK TO START" in the center. This message should display only when the shot clock is at zero, which will occur when the game is first loaded and every time the player loses. If the game is running, the message should be replaced with the sighting box. To create more tension, and to keep the player from having to divert their eyes to the shot clock, the rectangle turns red when only 3 seconds remain.

Listing 11.2 displays the code for the ScanTheSkiesDisplay class. It can be found on the CD as ScanTheSkiesDisplay.java.

LISTING 11.2 SCANTHESKIESDISPLAY (*SCANTHESKIESDISPLAY.JAVA*)

```java
package custom_nodes;

import shout3d.core.*;
import shout3d.*;
import java.awt.*;


public class ScanTheSkiesDisplay extends PostRenderEffect{


    final public IntField  score = new IntField(this, "score",
➥bField.NON_NEGATIVE_INT, 0);

    final public IntField  shotClock = new IntField(this,
➥"shotClock", Field.NON_NEGATIVE_INT, 0);

    //constructor
    public ScanTheSkiesDisplay(){

    }


    public void filter(Graphics g, int surface_pixel_bits[], float
➥z_buffer[], int deviceWidth, int deviceHeight){

        //initialize display strings
        String scoreString = ""+score.getValue();
        String clockString = ""+shotClock.getValue();
        String message = "CLICK TO START";


        //if shot clock is at zero
        //display CLICK TO START
        if (shotClock.getValue() == 0) {

            Font f = new Font("SansSerif", Font.BOLD, 30);
```

```
            FontMetrics fm = g.getFontMetrics(f);
            int stringWidth = fm.stringWidth(message);
            g.setFont(f);
            g.setColor(java.awt.Color.yellow);
            g.drawString(message, (deviceWidth - stringWidth)/2,
 ➥deviceHeight/2);

        }

        //if game is running
        //draw sight rectangle
        else {
            //red in final 3 seconds
            //as warning
            if (shotClock.getValue() < 4) {
                g.setColor(java.awt.Color.red);
            }
            //otherwise yellow
            else {
                g.setColor(java.awt.Color.yellow);
            }
            g.drawRect((deviceWidth/2)-25, (deviceHeight/2)-25,
 ➥ 50, 50);
        }

        //set up score and shot clock display
        g.setFont( new Font("SansSerif", Font.BOLD, 16));
        g.setColor(java.awt.Color.yellow);
        g.drawString(scoreString, deviceWidth - 50, 30);
        g.drawString(clockString, 50, 30);

    }
}
```

Note how the deviceWidth and deviceHeight arguments to the filter() method are used to center both the message and the sighting box. Look at the way in which the rectangle is drawn. The drawRect() method takes four arguments—the *x* and *y* pixel location of the upper-left corner and the width and height of the rectangle. As the rectangle is 50 pixels in width, its left side must be 25 pixels less than the pixel in the horizontal center of the screen. Vertical centering is computed in the same way.

Centering the text requires a FontMetrics object, which is used to compute the width, in pixels, of the text string when using the specified font. This is a basic Java graphics technique that can be found in any elementary book on Java.

We can test this display out all by itself by creating a text file containing only this node, as follows.

```
ScanTheSkiesDisplay {}
```

When loaded into the basic Shout3DApplet (using 320×240 dimensions), the default display is correct.

To see if the node properly responds to changing values, we can test it by typing in non-default field values.

```
ScanTheSkiesDisplay {
    shotClock 10
    score 6
}
```

When the edited file is loaded, the message is replaced by a yellow rectangle, and the two numerical values are correctly displayed.

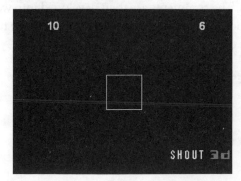

We can even test whether the rectangle turns red at the correct time with:

```
ScanTheSkiesDisplay {
    shotClock 3
    score 6
}
```

I'll spare you another black-and-white image, but this practice of testing nodes carefully by hand editing their fields in a scene file is basic and essential. You don't want to dump this node into the game scene file until you are convinced that it works correctly all by itself.

Building the Panel Class

The panel class *is* the game. Rather than just hand you the finished version, I'd like you to consider the process for developing the code that implements our design.

Mapping Things Out

Coding the panel class is fundamentally a matter of determining how the functionality of the game maps to the structure of the panel. We ask ourselves the following questions and plug the answers into the slots provided by the framework of a Shout3DPanel.

- What data needs to be stored by the game?
- What must be done to set things up before play can begin?
- What happens when the player presses, drags, and releases the mouse button?
- How does the game change while running (e.g., animating the missile)?

We can begin to build our code by organizing these decisions into comments within the various methods of the panel class. The comments are then developed into working code.

Listing 11.3 illustrates the process at a point at which almost all of the functionality has been mapped out, but not yet coded.

LISTING 11.3 SCANTHESKIESPANEL IN DEVELOPMENT

```
package applets;

import shout3d.*;
import shout3d.core.*;
```

```
import shout3d.math.*;
import custom_nodes.*;  //for ScanTheSkiesDisplay
import java.applet.*;  //for AudioClip


public class ScanTheSkiesPanel extends Shout3DPanel implements
➥DeviceObserver {


    //game state variables
    boolean started = false;
    boolean killed = false;


    //screen pixels
    int startPixelX;
    int startPixelY;

    //heads-Up display
    ScanTheSkiesDisplay display;
    int score = 0;
    double startTime;
    int elapsedSeconds;


    //missile
    int totalSeconds = 40;
    float distance;
    float speed = 10;  //10 meters per second
    float startDistance = 10.f * totalSeconds;
    Transform child;
    Transform parent;
    float[] missileAxisAngle = new float[4];
    float[] missileEulers = new float[3];
    Quaternion missileQ = new Quaternion();


    //gun
    Transform gun;
    float[] gunAxisAngle = new float[4];
    float[] gunEulers = new float[3];
```

```java
Quaternion gunQ = new Quaternion();
float headingSpeed = 0.0f;
float pitchSpeed = 0.0f;
Picker fire;

//animated explosion
TimeSensor detonator;
Transform explosion;
float [] intersection = new float [3];
AudioClip gong;


//the constructor
public ScanTheSkiesPanel (Shout3DApplet applet){
    super(applet);
}


public void customInitialize() {

    //get references to scene nodes

    //register observers

    //create a picker


}



protected void finalize()  {

    //remove observers
}



public boolean onDeviceInput(DeviceInput di, Object
➥userData) {
```

```
        MouseInput mi = (MouseInput) di;
        switch (mi.which) {

            case MouseInput.DOWN:

                if (started == false) {
                    //create missile to start
                    started = true;
                    newMissile();
                }

                if (killed) {
                    //if killed, reset score
        }

                //in any case, store start of drag

return true;

            case MouseInput.DRAG:

                //set gun rotation speeds
                //based on drag distances
return true;

            case MouseInput.UP:

                //store intersection point

                //compute center of window

                //fire the picker ray

                //if ray hits something
                if (results != null)  {

                    //move explosion to intersection
                    //and detonate with sound
```

```
                     //increment the score
                     //and update the display

                     //decrease missile start
                     //distance by 10, but not
                     //below 200 meters

                     //launch a new missile

                 }

                 //stop gun rotation


        }//end of switch

        return false;

    }//end of onDeviceInput()



    public void onPreRender (Renderer r, Object o) {

        //do nothing unless game is started
        if (started) {

            //compute current distance
            //of missile from player

            //end game if missile hits player
            if (distance <= 0){
                //do everything
    return;
            }

            //if missile still moving,
            //update its position
```

```
        //update gun rotation

        //update shot clock


    }//end of if started

    }//end of onPreRender()


    private void newMissile() {

        //set random heading and pitch

        //rotate missile to start position

        //reset clock


    }//end of newMissile()


} //end of class
```

It makes no sense to begin coding until we've defined the underlying architecture in this way. Note how I decided to isolate the process of launching a new missile in a separate method, named newMissile(). A new missile is launched in two situations: when the player presses the mouse button to begin a new game, and when a missile is destroyed during a game. Rather than repeat the same code twice, it makes sense to package it in its own method. This also makes the code more readable. The newMissile() method is made private. It can be called by other methods only within the Scan-TheSkiesPanel class.

Using the Picker

We will be using a Picker object as a gun. Look over the Picker interface in online Javadocs API documentation to get a feeling for this tool.

First, you must create a Picker. The `getNewPicker()` method of the Shout3DPanel class instantiates a Picker object and returns its reference, which we can store in a Picker variable.

```
Picker fire;
fire = getNewPicker();
```

Now we can use all of the Picker methods. A Picker can send a ray through the scene in two different ways. The ray can originate from the Viewpoint and be directed by specifying a pixel location on the screen. This is the method we will use in the game. The other method specifies a *from* and a *to* point within the 3D space of the scene, and the ray originates at the former and passes through the latter on its path. This technique is used in the Shout3D WalkPanel to test collisions.

By default, the ray will intersect all of the geometry in the scene, but you can choose to consider only a specified branch of the scene graph for ray intersection using the `setPath()` method. There's only one object in our particular scene that the ray can possibly intersect, so there's no need to consider this option here. And since the default permits intersection of the entire scene graph, we needn't bother explicitly calling the `setScene()` method, which includes all scene geometry in the ray intersection process.

You can use a Searcher object to determine a path to a specified item of scene geometry. That path then can be used in the `setPath()` method of the Picker. Look up the Searcher in your online Javadocs.

The Picker ray is fired by one of the four `pick()` methods. The `pickAny()` and `pickAnyFromTo()` methods return only a Boolean value (true or false) indicating whether any object was intersected. The `pickClosest()` and `pickClosestFromTo()` methods return the path to the first piece of geometry that is intersected by the ray. The path is an array of nodes. The first node in this array is the scene root and the last is the geometry node of the particular object. A typical path might be:

path[0] Transform (scene root)

path[1] Transform

path[2] Shape

path[3] MultiMesh (the geometry intersected)

The LightTestPanel in your Shout installation illustrates the use of the path returned by a Picker to find the Transform above the selected geometry. We have no need for the path to the intersected geometry in our game, and thus it would seem that we could get by with the pickAny() method to return a simple true or false. This would be so if we did not also need to determine the precise point of intersection. We need to be able to move the explosion object to that point before detonating it. To obtain this information, we must use a pickClosest() method. Thus we will use the path information only to determine whether anything was hit. If the return value is null, nothing was hit. If it is not null (if any path is returned), we must have hit our target.

A Picker is capable of storing the location point of the intersection if we so instruct it before firing, using the setPickerInfo() method. After firing, we can recover this information with the getPickerInfo() method. The entire sequence runs like this:

```
//store intersection point
fire.setPickInfo(Picker.POINT, true);

//compute center of window
int centerPixelX = size().width/2;
int centerPixelY = size().height/2;

//fire the picker ray
Node [] results =
fire.pickClosest(centerPixelX, centerPixelY);

//if ray hits something
if (results != null)  {

    //move explosion to intersection point
        intersection = fire.getPickInfo(Picker.POINT);


explosion.translation.setValue(intersection);

}
```

The ScanTheSkiesPanel

If all of the functionality has been properly mapped out, the coding will be remarkably easy. Listing 11.4 shows the completed panel class.

LISTING 11.4 SCANTHESKIESPANEL (*SCANTHESKIESPANEL.JAVA*)

```java
package applets;

import shout3d.*;
import shout3d.core.*;
import shout3d.math.*;
import custom_nodes.*;  //for ScanTheSkiesDisplay
import java.applet.*;  //for AudioClip


public class ScanTheSkiesPanel extends Shout3DPanel implements
➥DeviceObserver {


    //game state variables
    boolean started = false;
    boolean killed = false;


    //screen pixels
    int startPixelX;
    int startPixelY;

    //heads-Up display
    ScanTheSkiesDisplay display;
    int score = 0;
    double startTime;
    int elapsedSeconds;

    //missile
    int totalSeconds = 40;
    float distance;
    float speed = 10;  //10 meters per second
    float startDistance = 10.0f * totalSeconds;
    Transform child;
    Transform parent;
    float[] missileAxisAngle = new float[4];
    float[] missileEulers = new float[3];
    Quaternion missileQ = new Quaternion();
```

```
    //gun
    Transform gun;
    float[] gunAxisAngle = new float[4];
    float[] gunEulers = new float[3];
    Quaternion gunQ = new Quaternion();
    float headingSpeed = 0.0f;
    float pitchSpeed = 0.0f;
    Picker fire;

    //animated explosion
    TimeSensor detonator;
    Transform explosion;
    float [] intersection = new float [3];
    AudioClip gong;




    //the constructor
    public ScanTheSkiesPanel (Shout3DApplet applet){
        super(applet);
    }


    public void customInitialize() {

        //get references to scene nodes
        child = (Transform) getNodeByName("CHILD");
        parent = (Transform) getNodeByName("PARENT");
        detonator = (TimeSensor) getNodeByName("DETONATOR");
        gun = (Transform) getNodeByName("GUN");
        explosion = (Transform) getNodeByName("EXPLOSION");
        display = (ScanTheSkiesDisplay)
  getNodeByName("DISPLAY");
        gong = applet.getAudioClip(applet.getCodeBase(),
  "models/sounds/gong.au");

        //register observers
        addDeviceObserver(this, "MouseInput", null);
        getRenderer().addRenderObserver(this, null);
```

```
        //create a picker
        fire = getNewPicker();

    }



    protected void finalize()  {
        removeDeviceObserver(this,"MouseInput");
        getRenderer().removeRenderObserver(this);
    }



    public boolean onDeviceInput(DeviceInput di, Object
➥userData) {

        MouseInput mi = (MouseInput) di;
        switch (mi.which) {

            case MouseInput.DOWN:

                if (started == false) {
                    //create missile to start
                    started = true;
                    newMissile();
                }

                if (killed) {
                    //if killed, reset score
                    score = 0;
                    display.score.setValue(score);
                    killed = false;
                }

                //in any case, store start of drag
                startPixelX = mi.x;
                startPixelY = mi.y;
                return true;

            case MouseInput.DRAG:
```

```
                 //set gun rotation speeds
                 //based on drag distances
                 int endPixelX = mi.x;
                 int endPixelY = mi.y;
                 int dragDistanceX = endPixelX - startPixelX;
                 int dragDistanceY = endPixelY - startPixelY;
                 headingSpeed = dragDistanceX/150f;
                 pitchSpeed = dragDistanceY/70f;
                 return true;


          case MouseInput.UP:

                 //store intersection point
                 fire.setPickInfo(Picker.POINT, true);

                 //compute center of window
                 int centerPixelX = size().width/2;
                 int centerPixelY = size().height/2;

                 //fire the picker ray
                 Node [] results =
                 fire.pickClosest(centerPixelX, centerPixelY);

                 //if ray hits something
                 if (results != null)  {

                     //move explosion to intersection
                     //and detonate with sound
                     intersection =
     fire.getPickInfo(Picker.POINT);

                             explosion.translation.setValue
          (intersection);

                     detonator.start();
                     gong.play();

                     //increment the score
                     //and update the display
```

```
                    score++;
                    display.score.setValue(score);

//decrease missile start
                    //distance by 10, but not
                    //below 200 meters
                    if (totalSeconds > 20) {
                        totalSeconds-;
                        startDistance = 10.0f * totalSeconds;
                    }

                    //launch a new missile
                    newMissile();
                }

                //stop gun rotation
                headingSpeed = 0.0f;
                pitchSpeed = 0.0f;
                return true;


        }//end of switch

        return false;

    }//end of onDeviceInput()



    public void onPreRender (Renderer r, Object o) {

        //do nothing unless game is started
        if (started) {

            //compute current distance
            //of missile from player
            float delta = speed/getFramesPerSecond();
            distance = distance - delta;

            //end game if missile hits player
```

```
            if (distance <= 0){

                display.shotClock.setValue(0);
                killed = true;
                started = false;
                totalSeconds = 40;
                startDistance = 10.0f * totalSeconds;
                return;
            }

            //if missile still moving,
            //update its position
            child.translation.set1Value(2, -distance);

            //update gun rotation
            float headingDelta =
        headingSpeed/getFramesPerSecond();
            float pitchDelta =
    pitchSpeed/getFramesPerSecond();
            gunEulers[0] = gunEulers[0] + headingDelta;
            gunEulers[1] = gunEulers[1] + pitchDelta;
            gunQ.setEulers(gunEulers);
            gunQ.getAxisAngle(gunAxisAngle);
            gun.rotation.setValue(gunAxisAngle);

            //update shot clock
            double currentTime = getAbsoluteTime();
            elapsedSeconds = (int)(currentTime - startTime);
            display.shotClock.setValue(totalSeconds -
    ➥elapsedSeconds);


        }//end of if started

    }//end of onPreRender()


    private void newMissile() {

        //set random heading and pitch
        missileEulers[0] =  (float) (Math.random() * 6.28);
```

374

```
        missileEulers[1] = (float) (Math.random() * 6.28);
        missileQ.setEulers(missileEulers);

        //rotate missile to start position
        missileQ.getAxisAngle(missileAxisAngle);
        parent.rotation.setValue(missileAxisAngle);
        distance = startDistance;
        child.translation.set1Value(2, -distance);

        //reset clock
        startTime = getAbsoluteTime();

    }//end of newMissile()


} //end of class
```

After you've spent some time contemplating this code, reward yourself with a game of *Scan the Skies*. Copy the following files from the CD to your Shout installation:

ScanTheSkiesApplet.java

ScanTheSkiesApplet.class

ScanTheSkiesPanel.java

ScanTheSkiesPanel.class

ScanTheSkiesDisplay.java

ScanTheSkiesDisplay.class

scantheskies.s3d

scantheskies.html

Take some time to play this game and see how all of the code performs in action. Consider how you might improve the game and edit the code to implement your ideas. Think how you might parameterize certain fields so they can be customized in the <APPLET> tag to make the game easier or more difficult to play.

Adjusting Panel Dimensions

One of the biggest problems with Web gaming is that the audience is distributed over a wide range of platforms. A game that responds well on a late-model system may run miserably slow on an older machine. It would be terrible if we were always forced to develop games for the "lowest common denominator." Luckily, we don't have to.

The biggest factor in performance is the size of the panel. Shout provides some exciting tools to allow users to adjust their own panel dimensions to achieve the right balance of size and frame rate.

Resizing with JavaScript

The overwhelming focus of this book has been on using Java to implement user inter-activity. However, the JavaScript language can be used to call the Java methods in the Shout API. It's important to understand that this use of JavaScript is not universally supported by browsers and that, in particular, it does not work with Microsoft Internet Explorer for the Macintosh. Thus JavaScript is not a serious option for work intended for general publication on the Web. However, because it doesn't require compiling, JavaScript offers a great way to perform simple tests. You write simple JavaScript func-tions directly in the HTML source code and just load the Web page. Many of the demos in your Shout installation have been implemented in JavaScript for just this reason.

Let's say we want to be able to provide the game in two sizes—400×300 and 320×240 pixels. The Shout3DPanel class provides a reshape() method to adjust its dimensions on the fly. The method takes four arguments—the x and y pixel location of the upper-left corner and the width and height of the panel.

Listing 11.5 shows an HTML page that allows users to call two reshape() methods by clicking on text links.

LISTING 11.5 SCAN THE SKIES IN TWO SIZES (*SCANTHESKIES_TWOSIZES.HTML*)

```
<html>

<head>

<SCRIPT language="JavaScript">
function make320(){
  document.Shout3D.panel.reshape(40, 30, 320, 240);
}
function make400(){
```

```
        document.Shout3D.panel.reshape(0, 0, 400, 300);
    }

</SCRIPT>

</head>


<body>

<p>
<applet NAME="Shout3D" CODEBASE="../codebase"
➡CODE="applets/ScanTheSkiesApplet.class"
➡ARCHIVE="shout3dClasses.zip" WIDTH=400 HEIGHT=300>
    <param name="src" value="models/scantheskies.s3d">
    <param name="headlightOn" value="true">
</applet>
</p>

<A HREF="javascript: make320()">Set panel size to
➡320 by 240</A><BR>
<A HREF="javascript: make400()">Set panel size to
➡400 by 300</A><BR>


</body>
</html>
```

The two JavaScript methods are placed in the <SCRIPT> tag, and each of these calls the appropriate Java method from the Shout API. The Java method is addressed through the JavaScript document object. This object contains all of the component objects on the page, and thus to reach the applet, we must name it. Note how the <APPLET> tag now contains a NAME element.

```
NAME="Shout3D"
```

I named the applet Shout3D, but I could have named it anything I wished. This name is used in the JavaScript method to address the applet. Once in the applet, we use the applet's panel field to call the panel's resize() method.

Copy `scantheskies_twosizes.html` from the CD into the `demos` folder in your Shout installation and give it a try. The page first loads with the larger panel.

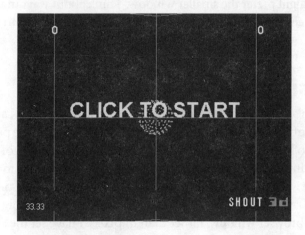

Set panel size to 320 by 240
Set panel size to 400 by 300

When the user clicks on the text link that calls the 320×240 resize function, the panel shrinks accordingly.

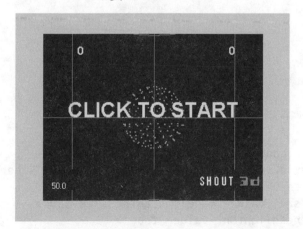

Set panel size to 320 by 240
Set panel size to 400 by 300

Note the striking difference in frame rate as displayed at the bottom of the two alternatives. Even the slower rate (33.3 fps) is plenty fast for this game, but on a slower machine than I used, the user might prefer the smaller window. Think about ways in which you could implement this choice in Java (rather than JavaScript)—perhaps with a button or a drop-down list.

Flexible Resizing

An even more powerful way to allow the user to resize the panel is as easy as can be. The `panelAutoFillsApplet` parameter in the `<APPLET>` tag produces a flexible panel that automatically adjusts to fit the browser window. The user can create a panel of any dimensions by simply stretching the browser. This is the ultimate in interactive customization.

Here is straightforward implementation in Listing 11.6 and available on the CD (`scantheskies_resizes.html`). Note how the applet dimensions are now expressed as a percentage of the browser window, rather than in pixels. I have set the applet to completely fill the window, except for a border of 30 pixels.

LISTING 11.6 USING A RESIZABLE APPLET (*SCANTHESKIES_RESIZES.HTML*)

```
<html>

<head>

</head>


<body>

<p>
<applet CODEBASE="../codebase"
➥CODE="applets/ScanTheSkiesApplet.class"
➥ARCHIVE="shout3dClasses.zip" WIDTH=100% HEIGHT=100% border=30
➥hspace=0 vspace=0>
  <param name="src" value="models/scantheskies.s3d">
  <param name="headlightOn" value="true">
  <param name="panelAutoFillsApplet" value="true">
```

```
</applet>
</p>

</body>

</html>
```

Copy `scantheskies_resize.html` to your Shout demos folder and play around with it a bit. Press the 'f' key to display your frame rate and resize the screen. If you have a powerful processor, you will be able to fill the entire monitor with the applet and preserve a workable frame rate. You can also change the aspect ratio if a wider screen appeals to you.

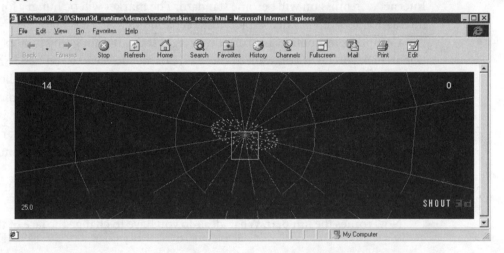

Take some time to experiment with different values for the border, vspace, and hspace attributes. Just type them into the HTML source and reload the file. You'll find that you have a lot a freedom to position the applet in the browser window.

Gaming is one of the most important applications for Web 3D. The Shout3D API is rich enough to provide compelling content that is consistent with the current limitations of Internet delivery. As these limitations evaporate with higher bandwidth and faster processors, the strengths of the Shout API will become even more apparent.

Some Final Words

We've come a long way in these pages. We started with the simplest scene graph, picked up some basic Java, and went on to build impressive interactive 3D applications with the Shout3D API. There's been a lot to learn.

The consequences of our new knowledge are profound, and the possibilities are limitless. Indeed, the greatest challenge in the rapidly emerging world of Web 3D is conceiving of vital and exciting new applications—projects that will reshape expectations about what is possible with a Web page. The field is wide open and ready for great ideas and large ambitions. A year from today, the average computer system will be far more powerful and capable of handling sophisticated graphical content. Broadband Internet transmission will become standard. The market will be hungry for powerful interactive 3D graphics that exploit these capabilities.

Computer technology is a barreling freight train. It's not going to stop at the station to pick you up. If you want to climb on board, you have to run beside it and jump on when you're moving fast enough. This means that you have to think ahead. If you start building your skills now, you'll be able to catch the Web 3D train some months down the road. Nor will it be the same train any more. The Web 3D scene is still very fluid, and it will change rapidly with new advancements. Shout3D 2 is a far more sophisticated package than Shout3D 1, and the next generation will certainly represent another quantum leap.

It takes energy, persistence, and passion to build the New World of interactive 3D graphics on the Internet. But with Shout3D, at least we have the tools.

Now comes the fun part. What ideas do you have to change the face of the Internet?

Index

Note to the Reader: Throughout this index **boldfaced** page numbers indicate primary discussions of a topic. *Italicized* page numbers indicate illustrations.

SYBEX BOOKS ON THE WEB

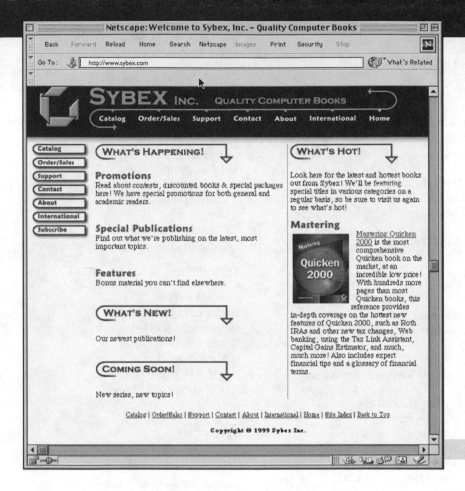

A t the dynamic and informative Sybex Web site, you can:

- · view our complete online catalog
- · preview a book you're interested in
- · access special book content

- · order books online at special discount prices
- · learn about Sybex

www.sybex.com

SYBEX Inc. • 1151 Marina Village Parkway, Alameda, CA 94501 • 510-523-8233

What's on the CD-ROM

The CD for *Interactive Web Graphics with Shout3D* contains everything you need for Shout3D development except for a 3D modeling package. If you don't have a 3D modeling package but are interested in programming interactivity using the Shout3D Java library, you can use the model files on the CD.

The CD contains:

→ A demo version of the Shout3D 2 Final Beta

→ Sun's Java Development Kit (JDK) 1.1.8 for Windows

→ All of the files for all of the exercises and projects from the book.

→ A directory of bonus projects not covered in the text.

The demo version of the most recent Shout3D 2 beta is ready for installation on your system. You'll want to go to the Shout Web site at www.shout3d.com where you can download the demo of the final Shout3D 2 release, or you can purchase the full Shout3D 2 software package.

The Java Development Kit (JDK) 1.1.8 for Windows from Sun Microsystems is the same package that is available free from the Sun Web site. Visit www.java.sun.com to make sure that you have the most recent version.

All of the exercise and project files are organized by chapter. The bonus projects contain all of the files used in their development, including the original 3D Studio MAX scenes.